WILDWATER TOURING

WILDWATER TOURING

Techniques and Tours

SCOTT ARIGHI
MARGARET S. ARIGHI

MACMILLAN PUBLISHING CO., INC.,
NEW YORK
COLLIER MACMILLAN PUBLISHERS,
LONDON

TO OSCAR—Who Taught Us of Safety

Library of Congress Cataloging in Publication Data

Arighi, Scott.
Wildwater touring.

1. White-water canoeing. 2. Canoes and canoeing–Oregon. 3. Canoes and canoeing–Idaho. I. Arighi, Margaret S., joint author. II. Title.
GV788.A74 917.95 73-21708
ISBN 0-02-503150-3

Macmillan Publishing Co., Inc.
866 Third Avenue, New York, N.Y. 10022
Collier-Macmillan Canada Ltd.

First Printing 1974

Printed in the United States of America

Preface

Why did we write a book on wildwater touring? There are really several answers to this question. For one, although there are many books on wilderness canoeing, the coverage which they give whitewater is usually either inadequate or nonexistent. The books on boating technique usually have a chapter or just a paragraph on touring—also inadequate. In fact, wildwater touring has a number of unique problems. We have found ways to deal with many of these problems which we believe will be of value to the fast-growing number of wildwater tourists.

A second answer to our question is conservation. Although we would like all the rivers in the guide section to be in a wilderness state, we are more concerned that they remain rivers, rather than ending up as sterile lakes behind dams. The only philosophy that seems to work at all in preventing more dams is "Use it or lose it." Even this philosophy has failed miserably in California and Colorado, both of which have been systematically raping their free-flowing rivers. We believe that the force of people who know, people who have been there, people who will use their political influence to keep rivers flowing will only be adequate if substantial numbers of people tour the rivers. Faced with this choice between more people or no rivers, we chose more people and wrote this book to encourage them to run, to see, to *protect* free-flowing rivers.

We wish to acknowledge the assistance of several people. Dave Bauman, of the River Forecast Service in Portland, has been extremely helpful to us over a period of years in providing water flow data and in suggesting a number of information sources. The other staff members of the River Forecast Service have also been very generous with their time in answering our requests.

We gratefully acknowledge the contributions of Trygve P. Steen both as a source of constructive criticism of the photographic work and as a source of some of the photographic techniques and equipment which were used to make the illustrations. We are also grateful to Robert Peirce and Bruce West for making available materials from which several of the illustrations in Tours 3, 4, and 6 were taken. We would like to thank Dr. Eric Jacobsen and Dr. Jay Nutt for their comments on the First Aid Kit listed in Chapter 6. Our thanks are also due to Professor Ken Davis for permission to use one of the Reed College darkrooms for much of the photographic processing.

Certainly too, we must acknowledge the valiant efforts of Jean Johnson in deciphering our nearly illegible scrawls while typing the manuscript and the efforts of Patsy Faulkner in drawing the final versions of the maps.

Scott Arighi
Margaret S. Arighi

Oregon City, Oregon
1974

Contents

PART TWO
On the River

PART THREE
River Tour Guides

Appendixes

Figures

Tables

Introduction

Freedom to drift with the current, to camp when you please, to decide to run a rapids—to us this is the essence of wildwater touring. Year by year this type of freedom has an increasing appeal, judging from our growing number of requests for information. Many people simply want information on a specific river tour while others, including experienced whitewater boaters, request hints on how to tour rivers. Some people cannot afford to hire a licensed guide to lead them by the hand down the river, and others would rather do it themselves. But all of the people making the requests have one thing in common—they do not want to make a wildwater tour without more information.

This book attempts to provide enough information for the would-be wildwater tourist to make a tour safely without hiring an outfitter or guide. It is a book on how and where to tour on wilderness whitewater for several days, not a book on how to maneuver a boat. We have tried to include enough information to allow the complete novice to prepare for and make a tour safely on one of the easier rivers in the guide section. But we have also tried to include enough technical information to make the book useful to the experienced whitewater boater who wishes to explore a river in the United States or Canada which is unknown to him.

The book was written for all whitewater boaters—whether they use rafts, wooden drift boats, canoes, or kayaks. Although we usually paddle kayaks, we have had some experience in all these boats and have accompanied all of them on tours. The problems encountered in wildwater touring do not depend strongly on the type of boat although some boats can handle certain problems better than others.

The first two sections of the book deal with the "how-to" aspects of river touring. The first section, Chapters 1–9, includes material dealing with planning a river tour (the hardest part!), while the second section, Chapters 10–13, discusses important techniques to use while on the actual trip. Thus Chapters 1–13 are applicable to any unknown river.

But for those who wish it, we have included a section on where to go and what to expect when you get there. Part III is a set of complete guides to nine wildwater tours of three days or longer. The tours range from those suitable for the novice to those suitable for experts only, and cover a season from March to September. (See Introduction to the Guides, page 151 for more information.)

Many of the great southwestern rivers have become so popular that severe restrictions have almost excluded their use by private parties without an outfitter. The new policies on the Middle Fork of the Salmon River mark the advent of restrictions for river runners in the Northwest—a trend that is certain to continue as the use of rivers increases. We hope that this book will encourage *competent* private parties to use these rivers. Then when the restrictions do come, a history of successful use by private parties should preclude the restriction of river use solely to parties with commercial guides. But please take note—if you run one of these rivers with an incompetent group and need rescue, you are increasing the chances that the river use will be restricted to commercially guided parties.

We wish to state here—and will repeatedly remind the reader throughout the book—that whitewater touring can be a very dangerous activity. Although this book will provide the reader with helpful safety advice and information, no amount of advice can eliminate the obvious potentially fatal dangers that may be involved in wildwater boating.

Our approach in this book is based on the assumption that if you don't want to make your own decisions on the river, you probably will hire a licensed outfitter. The book is not designed to make your decisions for you, but to give you enough information so that you can make your own.

Glossary of Wildwater Terms

BOILS: spots where the water surges up, usually in an unpredictable manner.

BRACE: see *high brace* and *low brace.*

BUSY: fast, tight maneuvering.

CLEAN: free of obstructions.

CHICKEN ROUTE: a relatively easy bypass route in a difficult rapids.

CHUTE: caused by the river constricting and dropping.

CONTINUOUS RAPIDS: unceasing rapids with few or no resting spots.

C.F.S.: cubic feet per second of water flowing past a given point. If the flow is 1,000 c.f.s., 1,000 cubic feet of water flows past a point each second.

DRAWSTROKE: a stroke that pulls the boat directly sideways.

DROPS: very steep, usually short rapids, such as 3-ft. falls.

EDDIES: spots where the downstream flow is very slight, or the flow actually proceeds upstream. Eddies are found behind rocks and often along the banks, and make excellent stopping or resting spots.

EDDY LINE: the turbulent, tricky area along the border of an eddy, where the current doesn't know *what* it's doing!

EDDY TURNS: turns into and out of eddies, a technique necessary for the safe boating of many rivers.

FERRY: a technique for moving the boat sideways across the river without moving downstream. A back ferry is done facing downstream at an angle and backpaddling, while a front ferry is done facing upstream at an angle and paddling forward upstream.

GRADIENT: the amount the river drops in a given length. A gradient of 10 ft./mi. means that the river drops an average of 10 ft. in each mile of its length.

HAYSTACKS: large pointed waves.

HEAVY RAPIDS: very turbulent with large waves and, frequently, holes. Heavy rapids are the most likely to occur at large flows.

HIGH BRACE: a stabilizing stroke made by extending the paddle with arms held high and pulling down on the water.

HOLE: a turbulent spot where the water flows down instead of downstream. Holes occur behind rocks when large volumes of water flow over the rock. Large holes can be very dangerous.

HYDRAULICS: turbulent phenomena due to water patterns, such as boils, holes, and violent eddy lines.

LINING: guiding the boat down the rapids by means of a rope.

LOW BRACE: a stabilizing stroke made by extending the paddle with arms held low, and pushing down on the water.

PLAY SPOTS: spots in the rapids that are well suited to practicing, experimenting, and just plain playing with various boating techniques. Kayakists are particularly partial to these.

POOL AND DROP: a type of rapids in which a quiet pool leads to a steep drop followed by another quiet pool.

PORTAGE: carrying boat and/or equipment around a rapids.

PUT-IN: the place where the boats are put in the river.

RIFFLES: very small shallow waves.

ROCK GARDEN: a type of rapids in which rocks are strewn throughout the rapids. These usually require skill in both water-reading and maneuvering.

ROLL: righting an upset kayak by using an appropriate paddle motion (without emerging from the kayak).

RUNOFF: water flow caused by melting snow or heavy rain.

RUNOUT: the area immediately below rapids. A good runout is a spot such as a long pool where rescue is easy.

SCOUTING: looking at a rapids from the shore.

SHUTTLE: driving the cars to the take-out or returning to the put-in to pick up cars.

SPRAY SKIRT: a waterproof covering that fits around a kayakist's waist and the opening in his boat to prevent water from entering.

SURVIVAL QUOTIENT: a measure of a person's ability to keep himself out of serious trouble.

SWIRLIES: small whirlpools, where the water is sucked down.

TAKE-OUT: the spot where boats are taken out of the water at the trip's end.

WATER-READING: the art of choosing the best spot to run a rapids.

PART ONE

PLANNING AND PREPARING FOR WILDWATER TOURS

ONE

The River Difficulty—Objective Evaluation

The central problem in planning any river trip is to determine whether the river and the boaters are well matched. Is the skill of the boaters adequate for the difficulty of the river? The answer to this question requires both a means of measuring a boater's skill and a means of measuring the difficulty of the river. Our measure of the boater's skill is discussed in Chapter 3. The present chapter deals with evaluation of the difficulty of the river itself.

The stakes in the game of judging river difficulty are high—your boat and your life. In 1970 a few boaters underestimated the difficulty of the Middle Fork of the Salmon River in Idaho in early July, a month when the river is usually runnable. Unusual runoffs that year made the river still dangerously high. The result was a number of drownings. We ran the same stretch somewhat later, after the water level had dropped. At the put-in we met a small party of rafters who told us that this was their first river trip. They laughed at our warnings about the difficulty of the

Middle Fork, and pushed merrily off. Fifteen minutes later, when we found them swimming and pulling their overturned raft to shore, they weren't quite so merry. We proceeded quite slowly, as we stopped to play in almost every rapids, so we encountered the raft group several times. For them, the rapids were a series of traumas: jumping out to pull the raft off rocks, overturning time after time, and swimming after lost gear. Our last encounter with these rafters was about one hour after they had put in. We passed them hiking back to the put-in, carrying the remnants of their gear. The raft was a total loss. If they had been further from the put-in, they might have lost more than their raft. So, if your life and your boat aren't laughing matters to you, you will need to judge river difficulty accurately.

The best way to evaluate river difficulty is through careful inspection of the river itself. A novice may have only a vague idea of what factors influence river difficulty, and thus may not know what features to look for on a river to estimate its difficulty. How much weight should be assigned to the various features to arrive at the overall difficulty? Difficulty can be a highly subjective term. The natural tendency is to call it easy if it looks easy to you. But what looks easy to an expert may look impossible to a novice, or vice versa, if the novice is the over-the-falls-in-the-barrel type. What is needed is a scale of evaluation that lists difficulties in terms of observable river features, not in subjective terms such as "easy," "difficult," etc.

For this reason, an International Scale of River Difficulty has evolved, based on observable river features. This rating system, using the Roman numerals I to VI to describe increasing difficulty of rapids, has been widely used in the United States, Canada, and Europe. There are several other rating systems in use in particular areas, e.g., the 1–10 or 1–12 systems used in the Southwest, but we will use only the more universally accepted international scale in this book.

The river features used to establish the difficulty ratings on the international scale are listed below in general terms:

CLASS I:

Moving water, perhaps a few small waves, few or no obstructions.

CLASS II:

Some eddies (see Glossary) small waves, and slight turbulence; some maneuvering required; some obstructions.

CLASS III:

Some fairly powerful eddies, medium-sized waves; considerable maneuvering required (at times fairly difficult); routes sometimes require scouting from shore.

CLASS IV:

Large and irregular waves; powerful hydraulics (see Glossary); routes that require precise maneuvering in such turbulence; runout (see Glossary) often poor; scouting from shore often necessary; rescue difficult.

CLASS V:

Either very long or very mean, usually wild turbulence capable, for example, of picking up boat and boater and throwing them several feet; extremely congested routes which nearly always must be scouted from shore; rescue difficult and some danger to life in event of a mishap.

CLASS VI:

Worse than Class V. If you are competent to handle this water, you can also identify it. Water of Class VI difficulty involves substantial hazard to life. Few people actually run this class of water.

The level of boater's skill needed to handle each of these classes of difficulty is given in Chapter 3.

Such a general description still presents some problems; for instance, at what height does a wave become large instead of medium sized? The Guidebook Committee of the American Whitewater Affiliation has designed a more specific table to use

Table 1-1 *River Rating Scale**
Factors Related to Difficulty of Negotiating and Safety

Points	*0*	*1*	*2*
Bends	few, very gradual	many gradual	few, sharp, blind
Length, ft.	less than 100	100–700	700–5,000
Gradient, ft./mi.	less than 5	5–15, even slope	15–40, ledges or steep drops
Obstacles (trees, rocks)	none	few; passage straight and obvious	some; courses easily recognized
Waves	few inches avoidable	low (up to 1 ft.) regular, avoidable	low to med. (up to 3 ft.) regular, avoidable
Turbulence	none	minor eddies	med. eddies
Resting or rescue spots	almost everywhere		
Water speed, mi./hr.	less than 3	3–6	6–10
Water speed, ft./sec.	less than 5	5–9	9–15
River width	narrow (75 ft. or less)	wide	narrow
River depth	shallow (less than 3 ft.)	shallow	deep
Water temp., °F.	over 65	55–65	45–55
Accessibility	road along river	one hour or less "out"	one hour to one day "out"
Total points		0–7	8–14
Difficulty rating		I	II
Approximate skill required		practiced beginner	intermediate

*Prepared by Guidebook Committee, American Whitewater Affiliation.

3	*4*	*5*	*6*
over 5,000			
over 40, steep drops, small falls			
maneuvering, courses not obvious	intricate maneuvering; course hard to recognize	course tortuous; frequent scouting needed	very tortuous; always scout from shore
med. to large (up to 5 ft.) mostly regular, avoidable	large: irregular, avoidable; or med. to large: unavoidable	large irregular, unavoidable	very large (over 5 ft.) irregular, unavoidable
strong eddies, cross currents	very strong eddies, strong cross currents, holes	large-scale eddies and cross currents, some boils	
good one below every danger spot			almost none
over 10 over 15 or flood			
wide			
deep			
less than 45			
more than one day "out"			
15–21 III	22–28 IV	29–35 V	36–40 VI
experienced	highly skilled several years with organized groups	team of experts	

in arriving at river difficulty, which we show as Table 1-1. It has one extremely important advantage. It is a means of objective evaluation, based on observable features such as actual height of waves and water temperature, not on subjective opinion.

Notice that safety factors such as water temperature and accessibility are included, as well as more obvious factors such as rocks and turbulence. The points related to actual difficulty are added to those related to safe rescue, and the total points are then used to give the difficulty rating. The safety factors are included because they do affect difficulty, by increasing the danger in case of accident. Greater skill is needed to reduce the possibility of accidents.

You must beware of changes in river conditions. River difficulty is strongly dependent on the flow, or volume of water passing a point, and a river that may have been a reasonable Class II when you evaluated it may become a raging Class IV at very high water levels. High flows often increase the size of waves, the turbulence, the water speed, width, and depth, and decrease the number of resting or rescue spots. Thus the difficulty often increases with the flow, and must be reevaluated at different water levels.

The river difficulty you observe will also be slightly dependent on the type of boat you use. For example, collisions with rocks are often terminal for wooden drift boats, thus making very rocky rivers more difficult for the wooden-boat operator than for the rafter or kayakist. Extremes in current velocity are more significant for boats that are designed for drifting, than they are for boats such as kayaks, that are designed for paddling. A high current velocity increases the river difficulty much more for a raft than for a kayak because the rafter has relatively little control of his boat at high current speeds. Very low current velocity is also important to drift-powered boats, of course, as their drift speed is directly related to the current.

River ratings estimated by using Table 1-1 seem to be representative of ratings assigned by experienced boaters, both nationally and internationally. Using the table should allow you to communicate river difficulty effectively to most experienced boaters. Never be afraid to disagree with the river rating of an "expert" if your own rating is based on objective observations. It is very easy for experts and novices alike to ignore the objective factors, and to rate rivers in terms of a subjective fright factor.

Direct evaluation is the best means of determining river difficulty, but unfortunately it is not always feasible, especially when the river is thousands of miles away. How can you objectively rate the difficulty of a river before you see it? Reasonable estimates of river difficulty can be made if you have the necessary information about river flow, in cubic feet per second passing a point, and gradient, the amount of drop of the river bed in feet per mile. Both flow and gradient data are available for many rivers (see Appendixes C and D). We have used these data to construct a simplified model shown in the graph of Figure 1-1. It is constructed on the basis of our experience in running a large number of rivers. We initially evaluated all the rivers in the guide section using this model, and then altered the ratings when we had actually run the rivers. If you are running only those rivers listed in the guides at recommended flow levels, you will not need the simplified model. For other rivers, or for those in the guide section at other than recommended flow levels, our simplified model may be helpful.

We will use the Grande Ronde River (Tour 2) as an example of how to use Figure 1-1. It is helpful to find both the average gradient and the gradient of the steepest section so that you can make estimates of both average and maximum difficulty. From maps we found that the put-in is at an elevation of about 2,500 ft. (feet) and the take-out is at about 1,600 ft. elevation. From the put-in to the take-out is 44 mi. (miles). Thus,

$$\text{gradient} = \frac{(2{,}500 - 1{,}600)\text{ ft.}}{44\text{ mi.}} = \text{about 21 ft./mi.}$$

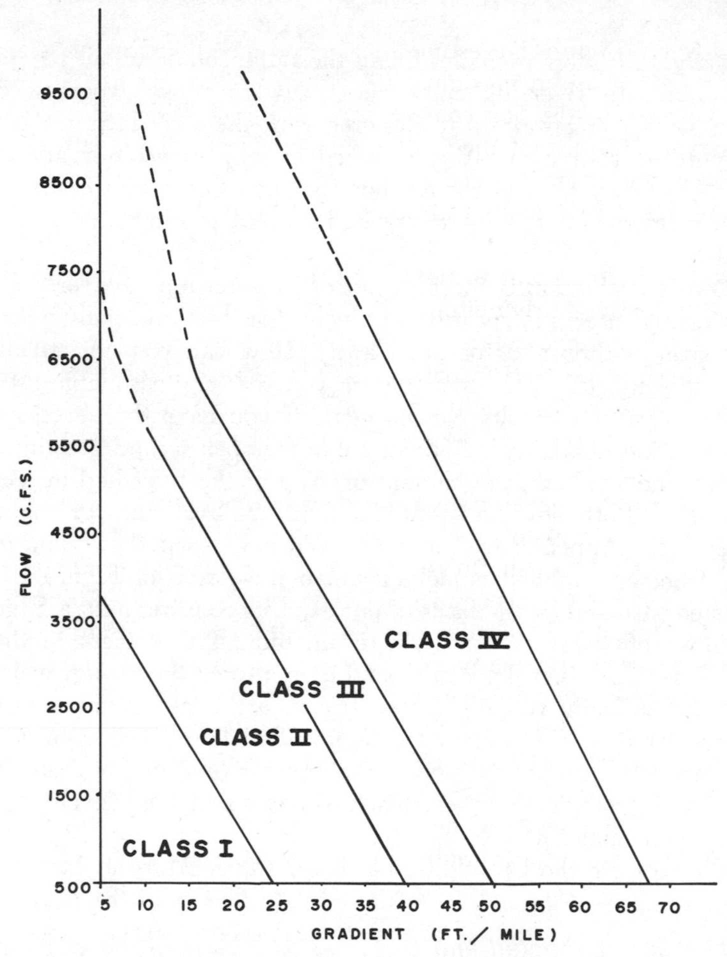

Figure 1-1 Graph for estimating river difficulty (assumes fairly even gradient and does not apply well to pool-and-drop rivers*)*

The steepest section, from the put-in to Rondowa, a distance of about 8 mi., has a gradient of about 27 ft./mi.

Flow levels (as suggested in Tour 2) of 1,500 cfs (cubic feet per second) to 4,000 c.f.s. fall in the moderate flow range for this river. Figure 1-1 estimates an average difficulty of Class II+ to III−, and a maximum difficulty of Class III to III+ for the Grande Ronde. This compares reasonably well with the actual observed difficulty of the Grande Ronde, as shown in Table 1-2.

Even this oversimplified model using only flow and gradient thus gives a reasonable estimate of river difficulty. It should be used only as a guide, of course, not as an infallible rating technique. It is important to note that Figure 1-1 only applies well to rivers with a fairly uniform gradient.

For some rivers, notably pool and drop rivers (see Glossary), this figure works very poorly. We know of one river that drops about 50 ft./mi. through a 1-mile section and has an average flow of about 900 c.f.s. According to the figure, this section of river should be about IV− in difficulty. In fact, it has five 10-ft., quite unrunnable waterfalls connected by pools.

Another example of a river to which Figure 1-1 does not apply is the Rogue River in Oregon (Tour 1). Its average gradient of 13 ft./mi. and the recommended flow range of 800–2,500 c.f.s. would indicate a difficulty of Class I according to Figure 1-1. But the rather extreme pool and drop nature of the Rogue leads to an actual difficulty between Class II and Class IV. As the character of rivers which you are examining goes from the extreme of even gradient to the extreme of pool and drop, Figure 1-1 becomes less and less helpful. We will make a few suggestions about ways you might use to detect a pool and drop character when we discuss gradient information in Appendix C.

Table 1-2 ***Expected and Observed Difficulty of the Grande Ronde River from Figure 1-1 and Actual Running***

	First 8 mi.		*Whole river*	
	(model)	*(observed)*	*(model)*	*(observed)*
1,500 c.f.s.	II	II+	II	II+
4,000 c.f.s.	III to III+	II+ to III−	II+ to III−	II+ to III−

Generalizations to be made about river difficulty from Figure 1-1 are as follows:

1. At higher flows, 5,000–10,000 c.f.s., even a rather small gradient, 15–25 ft./mi., can produce awesome difficulty.
2. At lower flows, under 1,000 c.f.s., a substantially larger gradient, 30–50 ft./mi. may be manageable.

At this point you have an idea of how to rate the difficulty of rivers from observation, and some idea of the meaning of the numerical ratings. Also, you know that you need information about flow and gradient to predict river difficulty in advance. In Appendix C we discuss both how to get these data and what to do with them. This information will be very useful to people who wish to run rivers of unknown difficulty.

TWO

The River Difficulty—Subjective Evaluation

A common source of river evaluations you may wish to use in trip planning is subjective evaluation by other boaters, fishermen, or local residents. For you as the "buyer" of such information, we recommend: Caveat Emptor. All subjective evaluations have to be treated with extreme caution. Blind faith in a verbal or written river description can be fatal. Even if the information is unusually accurate, log jams, rock slides, and record high flows can change a river beyond recognition, introducing new dangers or eliminating old ones. That is, your judgment is needed, too. And if you feel incapable of making good judgments on the river, perhaps you don't belong there without an outfitter.

Subjective evaluations of river difficulty may come from professional or amateur river runners (including passengers), from written guides, or from local residents. Let's look at some techniques for evaluating the evaluations. How reliable is the evaluation which you are getting from your subjective source?

Evaluations by River Runners

Professional river runners (outfitters) seem to vary widely in their attitudes toward amateurs who request river information and evaluation from them. Some professionals willingly and generously give rather detailed information about a river. The information from these people may be invaluable as it may be based on years of experience on the particular river at a wide range of water levels.

Other outfitters may actively discourage you from running the river, with the following reasons:

1. Many incompetent groups have gotten into serious trouble on the river and, as far as the outfitter knows, your group is also incompetent.

2. The river is "too difficult to run without a guide," according to the outfitter. You must be prepared to judge whether this comment is sincere or self-serving.

3. "This is our river. Stay off it." In the occasional cases when such hostile attitudes are expressed by professionals, the reason may be fear for their business or something inexplicable.

A few rather seedy types have even been known to give misleading or just plain wrong information about areas on the river that they run regularly and know thoroughly.

In all fairness to outfitters, we have had a number of rewarding and informative contacts with them. For example, we had the good fortune to talk to a local guide about Section I of the Owyhee River (Tour 8) just before we ran it for the first time.

Figure 2-1 Subjective evaluation—drift boat in Wild Sheep Creek Rapids, Hell's Canyon, Snake River, Oregon

His rather concise advice was, "You may want to carry five or six times." We carried five times!

One point about which you should be very wary, however, even with well-intentioned and helpful outfitters, is the gross difference between boats which amateur and commercial river runners use. Huge waves look a little different to an outfitter in his twenty-man raft than they do to you in a six-man raft or single kayak. Always inquire about the boats which the outfitter has used on the river so that you can guess whether his evaluation means anything for your craft.

You may be able to get information which is more directly applicable to your trip from other amateurs who have run the river. The quality of information from this source ranges, in our experience, from precise, relevant, and interesting to nearly disastrous.

When you try to get information from amateurs about a river which they have run, you will be faced with two major subjective problems. The first problem hinges on the competence and previous experience of your informant. If the river was substantially harder than your informant's group was competent to run, you may be treated to some choice horror stories about the river. Similarly, even competent boaters, thoroughly experienced on tortuous, intense, but small, Class IV rivers may be appalled at the size and ferocity of Class IV hydraulics on a big river. This effect works the other way, too. "Big water" boaters sometimes have great difficulty on small, busy rivers.

The second subjective problem which you have to face is memory. How well does the person remember the particular river which he is describing to you? Did he take written notes? Two people with whom we have toured come to mind as examples. Both are very competent boaters and both have extensive river experience. From one of these people a river description is minutely detailed and highly accurate, including the placement of obstacles in each major rapids. From the other person, you get a very vague and at times incorrect description.

How can you evaluate subjective river descriptions with one or both of these problems inherent in them? A good means of evaluation is to ask the right questions. Some of the questions which we have found useful are given below.

1. When did you run the river (dates) and what was the flow? This question should give you information about flow, either directly or through U.S. Geological Survey historical records (see Appendix D).
2. Where were the most difficult sections, why were they difficult (difficult water, log jams, etc.), and how long and difficult were these sections? If you can pinpoint the locations of the trouble spots with this question, you will have a head start on your further investigation of the river.
3. Were all the difficult sections visible far enough in advance that you could get to shore easily? Blind rapids are well-known disaster areas. An example of this type of rapids is China Rapids on the Lower Canyon of the Salmon (Tour 7), where some friends of ours lost a boat by recognizing the rapids only after it was too late to get to the proper side.
4. What kind of boats were you using? The river difficulties that are most troublesome for rafters and drift boaters (such as rock gardens) are sometimes trivial for kayaks (and vice versa).
5. You may find a polite inquiry about the person's previous experience very useful to assess the reliability of his information. A direct comparison to local rivers is useful in assessing the person's experience.

Your purpose in asking these questions, as well as others that may occur to you, is to get reliable information, not just random anecdotes.

Yet another group of river runners from whom you may be able to get information is passengers on commercially outfitted trips. If these people are river runners in their own right, their evaluation of the river difficulty may be useful to you. If the people have run few or no rivers before their trip on your river, you may still be able to extract some information by asking whether the passengers walked around any rapids while the boats were lined or run empty through the rapids. This may allow you to pinpoint the location of those rapids which the commercial groups consider difficult or dangerous. This information may be about all that you can get from an inexperienced passenger and it certainly may be all the information you can trust from this source.

Written River Guides

Written guides to a river tour seem to be at least as variable in quality as verbal reports. You will want to look for a number of items in a written map or guide to a river tour, including ours.

1. Are access points to the river listed in sufficient detail, including road conditions and type of vehicle needed, to tell you how to get to the put-in and from the take-out?
2. Are the length of the trip, average gradient or difficulty, gradient or difficulty of the steepest section, and approximate duration of the trip in days given?
3. Has the writer of the guide run the river more than once? This is a particularly important question for several reasons. First, we have found that a river seems more difficult the first time we run it, succeeding runs give a much clearer and more realistic perspective. Second, a run at only one water level can be very misleading. The difficulty of rapids does change with flow; some get easier at higher flows while others become more difficult. For example, Plowshare Rapids on the Rogue River (Tour 1) might well escape your notice at 900 c.f.s., while at 2,000 c.f.s. it is relatively challenging.

4. Is a range of water levels stated, as well as their source, for which the guide is valid? Such a range of levels is extremely useful if you want some flexibility in your vacation planning.

5. Is the approximate time of year stated at which the recommended flows occur?

6. Is there a description of landmarks which can be used for recognition of the major rapids?

7. Is any comment made about the suitability of various boats for the river at the recommended flows?

8. Last but really most important, is the difficulty of the most major rapids given on a clearly stated rating scale? Of course, this should also include comments about the change in difficulty with changes in flow if appropriate.

Outsiders' Evaluation

The most common other source of river evaluation is local residents, fishermen, etc. Local residents along a river often have horror stories about "the falls" or about a party that was nearly killed trying to run the river. Treat these tales with sceptical respect. Note the location of the disaster area and form your own judgment when you get there. We have had several experiences where "the falls" turned out to be 3-ft. drops of Class II difficulty. The locals are sometimes correct, however. We have also seen parties that were so incompetent that they could nearly have been killed on a lake on a calm day. The problem that faces you is that you simply know nothing about the validity of outsiders' evaluation.

To get information that you believe is valid you must evaluate critically. We have given you some tools that have been useful to us in critical evaluation of river information. A bit of ingenuity and flexibility on your part will suggest other tools as well.

THREE

The Party

In some respects the party involved in the whitewater tour is the most important single ingredient. The success of the tour will depend directly on the competence of the party, and the enjoyment of the trip will depend largely on the personalities and compatibility of the party members. Let's look at the party first from the viewpoint of skill, then compatibility, size, financial responsibility, and last from the viewpoint of leadership.

Boating and Related Skills

A technique which we have found very useful to determine whether a boater is sufficiently skillful and competent to join a specific whitewater tour is simply to class the boater on a I to VI scale related to the river scale. Presumably, a Class III boater should be able to handle a day trip or a tour on a class II+ river or on an easy Class III river without undue difficulty. We use a slightly different basis for evaluating people in slalom canoes and kayaks than we do for people with rafts or drift boats.

Boater's Skill Classification, Slalom Kayak and Slalom Canoe

Class I:
Capable of getting into and out of boat easily. Can paddle effectively forward and backward in a straight line and can do elementary turns. Has practiced getting out of overturned boat with spray skirt on. Knows how to rescue himself and his boat in case of a tipover.

Class II:
In addition to the above techniques, has practiced both upstream and downstream ferry technique. Can backpaddle effectively. Can do low braces and low brace turns. Has some successful experience on Class I+ rapids.

Class III:
In addition to the above techniques, he can do high braces and high brace turns, draw strokes, and eskimo roll. Should have practiced eddy turns, and upstream and downstream ferries in heavy currents. Should have demonstrated ability to read and to run, successfully, Class II+ water. Should be able to aid in rescues in Class II water.

Class IV:
In addition to above, should be able to eskimo roll reliably in turbulent water. In general, has excellent control of his boat in turbulent water. Has considerable experience in reading water from his boat and running successfully Class III+ water. Should be able to carry out a rescue in Class III water.

Class V (Equally applicable to all boats):
These boaters generally have superb control of their boats in very turbulent water, highly panic-resistant personalities, and

previously demonstrated good judgment of whitewater hazards. They are willing to take necessary precautions to avoid accidents. Generally, Class V boaters run in thoroughly competent teams and are capable of carrying out team rescues on Class IV water.

Boater's Skill Classification, Rafts and Drift Boats

Class I:
Capable of getting boat into the water at the river (assembling raft frame, etc.). Should be able to coordinate strokes to turn the boat in the intended direction.

Class II:
In addition, should have practiced rowing the boat in moving water. Should have at least some previous water reading practice. (Should not run rocky Class II without previous Class II experience.)

Class III:
Should be able to read water and should have reasonably good control of back-ferrying and holding in turbulent water. Should have substantial Class II experience.

Class IV:
Should be able to read water accurately and quickly from the boat, should have very precise control of his boat orientation and, in addition, should have good resistance to panic in tense whitewater situations. Should have a substantial amount of Class III experience, including experience in rescue.

Along with boating skill, a certain amount of swimming skill is necessary if you are going on a whitewater tour. It is not necessary to be an Olympic swimmer because it is nearly impossible to swim with Olympic form in whitewater. (In fact, it is nearly impossible to swim at all!) What is required in whitewater is a minimal level of swimming ability, a good life jacket (see Chapter 5), and a great deal of resistance to panic. A swimming test which we have found successful to weed out the potential problem people is five minutes immersion in 8 ft. or so of water in full clothes and shoes with the person swimming 50 yds. and demonstrating that he can do side stroke (useful for boat rescue). We quite unexpectedly eliminated two of the best boaters from one group in which we used this test. They were unable to stay immersed for five minutes without severe emotional stress. We were, of course, prepared to fish those being tested out of the drink at the first sign of a problem.

Outdoor and Related Skills

If boating ability alone were the criterion for a whitewater touring party, life would be much simpler for the leader of the party. However, if you want to lead an enjoyable trip, you will want to have some people in the party who have previous outdoor experience and some outdoor skills. Will there be several people on the tour who are competent to lead hikes, particularly if they involve nontechnical rock-climbing or difficult route-finding? Are there any other people in the party who could lead on the river if the leader were incapacitated? Are the individual members of the party, in terms of both physical condition and outdoor experience, capable of walking back to civilization should this prove necessary? Do the party members have camping experience in weather conditions comparable to the conditions which you expect? Are the party members sufficiently experienced at camping to adapt their equipment and techniques to much worse weather than expected? Is any member's equipment habitually in such poor repair that he will be a liability to the rest of the party on an extended trip? Such questions about the outdoor skills of the party members can become quite important to the strength of the party and its morale on an extended tour.

The importance of outdoor skills to a successful tour was etched in our memories by a six-day trip on the River of No Return section of the Salmon River in Idaho. We started the trip in the second week of August in 1968. Normally the weather in this area in August is clear and warm or even hot with, at most, occasional thundershowers. The various members of the group, all experienced outdoor enthusiasts, had all brought at least partial wet suits, sleeping bags, ponchos, and other suitable equipment. However, at the put-in, the temperature was about 95°F and the water warm. As a result, wetsuits were left behind and several members of the group even elected to experiment with "space blankets" in place of their sleeping bags. We had barely left the cars behind when the weather turned grim. For the next six days, we had heavy, nearly continuous rain (the most August rain in 55 years), temperatures in the 50's, and heavy wind much of the time. Furthermore, the river temperature dropped substantially from the melt coming from the fresh snow in the higher areas surrounding the river. The group came through with no more than minor discomfort, however, because they could start fires with wet wood, they could put up adequate rain shelters with ponchos and tarps, and because they were careful to keep essential equipment dry or to dry it at every opportunity. A group that was weak in outdoor skills might well have had a disaster result from such a poor decision at the put-in.

From this experience we did learn several things which you may note in Chapter 6. It is an excellent idea to take a paddling jacket or wetsuit jacket even on the most benign summer tours and if you do insist on carrying a space blanket, plan to reserve it for emergency use. Equip yourself for worse weather than you hope you will have.

We have found that some of the strongest contributors to the success of whitewater tours have been mediocre boaters who have had extensive backgrounds in mountaineering or rock-climbing, backpacking, and similar outdoor activities that require self-reliance. This comment does not suggest, however, that Class II boaters with a great deal of camping skill should be taken on Class IV tours.

Compatibility

A frequent problem that arises, not only on whitewater tours, but also during other extended outdoor activities which involve living in close proximity, is a clash of personalities among the members of the party. The presence of several strong and mutually antagonistic personalities may spell disaster for the morale of the group. The people in the touring group are going to be, figuratively, roommates for the three or four to ten days they are on the river. We find ourselves asking a number of questions about each individual with whom we plan to tour.

Does the person have a personality which is objectionable to many people? If so, will the other people on this particular tour get along with him?

Does the person have slovenly personal habits? Friction may arise between fastidious and slovenly people on extended trips.

Is the person highly emotional or quite easygoing? Will he become irritated at minor problems or inconveniences?

Does the person react calmly and intelligently in an emergency or does he panic or freeze? This question is usually very difficult but also very important to try to answer.

Does the person willingly share the work load, for example, cooking and gathering firewood?

Is the person insistent about doing his own thing without regard for the group? Does he, for example, go on playing in a rapids rather than helping with a rescue?

Does he habitually keep the rest of the party waiting?

Is he flexible in adapting to new plans or must he go to a certain campsite at a certain time because that was scheduled?

Clearly any one person may be strong on some of these points and weak on others. The relative importance of the questions will vary from person to person, too. With some additions of your own perhaps, the questions are a starting point for assembling a compatible as well as competent party.

A note of caution should be added here about party members and their compatibility. Major problems may occur with members of parties, spouses and children particularly, who are dragged along on a trip. We have observed, for example, several cases of hysteria among such unwilling victims. Be sure that these people are fully aware of the hazards and potential problems of the trip and that they seem to be compatible with the group too.

Once the group is selected there is little that you can do to change personal habits. You can help ensure an enjoyable trip by making very sure that all members of the group understand the overall plan of the trip.

Suppose you wish to spend five days on a 45-mile section of river to allow a great deal of time for fishing. The person who prefers to paddle 25 miles each day may be bitterly unhappy with this plan. Make it clear to each person what the average daily travel distance will be and by all means have the whole party in agreement about this point.

Each person should be aware of and in agreement with the emphasis of the trip, for example, that the trip is primarily a whitewater run with lots of time to play, or perhaps that the trip is a way to get into a prime rock-collecting or Indian relic area and the whitewater itself is secondary. Each person in the party should be aware of the possible whitewater difficulty, portages, and hazards from snakes, insects, or animals.

Finally, each person should be aware of his individual responsibility for providing some group equipment items, such as a repair kit or spare paddle, or a certain number of meals for the group and he should also be willing to accept his share of the group labor in cooking, dishwashing, etc.

Party Size

An often overlooked factor that is quite important in determining the nature of any wilderness experience is the size of the party. It is often blindly assumed that the more the merrier. A little experience with both large and small parties points out significant differences in the type of wilderness experience possible.

With a large party (fifteen or more), much of the wilderness aspect is lost; on the river or in camp, you often feel surrounded by a milling mob, and quiet contemplation of nature becomes very difficult. This is one reason that we avoid guided tours. The reasonably large party (eleven to fifteen) does, however, offer several advantages. First, the great variety of interests and personalities can provide a rewarding social experience. Second, the environmental impact per person is less since there are fewer latrines and campfires than for several, smaller parties. Nevertheless, the total impact on the environment is greater for larger parties due to more trampling of grass, etc., before it has time to recover. A final advantage: if a boat is irretrievably lost, it is easier for a large party to absorb the extra people and gear.

The small party (eight or fewer) offers a number of advantages. First, as already mentioned, it has less total impact on the environment than a large group has. Furthermore, it can co-exist in greater harmony with the environment, and its members will have more opportunity to observe wildlife, practice solitary fishing, etc.

Because it can use small campsites, a small party will have a greater choice of campsites than a larger party. Furthermore, organization in camp is much simpler with a small party. (The time it takes to get on the river in the morning seems to be directly proportional to group size.) On the river, it is easier to maintain contact with the entire membership of a small party, thus greatly increasing safety. Finally, flexibility increases as the size of the party decreases, whether it is a change in time of the trip due to high water, or a decision to camp early because someone is tired.

Our own personal preference is for a party size of four to six. The ideal party size for you will depend on which of these factors are most important to you.

Costs

An item of substantial importance to people on the tour is cost. Two categories of cost, normal and unplanned, should be considered, negotiated, and agreed on before the trip leaves home. Failure to discuss these items and agree beforehand often leads to bitterness and dissension in the party at a later time.

The first category, normal costs, includes transportation to and from the river, shuttle costs, and food costs, and may be managed in several ways:

1. Transportation to and from the river can be assessed at from 1¢ to 10¢ per passenger per mile, with the driver paying for all gas, oil, and routine maintenance from this money. Another alternative which we have found useful is to have the passengers, if there are several, divide the cost of gas and oil while the driver absorbs the cost of wear and tear, tires, and routine maintenance. There are many other possible techniques, but for all of them the principal criterion is that driver and passengers believe that the arrangement is equitable to all.

2. Shuttle costs will be widely variable depending primarily on whether you do your own shuttle or hire someone to do

it. We usually consider the shuttle costs as a group expense unless each driver is arranging to hire a shuttle driver for his car, in which case the passengers and driver work out the details. If this is a group expense, then we usually divide equally the cost of a shuttle driver and compensation for any extra mileage which cars accumulate because they are involved in the shuttle.

3. Food costs and their equitable division may be very readily managed by assigning each person in the group responsibility for a suitable number of meals for the whole group. For example, if six persons are going on a six-day tour, each person will furnish one day of food for six people. This technique not only assesses the costs equitably, but also distributes the labor of food planning and often results in some interesting new ideas for meals.

The second category of cost is unplanned cost arising from a rescue operation, from repairs to a vehicle, or from a car accident.

1. We have usually agreed in touring groups to have each person responsible for his own rescue costs. If someone is stricken with appendicitis and requires rescue by helicopter, he is expected to be responsible for its cost. The specter of high rescue cost may instill caution in even the most reckless individuals.
2. For vehicle repair, we hold the owner financially responsible for wear and tear repairs, such as fuel pump failure. A more difficult problem arises when a car is damaged in shuttle driving, particularly on back roads. Many mufflers have been lost and gas tanks punctured on shuttles. Our usual question here is whether the driver was taking reasonable care, a very subjective appraisal. If so, we consider this a group expense.

Similarly, in the case of an auto accident, all the passengers and owner are expected, if necessary, to pay their shares of the deductible amount on the insurance if the driver of their car was not at fault.

These methods have worked reasonably well for us. It is not important whether you adopt these particular ways of assigning costs to each member or not. What is important is that you agree beforehand on the possible liabilities of the drivers and others as assessed by some plan, formal or informal.

Leadership

A whitewater touring party is going to need leadership in three rather separate periods in its tour: in the planning period, on the smoothly running trip, and in case of emergency. The demands upon the leaders and qualifications for leadership will be markedly different for each period.

In the planning stage of a tour the leadership demands may be on one individual or on several persons. These demands will include selection of the river and the party for that river or vice versa; informing the members of their responsibilities and contributions to the group; picking a time at which to depart on the trip, with enough leeway to allow for changing water conditions; and arranging a shuttle if this is necessary. The leader at this stage need not be the best boater in the party, although he often is. If the leader does his work well at this stage, a party of adequate overall strength, reasonably similar purpose, and fair degree of compatibility will put in on the river.

Once on the river, the leadership may change to other hands depending on the size and composition of the party. With a minimum size of three persons, a party may find that no formal leader is necessary. Generally, with a party of six or more, a more formally designated leader is usually necessary.

When the trip is running smoothly, the main duties of the leader will fall primarily into two categories: river safety and pacing.

River safety techniques, such as appointing a lead, second, and sweep boater and keeping the party together, are discussed more fully in Chapters 10 and 11. Pacing the trip is quite an important function for a leader. The party will want to cover an average of, say, 10 to 20 miles per day on the trip. Flexibility is the keynote in leadership. For example, why paddle hard for 3 hours to cover your 15 miles for the day, passing hurriedly by Indian caves or rock-hunting areas? This kind of exercise may leave the party members cooking in the sun all afternoon in camp. On the other hand, spending all day at one point of interest may leave you with either a moonlight run or a 30-mile day tomorrow. A watch, repugnant though it may be to vacationers, is very useful to avoid these problems. If you know how far you have left to go for the day and how many hours of daylight are left, you will know how fast to push the group. We usually try to get to a camp 1 to 1½ hours before dark, at the latest. This allows a margin of safety for unexpected problems. This period of leadership is usually the easiest of the three.

The most difficult task of leadership occurs during an emergency, either one of a morale-shattering nature such as an unexpected waterfall, or one which requires serious reorganization of the trip such as serious illness or broken bones or boats. The first type of emergency, a severe unexpected river difficulty, is usually less severe physically than psychologically. The most important assets a leader can possess to deal with this type of problem are cautious optimism and practical problem-solving ability. The leader must keep the morale of the group to a functioning level with optimism, but at the same time must retain his credibility. In short, a cheery idiot approach often doesn't work. Actual leadership in crises often is transferred to one of the experienced outdoor people, even though he may be the poorest boater.

Leadership may change in the medical emergency, too. On river trips there are usually only three medical emergencies that require instant action—drowning, sunstroke, and exposure. For their treatment see Wilkerson's book *Medicine for Mountaineering* (mentioned in Appendix D.3). Nearly all the other medical emergencies which are repairable will allow several minutes of careful thought and discussion to avoid damaging treatments. A key point in handling a medical emergency is to minimize panic, either of the victim or, more commonly, of the other party members. Panic and resulting hysteria by someone other than the victim may require harsh words, a slap in the face, or having another party member lead the person away from the victim to control the effect of the display on the victim. If the victim is panic-stricken and his injuries allow tranquilizers to be used, they may prove helpful. For further information, we strongly recommend that you read and understand Wilkerson's book before going on extended tours.

Once the leader has done everything possible for the victim, he must decide whether, and to what extent, the trip plans will be modified. To make this decision, he will need to know both the nature and severity of the victim's injury. If you are uncertain, assume the worst. A life may hang on the leader's decision at this point. He should try to get as much objective and informed opinion from the group as possible and judge the best course of action on the basis of this information. He should try to get concurrence of the group in his decision, not just to flatter his ego, but because the party will be involved in the rescue.

Several questions to be answered by the leader and group are:

1. Can the victim be moved? If not, where can a rescue plane, helicopter, or other vehicle be reached?
2. If the victim can be moved, can he walk out or be taken out in a boat?
3. Would a stay of several days be helpful to the victim (e.g., in the case of flu), and, if so, is it feasible in terms of food supply?

In particular, if the victim can't be moved, the leader will have to decide how many persons will go for help (preferably two), who will go, and whether they will walk or go by river. Clearly, the leader must be sure that the persons going for help are likely to succeed without requiring rescue themselves, that they know the nature of the injury, and that they are able to describe the location of the party. Although this may seem obvious to you, the history of back country rescue operations is rich with examples of party members going for help and getting lost or injured themselves or being unable to describe the victim's injury.

The leader also must be sure that those staying with the victim have been instructed in ways to keep the victim comfortable and in what to do if his condition deteriorates. In the case of the broken boat, many of the same kinds of questions must be asked. For example, can the victim, in this case the boat, be repaired in a length of time for which the food supply is sufficient?

This awesome set of responsibilities illustrates the depth of experience and common sense required of a leader. Lest you begin to worry that every trip ends in a major emergency, we should mention that emergencies happen very rarely on well-planned trips. Nevertheless it is worthwhile to ask yourself "What if?"

ABOVE: *Figure 4-1 Wooden drift boat and kayak*
BELOW: *Figure 4-2 Typical raft with frame and oars*

FOUR

Wildwater Boats

This chapter is sure to arouse the passion of advocates of each of the kinds of boat we will discuss. Our comments are based on our own use of the boats and on observation of each of these types on wildwater rivers. Basic boat types will be distinguished on the basis of predominant technique of whitewater use, contrasting drift boats, including rafts, with paddle-powered boats, including canoes and kayaks.

Drift Boats

Rigid drift boats, such as the one shown in Figure 4-1, are typically 12 to 16 ft. long, about 5 to 6 ft. across the widest point, and heavily rockered. The rocker, or curvature along the bottom from bow to stern, allows quick turning of the boat. Typical prices for these boats range from $150 to $450 in plywood or $500 to $950 in aluminum, depending on size and luxury. The boats are virtually always rowed or run with a motor.

Rubber rafts, the other major drift boat class, for reasonable private whitewater use range from 8 to 14 ft. in length and from 5 to 8 ft. in width. They cost from $50 to $700, with the price determined by quality and size. A typical raft, with frame and oars, is shown in Figure 4-2. Rafts are sometimes paddled with canoe paddles by church groups out on a lark, but experienced whitewater boaters commonly row with oars attached to oarlocks set in a wooden frame which is attached to the boat. These rafts are occasionally fitted with a motor bracket so that a small outboard motor may be used.

The mode of operation in whitewater is similar for each of the various drift boats. The oarsman faces downstream at the top of a rapids and back-ferries (see Glossary) his boat to a position from which the current will take him down the rapids in a suitable channel. Generally obstacles in a rapids are avoided by rowing backward away from them. Forward acceleration of the boat is difficult with a rigid boat and nearly impossible with a raft.

Drift boats have many advantages. One major advantage of these boats is the good visibility of a rapids as you approach it. You can even stand up to look at a rapids before running it. The large size of the boats allows both more people and more goodies to be carried on a trip. Also, these boats do allow you to take nonboating passengers, and, in an emergency, to take out people who have wrecked their own boats on the river. Beware of the common tendency to overload drift boats. Conservative maximum loading of rigid boats is three persons with gear in a 16-ft. drift boat on easier rivers, and a maximum of two persons with gear on rivers of Class IV and above. For rafts, the typical 10-ft. raft, often called a six-man raft, is suitable for a maximum of three persons with gear on easier rivers and two persons with gear on more difficult rivers. Three to four persons with gear can be carried by 14-ft. rafts on reasonably difficult rivers. It is possible to fish from either rigid boats or rafts, a near impossibility from the paddle-

Figure 4-3 Raft in use at Halfmile Rapids, Owyhee River, Oregon (Tour 8)

powered boats if they are enclosed. Finally rigid drift boats but not rafts remain relatively dry, a real advantage in cold weather!

Disadvantages of drift boats are also numerous. These boats are heavy and awkward to transport to the river and to carry during portage. Second, these boats allow you only one opportunity to run a rapids, whereas the paddle-powered boats allow you to play in a rapids for hours if you wish. Third, the drift boats are horribly sensitive to upstream winds and lack of current, requiring backbreaking work to keep them moving downstream. In addition, the wooden boat is easily broken on impact with rocks, although aluminum boats are less so and the raft is relatively insensitive to this danger.

Paddle-Powered Boats

Canoes as discussed here are decked whitewater canoes, specifically C-1's and C-2's to use slalom racing designations for one-man and two-man canoes. If you wish to take open, undecked canoes on whitewater, that is up to you, but we don't recommend them. We used open canoes for six years on whitewater and believe that these boats are a poor choice for whitewater.

One-man, or C-1, canoes are excellent whitewater boats in many respects. A typical C-1 is 13 ft. long and 27 to 31 in. wide. Typical cost ranges from $175 to $300. A 31-in.-wide boat is shown in Figure 4-5. The usual construction uses glass-reinforced plastic (fiberglass). C-1 canoes combine high buoyancy and reasonable visibility with excellent maneuverability. The boats can carry a substantial amount of gear, although not as much as drift boats. These boats would be ideal single touring boats but for three disadvantages: 1) the high profile and maneuverablity make the boats damnably wind sensitive; 2) learning to use them well is very demanding; and 3) the single-bladed paddle used with these

Figure 4-4 C-1 in use on Lower Salmon (Tour 7)

ABOVE: *Figure 4-5 C-1 (right) and K-1*
RIGHT: *Figure 4-6 C-2 (left) and K-1*

boats makes playing in rivers that have fast currents brutal work. Also, the boats are uncomfortable for some people.

The two-man, or C-2 canoe, should be modified for touring by adding a center cockpit, both to make packing gear easier and to allow the option of paddling the boat single. Modified C-2's range from 15 to 17 ft. in length and from 31 to 37 in. in width. A C-2 designed primarily for wildwater touring is shown in Figure 4-6. The typical cost of these boats is $225 to $450. Glass-reinforced plastic is the most common construction material. These boats are highly maneuverable, have large volume, good visibility, particularly for the bowman, and for their size remarkably little sensitivity to wind. In our opinion, the C-2 is potentially the best overall touring boat available. Unfortunately two competent paddlers are required to make full use of the potential of a C-2. This requirement has rarely been met in our touring experience with

C-2 teams. C-2's are also notably uncomfortable on extended trips.

Kayaks, specifically K-1 whitewater kayaks as discussed here, are one-man boats which have been designed for slalom racing. Most of the K-2's, or two-man kayaks, available in the Western Hemisphere are not, in fact, whitewater touring boats, but flat-water touring boats. K-1's as whitewater touring boats have several distinctive features; they are small (13 ft. long, 24 in. wide), lightweight (25–40 lbs.), and relatively inexpensive ($150 to $275). The usual construction material for kayaks is fiberglass, although some folding K-1's made from impregnated cloth and wooden frame are still used. A typical K-1 is shown in Figure 4-6. Kayaks have a number of advantages including high maneuverability, very slight wind sensitivity, minimal work in paddling

either upstream or downstream, and the ease with which they may be transported or portaged. Countering these advantages are a few negative features: poor visibility, poor stability, very limited storage space, and an interesting tendency to "submarine," or go under water in large waves. We have also found that persons who weigh more than 200 lbs. have a great deal of trouble using a K-1 as a touring boat. No severe limitation of this sort exists with the other boats we have discussed.

Paddle-powered boats have no single method of running rapids. They may be run forward, backward, broadside, or even upside down through rapids. In the hands of skilled paddlers, the boats have nearly unbelievable maneuverability compared to rafts. These boats have another distinct difference from drift boats in their capability to be rolled up, boater inside, after a tipover; a physically impossible task with a drift boat. In all fairness, you should

Figure 4-7 C-2 in use at unnamed rapids on Lower Salmon (Tour 7)

be aware that the success of an attempt to eskimo roll a canoe or kayak depends on the skill of the paddler rather than some magical property of the boat and that the paddlers of canoes and kayaks have ample opportunity to use their rolls. (Drift boats are much more stable.)

Inflatable Kayaks and Canoes

These boats are a recent innovation on whitewater rivers. They are rather wide, flat-bottomed, inflatable boats with open cockpits and are usually paddled with a double paddle. Although our initial reactions to these boats were negative, we have since used them on the Grande Ronde River (Tour 2) and seen them on several wildwater rivers of substantial difficulty. We now believe that they are excellent wildwater boats for beginners. The flat bottom and width (about 3 ft. for a 10- to 11-ft. long boat) give the

boat excellent stability. Further, we have found that the boats are relatively maneuverable.

We have one observation about the use of these boats on wildwater, particularly for wildwater touring. In common with other small, undecked boats, the inflatable kayaks and canoes swamp easily in heavy rapids. When the boat swamps, it becomes nearly unmanageable—potentially a very dangerous situation in continuous rapids.

This type of boat may serve a valuable safety role as a spare in kayak or canoe parties. The boats are fairly light (15–20 lbs.), fairly inexpensive ($80–$100), and could be paddled out by persons who had lost or destroyed their own boats.

A comparison of the important features of the various wildwater boats is given in Table 4-1. Although there may be some argument about the choice of adjectives in the Table, the ordering of these boats in the various categories conforms well not only to our own opinions but also to the opinions of a few others who have had extensive experience with all of these craft.

It is important to remember when reading Table 4-1 that there is no best whitewater boat. The best boat to use on a whitewater tour is the one that suits your needs and interests in the best way. With the exception of the inflatable kayaks, the boats we have listed are all proven whitewater boats, which have been used on all the tours in the guide section and which, in the hands of an expert who not only knows his own boat but understands rivers, can be run successfully on some incredibly difficult rapids.

Specific Boat Recommendations for Wildwater Touring

This section is presented only with considerable hesitation. First, we should comment that we have no financial or other interest in any of the boats we are recommending. The recommendations are based on either experience or observation of the boats on whitewater rivers. By observation the boats are functional for touring, and by test, they are suitably constructed to handle whitewater. The list is not comprehensive and makes no attempt to be.

Kayak:	Lettman "Olymp" series HIPP "Vector" Old Town "Slalom Kayak" Hahn "Augsburg" (Easy Rider)
C-1:	Lettman "Mark II" Hahn "Munich" (Easy Rider) These are both the new, narrow (70 cm.) boats. An older C-1, the Bone, is available via private molds in many areas of the country and is excellent for touring.
C-2:	Either Lettman or Hahn C-2's are usable for touring if modified by addition of a center cockpit. For long trips, the Easy Rider Touring C-2 is a good though expensive choice.
Raft:	The Avon (Redshank, Redseal, etc.) series are premium rafts at premium prices. Inflatable Boats Unlimited makes quite sturdy larger rafts. For lower-priced rafts, World Famous, a Japanese import, seems to be fairly sturdy.
Wooden drift boat:	Eastside Boats, "McKenzie" (available in 12 to 16 ft. lengths). This particular design is quite similar to the design of the boat in Figure 2-1.
Aluminum drift boat:	Alumaweld Boats, Inc., "McKenzie" (12- to 16-ft. boats available).

In addition to these rather high-priced sources of boats, you may wish to investigate building your own. This is an entirely

Table 4-1 *Comparative Features of Wildwater Boats*

	K-1	*C-1*	*C-2*
Length, ft.	13	13	15–17
Width, ft.	2	2½	2½–3
Weight, lbs.	30–45	35–50	50–80
Is trailer required?	no	no	no
Can passengers be carried?	no	no	only on very easy rivers
Required maintenance	none	none	none
Cost (new)	$150–$300	$200–$300	$225–$450
Load capacity	small	medium	medium (for two people)
Wind sensitivity	slight	severe	moderate
Maneuverability	very good	excellent	excellent
Ease of acceleration	excellent	moderate	very good
Ease of upstream or cross-stream use	excellent	poor upstream good cross-stream	excellent
Stability	poor	slightly better than C-2	fair
Visibility of rapids from above	miserable	fair	medium
Skill required in Class III water at:			
1) Water reading	moderate	a little more than with K-1	a little more than with K-1
2) Boat control	considerable	considerable	considerable

Raft	*Wooden drift boat*	*Aluminum drift boat*	*Inflatable canoes and kayaks*
8–14	12–16	13–16	8–11
6–8	5–6	5–6	2½–3
30–105	140–350	170–250	12–20
no	yes	yes	no
yes	yes	yes	not with much safety
slight	at least yearly	none	slight
$70–$800	$200–$500	$500–$950	$50–$100
medium-large	large	large	small
very severe	very severe	very severe	severe
poor	good	good	good
terrible	poor	poor	moderate
very poor	medium to poor	medium to poor	fair
very good	very good	very good	good
reasonably good	good	good	poor
slight (but some)	considerable	considerable	like raft
fair	considerable	considerable	fair

feasible, although time-consuming project. Kits or plans are available for some rigid drift boats and a large number of private rental molds are available for the fiberglass boats. To find out the location of molds and the addresses of their owners, write to the whitewater club (see Appendix E) nearest to your home. Often the mold owner will in self-defense give you instructions on construction of the boat. Boat building instructions for fiberglass boats are available in *Living Canoeing*, referred to in Appendix D.

Characteristics to Look for in Whitewater Touring Boats Before You Buy

You may have an opportunity to purchase boats other than the ones we have listed. The characteristics that you will wish to look for in whitewater touring boats, aside from the obvious requirements that they be leak-tight and built in a craftsmanlike fashion, are characteristics related to function. Specifically, you will wish to look for maneuverability, buoyancy, and convenience, which are design features, as well as strength or durability, which is primarily a construction feature.

Maneuverability

The prime design feature which determines maneuverability is rocker, or bow to stern curvature. On wooden drift boats this curvature is usually fairly severe; on rafts nonexistent. Paddle-powered boats have variable rocker; the rocker changes when the boat is leaned on its side. For all these boats except rafts make sure that the boat has some rocker, otherwise it will be a beast to turn. But you can have too much of a good thing. Some C-1's, in particular, have so much rocker that they seem to do nothing but turn even when an experienced boater paddles them. If possible, try the boat on flat water before you buy it to find out about maneuverability.

Buoyancy

From a practical viewpoint, buoyancy in whitewater is the ability of the bow of a boat to rise quickly after plunging down into turbulent water. This ability is determined by the rate at which the volume of the boat under water increases as the boat is driven down. A kayak with a long, narrow, needle-shaped nose will dive more deeply and rise much more slowly than a kayak with a blunt nose. Wooden drift boats are often flared severely from a small bottom to wide top (gunwale) to enhance their buoyancy. With kayaks and canoes, you will want to look for boats that retain their volume well out to the bow, unless you like to run with your boat under rather than on whitewater. In rafts, most of the buoyancy will come from the front air chamber, which should be larger in diameter than the side chambers.

Convenience

In the various drift boats, the key questions to ask are: Is there a convenient place to put gear as well as passengers and is there something to which gear or a frame can be tied? For the paddle-powered boats, the key questions are:

1. Does the boat fit you reasonably? (Kayaks and canoes should fit you like a glove.)
2. Are the size and shape of the boat, as well as the openings in it, particularly the seat back, cockpit, and bracing, both reasonable and large enough to put in the gear which you wish to carry? It's no fun if you need a hydraulic jack to get gear into a boat and even less fun to get it back out. In short, think about the uses to which you are going to put your boat before you lay out hard-earned bucks for it.

Durability

We should cast some doubt immediately on one prevalent notion. Heavier is not necessarily stronger in rigid boats. Although controlled experiments are nearly impossible to perform under whitewater conditions, a number of observations suggest that flexibility in a boat can offset heavy structure, i.e., thicker, more rigid structure, in a disaster situation. Sharp rocks have more tendency to punch through a rigid, heavy construction, while a thinner, more flexible construction bends around rocks and then returns to its original shape. Obviously, boats (except rafts) must be rigid enough so they don't behave like rubber bands in turbulent water. The main point we are making here is that a tank may not be the best choice for your whitewater use.

Tested and suitable constructions for whitewater use for the various boats are shown below. We give these as *guides, not as the only possible constructions.*

Wooden drift boats: Three-eighths-in. marine plywood bottom (sometimes with an additional 1/4-in. replaceable sole and sometimes fiberglass treated), 1/4-in. plywood sides, oak or mahogany bumper areas. These figures would be typical for the 14-ft. to 16-ft. boats.

Aluminum drift boats: 6061-T6 or 5052 alloy, at least 0.060 in. thick on sides and 0.080 in. thick on the bottom. Welded or riveted.

Rubber rafts: usually impregnated nylon with additional layer(s) around the boat to resist abrasion. The weight of the fabric for these boats will determine durability, assuming the boats are well-made. You normally choose the weight of fabric by the size of your bank account and the strength of your back.

Canoes and kayaks: usual construction of these is glass-reinforced plastic. Such boats are far more durable than boats with wooden frame and treated canvas covering. There is no single basic construction for these boats, but we will give several variations which have been well proven in whitewater use. These boats are most commonly made in two halves, top or deck and bottom or hull, and then joined internally.

If we code the fiber materials in the following way:

C = 10 oz./sq. yd. glass cloth
R = 24 oz./sq. yd. woven glass roving
M = $1\frac{1}{2}$ oz./sq. ft. glass mat

we could have the following laminations, where the code letters reading from left to right correspond to the laminations from the outside of the boat to the inside:

	Hull	*Deck*
K-1	CCR	CCC
	CCCC	CR
	CCRC	CM
	CMR	
	Seam is two or three layers of C.	
C-1	CCR	CCR
	CCCCC	CCCC
	CCMC	CMC
	CRR	CCC (light)
		CR (light)
	Seam is three or four layers of C.	
C-2	CCR	CCCC
	CCCCC	CMC
	CMRC	CCR
	CCRC	
	CRR	
	Seam is three or four layers of C.	

The outermost layer in the hull only is sometimes replaced with 4–5 oz./sq. yd. polypropylene cloth to give better abrasion resistance. The most commonly used plastic in the laminate is a polyester, either used directly or mixed with about 10 percent of an isophthalic (high impact) resin to give slightly better flexibility. Epoxy resins have been used successfully in these boats but tend to be expensive.

Plastic resins are made by many manufacturers and vary considerably in their properties. Since we have had success with randomly obtained varieties from plastics shops, we suspect that the choice of resin is not crucial to building a serviceable boat.

A word of warning: building kayaks and canoes requires a very low initial investment for professional fiberglass shops. As a result, large numbers of boats, "professionally built" by persons with no idea of the structural demands imposed by whitewater use, are totally unsuitable for such use. The boats are simply built by the most economical production techniques available. In particular, be wary of spray mat (i.e., chopped fiber) boats or boats made primarily of glass mat. Both of these construction materials seem to break very readily when a boat crunches down on a rock. We have noted this defect in a number of boats manufactured by so-called professional fiberglass shops. We have made construction recommendations involving mat in the preceding table because it is commonly used, although our own opinion is that little or no mat should be used in the main laminations of the hull and deck. This information may be helpful to you even if you don't choose to build a boat. In particular, before you buy a kayak or a canoe, demand to know what the construction is, in detail. If the retailer won't or can't tell you, don't buy the boat from him. This way you may avoid some of the lemons sometimes appearing on the market. With this chapter in mind, you should be able to make a rational decision about what type of boat you want for your whitewater tour, and you should also have some criteria (other than the pretty color) to use for selecting one craft within the type.

FIVE

Boating Accessories and Boat Repair

Once you have chosen the type of boat you wish to use, you will need to equip it properly for river use. Let's look at the accessory needs of the two classes of boats.

Drift Boats

For either rigid drift boats or for rafts with wooden frames, oars about 7–8 ft. long will be needed. (Remember that we are talking about rafts 14 ft. or shorter.) Normal availability usually dictates that you must choose between spruce and ash as the material for oars. Spruce oars are lightweight and pleasant to use, but are more prone to breakage than the heavier ash oars. Ash oars are a more sensible choice for extended touring. Make sure that you have at least one spare oar for easy trips or more for difficult or long trips. Rubber or nylon stops permanently mounted on the oars will prevent the oars from slipping through the oarlocks.

To use the oars, you will need oarlocks to fit the fittings or oar deals, in the gunwale, or frame, of the boat. Oarlocks are available in open U form or closed O form types. The closed form is favored by many drift boaters because its use precludes the possibility of an oar being lifted from the oarlock in the middle of a rapids. If possible, get solid cast bronze rather than potmetal oarlocks to avoid unpredictable breakage. At least two spare oarlocks should be carried on the tour for each boat. You may also want to carry either bailing wire or metal shower curtain rings to fasten the oarlock itself to the boat or frame. You will need pliers to do this, a must item in the drift boat equipment box.

For both rafts and rigid drift boats, a 25–30 ft. length of dacron or nylon rope can be permanently attached to the bow for mooring the boat. In addition, one or more 120-ft., 3/8-in. nylon climbing ropes should be carried for lining around rapids. For both rafts and rigid drift boats you will need either a foot-operated bilge pump or a plastic bucket to bail out water that splashes into the boat.

Raft frames are simple, do-it-yourself projects, unless you wish to build a baroque frame, the kind with hinges, etc., that requires many hours to assemble. The raft shown in Figure 4-2 is approximately 5 ft. × 10 ft. and the frame on it is about $4\frac{1}{2}$ ft. × $4\frac{1}{2}$ ft. The frame itself is made from 1 in. × 10 in. painted fir and the oarlocks are set in hardwood oak blocks about 6 in. high. The oar blocks are bolted (not screwed) to the frame. Plated 1/4-in. bolts and wing nuts are used to join the frame at the corners. This particular frame takes about 20 minutes to assemble at the river. A detailed view of the frame is shown in Figure 5-1. Some rafters use an old piece of rug under the frame to protect the raft from abrasion by the frame.

Six or eight 1/2-in.-diameter holes drilled in each of the boards of the frame will serve as convenient tie points for lashing your gear to the frame. In a raft, gear is tied to the frame or hung from it rather than placed directly on the floor. Placing gear on the floor will cause undue wear to the floor when the raft slides over rocks.

Each raft in your group should also have an air pump and a patching kit. The patching kit should have several large pieces of rubber and a half pint or more of contact cement. The patching kit supplied with most rafts is simply too small to do an extensive patch. The type of patching which may be required was illustrated on a trip on the Grande Ronde River (Tour 2) in 1967. The lead raft, landing hurriedly after another raft had tipped over, ran over a partially submerged fence post near shore. The 2-ft.-long tear that resulted had to be patched using the whole rubber seat of the boat as patching material. Fluke accidents of this sort occur surprisingly often even on easy rivers like the Grande Ronde.

Figure 5-1 Detailed view of raft frame

For wooden or metal drift boats the repair kit will be both heavy and bulky. Fortunately, these large boats can carry the necessary items quite easily.

For wooden boats, several $1\frac{1}{2}$ ft. × 2 ft. pieces of 1/4-in. marine plywood, bronze nails or brass screws (about 3/4 in. long), and caulking material can make a suitable patch. Either fiberglass auto body putty or roofing tar will serve as caulking compound. Patches below the waterline should be done from the inside to prevent loss of the patch by abrasion against rocks. The caulking compound will give a reasonably smooth, although ugly, exterior surface.

For repair of aluminum drift boats, several sheets of 1 ft. × $1\frac{1}{2}$ ft. of 6061-T6 aluminum (if you can't get this alloy, hardware store aluminum sheet will work) should be carried, as well as a supply of small rivets and a rivet set. Caulking materials are handy for patching metal boats also, since riveted patches done on the river seem to leak without caulking.

To repair either a wooden or a metal drift boat that has a major hole, cut a patch of material slightly larger than the hole, smear it with caulking material and lay it into the boat. Drill holes for screws or rivets and place these fasteners. Once the patch is in place, caulking material can be smeared onto the outside over the patched area to make the patch more watertight and to give it a smoother exterior surface.

For small breaks or holes, 2-in.-wide heating-duct tape (available in building supply stores) is excellent. If this tape is applied to a dry surface initially, adhesion is excellent and the material is very durable. To avoid cheap imitations of this tape make a simple test to check the quality of the material before taking it on the river. For example, firmly smooth down a piece of the tape on a clean, dry wood or metal object, then immerse it in water for two hours and see if the tape peels off easily. If it peels easily, buy another brand of tape.

From these rough descriptions, we can formulate the tool and repair kit for rafts and rigid drift boats, as listed in Table 5-1.

Table 5-1 *Repair and Tool Kits for Rafts and Rigid Drift Boats*

Raft	*Wooden boat*	*Metal boat*
Rubber material (from truck inner tubes)	Marine plywood	aluminum sheet
Contact cement	caulking material	caulking material
	brass screws or bronze nails	rivets
	small saw	rivet set
Wood rasp (for roughening rubber surface)	wood rasp	hammer
	hammer	

For all of these boats, the following equipment: Pliers, metal file, screwdriver, hand drill and suitable bits, bailing wire, spare nuts, bolts and small metal fittings, coarse sandpaper, crescent wrench, heating-duct tape.

An additional accessory which some owners of rigid drift boats carry is a pair of heavy duty inflatable cylinders about 10 in. in diameter and 2 ft. long on which they may roll the boat along shore. These cylinders are particularly helpful to avoid boat damage when the boat is beached on a rocky shore at night.

Paddle-Powered Boats

Paddles suitable for touring should be strong, should float, should be the proper length, and should have a large blade area. The paddle should be strong to prevent breakage and help you maintain your margin of safety. Either wood or aluminum with fiberglass will provide sufficient strength if the paddles are decently made. The suppliers in Appendix A sell a wide variety of paddles of either type. We usually use one-piece kayak paddles and carry one or more two-piece paddles as spares. The one-piece paddles have one less thing (the joining ferrule) that can go wrong than two-piece paddles.

The requirement that a paddle float helps prevent the permanent loss of a paddle in an upset or other mishap, as occurred on Section I of the Owyhee (Tour 8) in 1969. In the course of a portage around Widowmaker Rapids, one of our paddles fell out of the boat and into the river. We watched it disappear over the Class VI drop, but didn't feel inclined to swim after it. When we didn't find the paddle below the drop, we broke out the spare and continued. The next afternoon, a cry from the lead boater called our attention to the paddle, which was floating in an eddy 8 miles downstream from the place where we had lost it. Both wooden and fiberglass-aluminum paddles float, the latter only if there is a sufficient volume of air inside the hollow shaft.

The length and blade area requirements are designed to give a paddle which is admirable for bracing although it would be a bit clumsy for slalom racing. What length should a kayak paddle be? Arguments arise about the merits of long *vs.* short. One historical technique to determine "correct" paddle length is to find a paddle which is long enough so that you can just close your hand over the top of the paddle blade when it is standing next to you. Most paddlers in real life find that they can use a range of lengths without any problem. [This is true of the authors. Margaret, who is 5 ft. 2 in. tall, has used 74- to 84-in. paddles and prefers 78- to 82-in. paddles; Scott, who is 6 ft. 1 in. tall, has used 76- to 88-in. and prefers 80- to 86-in.] If you are able to examine paddles in a store before buying, test them for comfort. If your hands touch the blade in your normal grip position, the paddle is a bit short. If the paddle feels like a club compared to the shorter ones, it probably is too long for you.

The length of canoe paddles is as controversial as that of kayak paddles. A historic means of choosing the right length was to choose a paddle long enough to reach your chin. Although this means of choosing length gives a rough figure, comfort is again the dominant criterion. [Again, for comparison, Margaret has used 4 ft. 4 in. to 5 ft. 1 in. but prefers 4 ft. 6 in. to 4 ft. 8 in., while Scott has used 5 ft. to 5 ft. 9 in. paddles but prefers 5 ft. 2 in. to 5 ft. 6 in.]

Blade areas on the paddles we have used range from 120 sq. in. (small) to over 220 sq. in. (large). Normally the kayakist uses blades with somewhat smaller area than does the canoeist to avoid having his twobladed paddle become horribly heavy. For touring, we recommend blade areas about 140–170 sq. in. for each blade of a K-1 paddle and 160–200 sq. in. for the blade of C-1 or C-2 paddle, with the smaller end of the range for short paddles often used by women.

For kayak paddles we strongly recommend feathered blades, that is, the two blades at right angles to one another. You will need these to fight upstream winds which commonly occur on rivers. Should kayak blades be flat or spooned? We have heard arguments for the merits of both types, have tried both, and have found both usable, although using the spooned, or curved, blade requires more practice. The most important point about paddles, whatever their length or construction, is that you must learn to use, and use well, the paddle you buy.

Spray skirts are an essential item for whitewater touring with paddle-powered boats. The function of a spray skirt is to seal the boat enough to prevent water from entering when the paddler is sitting or kneeling in his boat. The spray skirt fits loosely enough to come off when necessary and the design is simple. For example, the skirt might have a flat deck attached to the coaming (cockpit rim) with a sewn-in elastic cord and covering all but a 10- to 12-in.-diameter hole at the paddler's post. An upright tube, 8- to 12-in. long, is sewn or glued to the edges of the hole, which is designed to fit snugly around the paddler's body, both to prevent leakage and to make sure that the skirt comes off the boat with the paddler if he bails out. We have observed many near disasters happen because spray skirts fit so tightly around the coaming that exit from the boat was possible only by squirming out through the sleeve. We call this design the suicide sleeve. To avoid this problem, simply try to lift your boat by the spray skirt. If you can lift the boat off the ground by its skirt, the skirt is far too tight, and you should either adjust it or replace it. Your life may depend on it.

The usual construction materials for spray skirts are neoprene foam (wetsuit material) or vinyl-coated nylon. (See Figure 5-2.) However, even a closely woven, nonwaterproof cotton duck can be used to make a spray skirt.

We find two more items essential on kayaks and canoes. One of these items, grab loops, is nearly essential for rescue and very useful for portaging. About 3–4 in. in diameter, these loops are put through holes drilled in the solid end plugs at each end of the boat. The best material that we have found for the grab loops is flat nylon tubing either 1/2-in. or 1-in wide, available through climbing equipment stores. This material is strong and fairly easy on your hands if you have to carry a loaded boat.

The other item which we find very useful for touring is a single rope, 1/4- to 5/16-in. nylon, just long enough so that one end hangs 6 in. or so into the cockpit when the other end is tied to the stern grab loop. This rope is useful for rescue, mooring, and for helping to guide the boat through rocks while lining sections of the river. Beware of either too long or too many ropes! (More

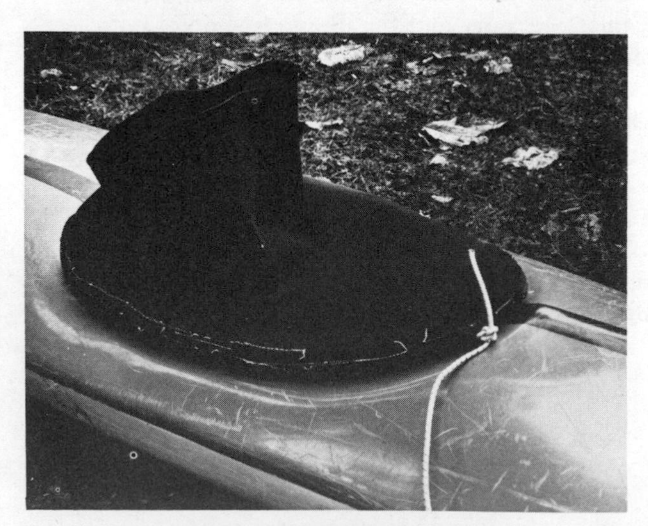

Figure 5-2
Neoprene foam kayak spray skirt

than one is too many.) One of us, like a number of other boaters, has had the frightening experience of being dragged through a rapids by his boat because a too-long rope had tangled around his foot. Tuck the rope in under your spray skirt so that it will only come out of the boat if you do. (Ropes left dangling in the water have a habit of getting caught under rocks in the middle of rapids while you dangle helplessly at the other end.) If you have any rope on the boat you can get tangled in it while swimming, but the chance is small with the arrangement we have suggested, and the benefits of the rope seem to be worth the slight risk.

In some areas another widely used method of attaching lines to boats is to place the line or lines the full length of the boat, one end tied to a grab loop, the other to a small hook of copper wire. Presumably this system allows release of the line only if it is jerked loose, but we have not been favorably impressed by the system in use. The line tended to release accidentally or, in too many cases, required a knife to loosen it. We do not recommend this system, but mention it only for completeness.

To repair fiberglass boats on the river, heating-duct tape will be needed for minor repairs and a fiberglass repair kit for major repairs. Heating-duct tape was discussed earlier in the chapter. For a fiberglass repair kit we use the following criterion for a party of six: there should be enough material to repair two kayaks which have been broken in half. A typical repair kit for a party of six is given in Table 5-2. All these items should be enclosed in a triple thickness of plastic bags and stored in a separate wetpack. Be careful to avoid placing food near your fiberglass kit. Oily foods pick up some very unappetizing flavors when they are placed in the same wetpack or even the same car trunk as polyester resin.

To do a fiberglass repair, you must first get the damaged area thoroughly dry, then attack it with the rasp and sandpaper to clean and to roughen the surface. Roughen the area around the break and for 1–2 in. out from all sides of the break. You normally

Table 5-2 *Repair and Tool Kit for Fiberglass Boats*

3 ft. × 3 ft. piece of 10-oz. glass cloth
1 ft. × 2 ft. piece of 24-oz. glass roving
2 ft. × 2 ft. piece of 1½-oz. glass mat
1 qt. polyester resin (in polyethylene bottle within double plastic bag.
Be sure to get bonding or laminating resin, not surfacing resin.
4 oz. catalyst in plastic bottle within plastic bags
2 oz. container asbestos fiber or Cab-O-Sil for making putty
8 oz. acetone for cleaning
dull table knife
razor blade
several small wiping rags
scissors
combination rasp
coarse sandpaper
teaspoon or eyedropper
3 2-in. paint brushes
3 8-oz. waxed paper cups }
4 4-oz. waxed paper cups } for mixing resin

will put the patch on the inside of the boat if you can reach the damaged area from the inside. Fill big holes by putting tape on one side and fiberglass putty on the other. Make the putty by adding asbestos or Cab-O-Sil to resin until it is thick enough for your job; then catalyze the mixture and apply it with the table knife. As a first guess, use about 1/4 teaspoon or 1–1½ eyedroppers of catalyst for each 4-oz. container of resin at 80°F. At 60°F use twice this amount of catalyst, and at 100°F use half this amount. You should try out your particular resin and catalyst at home to avoid wasting precious resin when you have major repairs to do on the river.

Once you have filled the big holes so that your resin won't simply run through the holes, you are ready for the main patch. Cut three pieces of cloth, or one piece of cloth and one piece of roving, each 1–2 in. larger than the damaged area on all sides. Cut a piece of mat slightly larger than these pieces to cover them.

Then lay these layers down with the cloth next to the boat surface and mat on the side exposed to the air and, using your paint brush, saturate all layers completely with catalyzed, thoroughly stirred resin. If white spots of glass fiber show, the material probably isn't saturated. You can poke and prod with the paint brush until slimy lumps begin to form or the material becomes jelly-like. When the resin reaches this stage, quit. This gel time, the time between addition of the catalyst and formation of jelly-like consistency, is determined by temperature and amount of catalyst. For a given amount of catalyst, the gel time is shorter as the temperature increases. Realistically though, you usually have little or no control over temperature when you are repairing a broken boat on the river. Thus, the amount of catalyst you add will be your only variable. At one temperature, doubling the amount of catalyst will double the rate of the reaction, that is, cut the gel time in half.

Once you have saturated the patch and the resin has cured until it is hard to the touch, you can sand or file away any sharp spikes. Using mat as the outside layer minimizes the number of these hazardous spikes but doesn't eliminate them. If possible, let the patch cure overnight; if not, let it cure for at least one hour after it becomes hard to the touch. Acetone can be used to dissolve resin on brushes or hands until the resin becomes hard. We usually consider the paper cups and paint brushes expendable items, carrying them out in our garbage sack.

If you have never done any fiberglass work before, try it out at home before you go on a river tour. Mistakes made at home can be very informative and can help give you much-needed confidence to attempt repairs on a boat that looks as if it had been run over by a Sherman tank.

Flotation in Drift Boats and Paddle Boats

Flotation, the space filling that is added to a boat to make it float adequately in case of an upset, is an item of the utmost importance to owners of rigid boats. (Rafts, with their built-in adequacy of flotation, are excluded here.)

Let's look at some boat manufacturers' advertising literature, as a start. To paraphrase a common advertising claim, "Our boats are unsinkable because they have 1 cu. ft. of polyurethane foam (or sealed air chambers, etc.) in each end." In the strict sense, the claim may be true. If the boat is filled with water on a quiet lake, it may not sink out of sight. Unfortunately the claim though true is utterly worthless for whitewater use.

To defend these comments, we can start with the following observations:

1. A boat filled with water has a larger area under water that can come in contact with subsurface rocks.
2. A boat filled with water is heavy. This means that a filled boat has more momentum in moving water than an empty boat. This added momentum both greatly increases the chance of damage if the boat hits rocks and makes the boat much less manageable in rescue operations. To illustrate, a 13-ft slalom kayak, the smallest boat discussed here, will hold over a half ton of water when it is full of water.
3. Turbulent, or aerated, water is less dense than still water, and thus is less effective in supporting a boat, particularly one which is filled with water. Further, the power of the river hydraulics may force the boat under water for short periods even if some flotation is present.

These three observations point to an obvious conclusion: you must keep the boat from filling with water. The aim will be to exclude water from the boat by occupying the space with something else. Thus, you should cram gear in waterproof containers, inflatable bags, inner tubes, etc., into all the space that you yourself aren't occupying in the boat. Another way to exclude water is to use bulkheads in the boat. As long as the bulkheads don't leak, they are excellent for excluding water. We have watched dozens of boats be damaged badly that did not have adequate flotation, but have seen this happen to very few boats that did have adequate flotation.

Although many owners of paddle boats are aware of the virtues of maximum flotation, this concept seems to be nearly unknown among owners of wooden drift boats. Figure 5-3 shows one form of flotation for a drift boat, $5 inflatable vinyl chairs. The 14-ft. boat shown in Figure 5-3 flipped in a Class V rapids (shown in Figure 2-1) in Hell's Canyon. The owner was able to tow it to shore, swimming without help, and the boat suffered no damage because the boat floated very high, with water excluded from a substantial percentage of its volume.

A common attitude among owners of wooden drift boats is, "If I tip over, I'll lose the boat, so I won't run anything in which I'll tip over." This attitude is a fine, conservative attitude—if you never make a mistake. But if $10–$15 worth of inner tubes, vinyl chairs, or similar objects might prevent the loss of a $200–$400 drift boat when you do make a mistake, why not buy some of this cheap insurance? Remember too that when you are touring in a remote canyon loss of a boat may mean more than money.

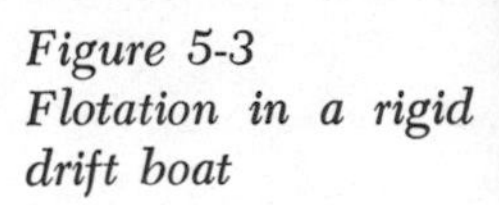

Figure 5-3
Flotation in a rigid drift boat

SIX

Camping Gear and Personal Equipment

The following is a minimal list of equipment needed in the summer on the rivers discussed in our guide. We have found it to be adequate for trips as long as thirteen days, and quite manageable on all-kayak trips. Of course larger boats can carry more luxuries. Certain of the items are discussed in more detail in the pages following the list.

Community Equipment

cooking equipment: 3 assorted pots with covers (one cover should double as a frying pan). If the largest pot has a 1-gallon capacity, the set can serve a group of up to six people. 1 spatula, 1 long-handled wooden spoon, 1 can opener, 1 fork, 1 spoon and cup per person, 1 extra cup and spoon. Optional: 1 lightweight grate, 1 reflector oven and baking pan.

food: $1\frac{1}{2}$–2 lbs. per person per day stored in waterproof wetpacks. See Chapter 7.
first aid kit: complete. A discussion of its contents follows this list.
matches and firestarters, such as Hexamine, candles, or waxed paper, in waterproof containers
maps and information on the river packaged so that they can be used *while boating*
water jugs: 1 gallon per person on rivers where water must be carried
rescue rope, long and sturdy
technical climbing gear where appropriate
flashlight and spare batteries
spare spray covers and paddle for kayaks. We use collapsible paddles as spares and try to carry two on long or difficult trips.
spare oars and oarlocks for drift boats or rubber rafts
waterproof containers (wooden pantry boxes for drift boats) or rubber wetpacks. (See discussion following this list).
repair and tool kit. (See Chapter 5).

River Gear

hat or helmet
cotton shirt for sun protection
lifejacket. (See Chapter 11).
bathing suit
tennis shoes and socks
light wool sweater and waterproof jacket
lightweight wetsuit top if water temperature is cold (for kayaks or rafts; see Chapter 11).
lightweight wool pants or wetsuit shorts if cool weather is expected
two pairs of gloves for rafts and drift boats; one for rowing, one drying

bailing bucket for rafts and drift boats
sponge
air pump for rafts

Other Personal Gear

plastic or rubberized nylon tarp for shelter and cord or rope for rigging it, 5 ft. × 7 ft. for 1 person, 9 ft. × 12 ft. for 3 persons. Plastic is less expensive, but nylon is more durable.
lightweight rain poncho to double as ground cloth
sleeping bag, compressible, summer weight. A more complete discussion follows this list.
shortie air mattress or sleeping pad gives additional warmth as well as comfort. A more complete discussion follows this list.
1 pair of lightweight shoes suitable for hiking
2 pairs of socks
1 set of underwear
1 light cotton shirt
1 light pair of long pants
1 bandanna
1 light wool shirt or sweater
1 nylon ski shell

You can wash them when they get dirty! A more complete discussion of clothing follows this list.

sewing kit: needle, thread, small cloth scrap, a few buttons, safety pins
Chapstick
suntan lotion
insect repellent
toilet paper
soap, small cake
knife
sunglasses with tie down
toothbrush

comb
wet packs
matches
money
Optional: camera and film, fishing gear

First Aid Kit

First aid kits for river touring trips should include the normal items listed below and the special items, which are not included in most first aid kits. You need them because you can't just pick up the phone and call the doctor when you are halfway down a 100-mile stretch of wilderness river. Some of these special items are obtainable only with a doctor's prescription, but if you explain why you need them, your doctor will probably give you prescriptions and instructions for their use.

For a party of six on a six-day river trip:

Normal Items

aspirin	50 tablets
Band-Aids: large size	30
small size	10
sterile gauze pads	12
butterfly bandages	12
triangular bandages	3
adhesive tape	1 roll
fever thermometer	1
elastic bandage (3″ Ace)	1 or 2
scalpel blade or new razor blade	1
needles	2
tweezers or splinter forceps	1
Phisohex (disinfectant)	several oz
moleskin (for blisters, 4″ × 4″)	3
safety pins	6

Special Items

Item	Quantity
*Codeine 30-mg tablets (for mild pain)	18
*Demerol 50-mg tablets (for severe pain)	12
*Lomotil (for diarrhea)	12
*Tetracycline (broad-spectrum antibiotic)	24
*Compazine 5-mg tablets (for nausea & vomiting)	4
*Polysporin ointment (for bad burns)	small tube
*Cortisone cream (for poison oak, ivy, rashes)	small tube
antihistamine Teldrin, Benadryl*, etc. (for hayfever and allergies)	20
salt tablets (for heat exhaustion)	24
laundry soap, strong, nonabrasive (for washing after exposure to poison oak or ivy)	1 small cake
antivenin kit†	1
suction cup snakebite kit†	1

*Requires a prescription.
†Take both of these kits if you will be in a rattlesnake area.

All medicine containers in your first aid kit should be clearly labeled with the name of the medicine, directions for dosage and usage, and expiration date (if perishable). At least one member of the party should be quite knowledgeable about first aid. An outstanding book on the subject that is small enough to be carried on tours is Wilkerson's *Medicine for Mountaineering* (see Appendix D.3). In particular, be familiar with the symptoms and treatment of heat exhaustion, sunstroke, and hypothermia, commonly called exposure.

Waterproof Containers

Wetpacks are simply waterproof containers for carrying gear. They are, of course, vitally necessary on river trips, for which they must be sturdy and completely waterproof. Several types are

Figure 6-1 Assorted wetpacks

available commercially through boating equipment mail-order stores (see Appendix A). Occasionally army surplus stores will carry very sturdy, black, box-like bags made out of heavy duty rubber. These are completely waterproof and come in a variety of sizes, but are rather heavy. See Figure 6-1.

Other satisfactory homemade arrangements include large plastic screw-top jars for small crushable items, and a combination of a heavy polyethylene bag with a sturdy outer bag to protect it from abrasion. Of course all waterproof containers should be attached to the boat to avoid their loss in case of an upset.

In larger rafts and drift boats, wooden pantry boxes or commercial ice chests can be carried, which not only furnish such gourmet delights as fresh eggs and fresh meat, but also serve as tables for meal preparation. In addition, military surplus ammunition cans may be used, but they should be tested by immersion before you use them on a tour.

Sleeping Bags

Before purchasing a sleeping bag for river use you will need to consider three factors: the overall design, the construction, and the filling.

The most efficient and warmest design for sleeping bags is the mummy style, where the bag is broad at the shoulders and tapers at the feet. Some people find the mummy style too restrictive, and prefer the roomier rectangular design. The least expensive but least efficient type of sleeping bag construction has sewn-through seams, where the inner covering is sewn directly to the outer. Bags using other types of construction such as box or overlapping tube (see catalogs of the equipment suppliers listed in Appendix A) are more costly but warmer.

The type of filling used in your bag is extremely important. For convenient carrying on rivers, you will need a lightweight, fairly compressible bag. Because down bags are highly compressible and very light considering their warmth, they make excellent river bags. But, you don't need the arctic expedition type for United States rivers in normal summer months. A bag stuffed with 3½ lbs. of goose down is overdoing it when nighttime temperatures don't get much below 50°F—you would probably spend most of your time on top of the bag instead of in it. Most people find bags stuffed with 2 to 2½ lbs. of down adequate on summer river trips. Down bags are expensive, and difficult to dry out when wet, and wet down is *not* warm.

Polyester-filled bags are lightweight, but not very compressible although commercially available compressor bags do make it possible to compress them to a usable size. The typical polyester bag is not as warm as a down bag, but is usually warm enough for summer river trips. Polyester bags have the advantages of being relatively inexpensive and easy to dry even if thoroughly soaked.

The polyurethane bags that have recently come on the market sound promising for river use (*Wilderness Camping Magazine*, Sept.-Oct. 1971, pp. 8–12, see Appendix D). They are reputed to be warm even when wet, to dry quickly, to give uniform cushioning, to be nonallergenic, and not to require a sleeping pad. Disadvantages cited are stiffness and bulkiness.

Kapok and wool-filled bags are not recommended, as they are relatively heavy, not very compressible, and very difficult to dry.

Sleeping Bag Accessories

An excellent addition to a sleeping bag is a liner to protect the bag and lower your cleaning bill while providing additional warmth. And most useful of all for summer trips, it adds flexibility to your sleeping arrangements. Early in the evening, lying in the sleeping bag is frequently too hot, but lying on top of it is too cool. At times like this, the liner gives just the right amount of warmth for lying on top of the sleeping bag. Instead of the commercially available cotton liners, which are heavy and fragile, we sewed simple rectangular liners of lightweight nylon, and find them just as warm, but much lighter and more durable than cotton liners.

Occasionally we meet a rugged he-man type who places his sleeping bag directly on the rocks or sand and claims that he is sufficiently warm and comfortable. On the next trip he quietly lays out his sleeping bag on some sort of a pad. A pad or air mattress not only provides much-needed comfort when you are bedding down on an uneven surface, but also gives insulation from underneath. You will find that the coldest part of your body is usually the portion that is in contact with the ground. A full length mattress is not really necessary. One that extends from your hips to your shoulders is adequate. Air mattresses in general are comfortable and compact; nylon air mattresses have the added advantage of durability. A variety of sleeping pads made out of good insulating materials such as ensolite are also commercially available. One quarter inch will provide insulation, but not much comfort. Thicker pads are more comfortable, but compressibility becomes a problem.

Clothing

Space and weight limitations on boating trips dictate a limited but functional wardrobe. How limited depends partly on the size of the boat. A kayak can carry only the absolute minimum needed to maintain protection from the elements with some degree of comfort. Larger boats can handle a little more, but all boaters should restrict themselves to clothes that are really necessary. For example, there is no real need for pajamas on any camping trip—ordinary clothes or underwear can fulfill the same function as pajamas. Nor is there a need for more than two changes of clothes, since one can be dried over a fire or in the sun while you are wearing the other.

Of course the weather expected on the trip should influence the choice of clothing. We are discussing pleasure trips, and it is unlikely that many people are going to take pleasure whitewater trips in areas where or at times when daytime temperatures are expected to be near or below freezing. (Such trips would be dangerous as well as uncomfortable.) However, even on summer trips in hot areas, you should have clothing adequate to give you safe protection from wet weather and daytime temperatures as low as 50°F. This was made painfully clear to us on the ill-fated August trip mentioned in Chapter 3, on the No Return section of Idaho's Salmon River. Our clothing had been planned for normal hot weather, and although it would have sufficed for a short period of cold rainy weather, it was not suited for the six-day siege. Since then, we have modified our list of clothing so that it will provide some degree of comfort even in these circumstances. The clothing given in the equipment list should provide at least minimal protection at temperatures encountered on midsummer river trips in most of the United States. If you are planning a trip in April or May, or a summer trip in parts of Canada, you will want to provide more warm clothing. But in any case the clothing you do take must be functional and must provide adequate protection from cold, wind, rain, and sun.

Clothing for Warmth

As mentioned in the sleeping bag section, down has the highest warmth-to-weight ratio. But just because we recommended down sleeping bags for these trips doesn't mean we recommend down clothing. The warmth of down sleeping bags is very pleasant at cool predawn temperatures when you are sleeping. But clothing will be worn at warmer daytime and early evening temperatures while you are active, and down will usually be too warm. Furthermore, clothing worn on boating trips often gets wet or at least damp, and damp down is cold down.

Instead of down we recommend wool clothing to provide warmth. Several lightweight layers of clothing provide more warmth and flexibility than one heavy layer. One or two lightweight wool shirts or sweaters worn under a windproof shell provide all the warmth necessary at normal summer temperatures. As most campers know, wool has a great advantage over other fabrics in that it provides some warmth even when wet.

We also have found that underwear-type jackets insulated with dacron are excellent on trips, as they are lightweight and very quick drying. A light quilted dacron jacket and light wool sweater make an excellent warm combination. One pair of long pants will keep your legs warm and bug-free. Lightweight wool is best, but cotton will do.

Since hiking out is always a possibility, at least one extra pair of socks should be carried (again lightweight wool is the best choice). The socks should be free of holes and kept unused unless it is necessary to hike out. Be sure your shoes are adequate for hiking. The type of shoe needed depends on the length and ruggedness of the potential hike. On a river such as the Rogue (Tour 1) where an excellent hiking trail parallels the river, a sturdy pair of sneakers may give you blisters, but will get you out. On the other hand, climbing out of the Owyhee River (Tours 8 and 9) involves a long, rugged haul over cliffs and trailless desert, so a sturdy shoe is needed. Lightweight hiking boots or klettershoes are an excellent choice.

Clothing for Wind Protection

Because wind conducts heat away from the body, it has a tremendous cooling effect. This wind chill factor effectively lowers the air temperature as far as the body is concerned. For example, actual daytime temperatures as low as 50°F can easily be encountered on summer trips, but a temperature of 50°F combined with a 10 mi./hr. wind gives an effective temperature of 40°F. And combined with a 20 mi./hr. wind, the actual 50°F temperature acts like 32°F as far as the body is concerned (information from *Outdoor Living*, published by the Tacoma Unit, Mountain Rescue Council, Tacoma, Washington). So keeping the wind away from your body can be extremely important. There are a number of lightweight, compressible windproof jackets on the market. Those with hoods are preferable. Unlined nylon ski shells are an excellent choice. Remember that heavy jackets are not necessary; your lightweight wool layer will provide warmth if it has a thin windproof layer over it.

Clothing for Protection from Water

Even on rainless river trips, protection from water is needed because of splash from rapids. On cool, windy days, running rapids can be very unpleasant if you are not adequately dressed. Wet clothing conducts heat away from the body, so water combined with wind can be a dangerous combination, as the body is losing heat very rapidly from both convection and conduction.

Light wool underlayers topped by waterproof-windproof garments such as rain suits should give adequate protection under most conditions. We have found the "paddling jacket," a waterproof jacket with elasticized collar, cuffs, and waist, to be highly effective when worn over a light wool sweater. These jackets can be obtained through some sporting goods stores, where they are sold as wrestling jackets, a kind of sweatsuit for wrestlers, or through advertisements in the *American Whitewater Magazine* (see Appendix D). If the water temperature is below 60°F, a wetsuit jacket will add immeasurably to the comfort of kayakists and rafters. At water temperatures below 50°F, the wetsuit jacket is needed for safety as well as comfort. One-eighth-in. neoprene wetsuits are usually adequate for summer boating, although at water temperatures below 45°F, 3/16-in. thickness is preferable. Wetsuits, and the hazards of cold water are discussed more completely in Chapter 11. River clothes should not double as camping clothes. You will want dry clothes to wear in camp.

Clothing for Protection from the Sun

Sun and heat are encountered much more often on summer river trips than rain or cold, and can be just as severe a problem. All boaters should have and wear headgear to protect them from the sun. Wide-brimmed hats that can be secured in a wind are the most effective protection, but the kayaker's crash helmet will do. And everyone should have a shirt readily available for sun protection. Sunglasses help prevent discomfort and headaches caused by glare.

SEVEN

Food

Organizing the Planning

On most camping trips mealtime assumes an almost ridiculous importance due to sharpened appetites, but also to a psychological factor. On camping trips life is reduced to the basics—eating, sleeping, and keeping warm—so people are much more concerned with them than they are at home. Since food will be an important aspect of your whitewater tour, it is worth spending some time in the careful planning of good meals.

Planning food is often really pleasurable if you allow yourself enough time to enjoy it! We always cook communally on our trips, finding it more efficient in terms of gear and food and certainly more enjoyable than cooking individually. Mealtime is the time to get together and relax around the fire after a hard day's paddling. After trying a variety of methods, we find that we prefer dividing the food planning and purchasing duties equally among the party members, with each person responsible for a certain number of meals. This method has three advantages. First, it simplifies trip finances since each person pays for the same number of meals. Of course, some people are more extravagant than others; but that is their option. The more affluent members may serve you a luxurious and expensive meal of freeze-dried beefsteaks and ice cream, whereas the penniless student may serve you an equally delicious but more economical meal based on jerky prepared in his own oven. The second advantage of sharing is that it provides variety, an important factor on a long trip. If one person plans all the food, it reflects his personal tastes, and after a few meals, others may find it monotonous. On one of our overnight camping trips the apples 'n cinnamon oatmeal was a great success. So the person buying food supplied us with five days' worth of it for our next five-day trip. By the fifth day, none of us would touch it. Finally, this method saves any one person from having an overwhelming planning job, and gives people time to enjoy their planning.

Food Quantity

Estimating the quantity of food needed is very touchy. You don't want to overload your boats with vast piles of unneeded food; yet you don't want people to go hungry. If you must err, do it on the heavy side. We have found the following guidelines extremely helpful:

100 percent special backpacking foods: 1–1½ lbs. per person per day.

50 percent backpacking foods and 50 percent homemade and grocery store dried foods: 1¼–1¾ lbs. per person per day.

100 percent homemade and grocery store dried foods: 1½–2 lbs. per person per day.

These amounts have proved adequate for groups composed of young people in their twenties and thirties with an approximately equal distribution of sexes. Groups including a large proportion of big men or several teenage boys may need slightly more food. Predominantly female or older groups might not need quite as much food.

One interesting effect of the democracy of these trips pertains to food distribution. Out of curiosity all members have weighed themselves immediately before and after several of our trips. In all cases, each woman's weight either remained constant or went up, and each man's weight dropped 2–10 lbs. The reason seems obvious: around the campfire the food is doled out equally, regardless of the diners' size. After discovering this fact the lighter members of our parties haven't worried about getting every bite of their share, except when it comes to dessert.

Food Cost and Sources

Common sources of trip food are mail-order outdoor supply stores (Appendix A) or local stores carrying backpacking equipment. They usually carry a good supply of dried and freeze-dried foods. These have the advantages of being extremely lightweight, easy to prepare, and tasty, but they have the disadvantage of being expensive. Unless you can afford to pay for the convenience, avoid the complete meal packages. You can package your own biscuits, pancakes, cereals, and drinks for a fraction of the price. Be careful about the claims on packages concerning how many people they will feed. Occasionally a so-called four-man dinner really is adequate for four, but sometimes it will barely feed two, and we've never seen one that had too much food. If you have any doubts about quantity, try the dish out at home before the trip, and remember that on trips most people will eat at least two cups of the main course.

A convenient and often neglected source of trip food is the

local grocery store. There you will find a variety of easy-to-prepare dried foods that can be quite good and that are very reasonably priced. They have the disadvantages of being slightly heavier than many of the special backpacking foods, and usually requiring additional packaging. Not only can the grocery store supply your drinks, dried soups, cereals, rice, noodles, desserts, biscuit and pancake mixes, candy, crackers, and dried fruits, but also the main dishes for dinner. In the last few years a variety of dried dinners, such as those by Lipton's and Kraft, have come on the market that require no additions but water. Furthermore, if you buy a little freeze-dried meat, some imitation bacon bits, or a small can of chicken or tuna, you can make an excellent "glop" for four using some rice or noodles and one of the dried packaged sauces available in the grocery store.

A third source of trip food is your own kitchen. With a little ingenuity you can duplicate some of the commercial backpacking foods such as jerky in your kitchen at a very low cost. We include several recipes in Appendix B.

We have found it possible to supply an adequate quantity of food at a cost of $1.50 to $2.00 per day per person if most of the food was purchased at the grocery store. Commercial backpacking food usually will cost significantly more.

Nutrition

On trips of less than a week, an unbalanced diet probably isn't going to do any permanent damage. But even on short trips most people are happier if they think they're getting a balanced diet, so some efforts should be made along this line. On very long trips menues should be carefully planned to give a well-balanced diet perhaps including viatmin supplements. Following the guidelines in the menu pages will probably keep your menues balanced enough to satisfy the members' psychological needs and at least most of their physical needs. If you need more information on this subject consult some of the books listed in Appendix D.

Packaging Food

Trip food must be carefully packaged to keep it dry and convenient to use. Each item of food should be individually wrapped to be waterproof, then carried in a waterproof wetpack (discussed in Chapter 6). The wrapping of the individual items need not be particularly sturdy, since they will be carried inside a sturdy waterproof wetpack. The individual wrapping serves to keep the food dry if a few drops of water leak into the wetpack and to keep the items convenient to find and use. Plastic sandwich bags or the larger quart bags do very well for powdered items, but use two bags for each item as they tear readily. Staple items such as coffee or sugar should be triple-bagged. Be sure to squeeze all the air out of the bags before fastening them; not only will they take up less room, but also they will be more resistant to puncturing. Foods should be removed from boxes and repackaged in plastic bags to save both weight and space.

Some items, such as honey, margarine, and peanut butter, obviously need containers other than plastic bags. Wide-mouth, screw-top plastic bottles or plastic squeeze tubes (both available at backpacking stores and mail-order houses) work admirably for such foods. You may wish to enclose containers of particularly messy items in plastic bags.

Once the items are individually wrapped, they should be grouped in some logical fashion to avoid the need for groping at mealtime. We have found that the most effective method for us is to place all the items for one meal in a large plastic bag, such as a garbage bag, labeled to show whether it is the second breakfast or the third dinner. Finally the big bags are placed in order in wetpacks, the ones to be used last at the bottom. The staples bag discussed later in the chapter is always carried near the top, and the lunch of the day is carried in an accessible spot. The food should not all be carried in one boat (putting all your eggs in the same basket!), but should be distributed among most of the boats.

Breakfast Foods

Some parties prefer a quick, light breakfast on trips, while others opt for a more leisurely and substantial affair. If you plan to get on the river immediately after breakfast, it should be easy to digest and should include both short-range energy foods, such as honey or sugars, and long-range ones, proteins or fats. Even if you plan a leisurely trip, a couple of quickie breakfasts may come in very handy, as the trip won't always go exactly as you planned! If you are on a good fishing river, you may supplement some of your breakfasts and dinners with tasty trout. But from our experience we advise you not to count on it. On good fishing rivers we usually plan a few meals to accompany fish, but have enough food in them so we won't go hungry if the fish don't cooperate! (For recipes for preparing fish, see Appendix B.)

Our breakfasts contain:

1. a source of quick energy
2. a hot drink
3. a fillor
4. a source of protein (long-range energy)
5. fruit or juice if there is none in the lunch or dinner

Specific items are chosen from the following table:

Type of Food	*Provides components in the preceding list*	*Available from B, backpacking stores, and G, grocery stores*
coffee or tea (with sugar)	1, 2	G
hot chocolate	1, 2	G
hot liquid Jello[a]	1, 2, 4	G
hot instant breakfast (made with dried milk)	1, 2, 4	G
vitamin C drink such as Start, Tang	1, 5	G
dried fruit	5	G
hot cereal with sugar, raisins, and milk	1, 3, 4, 5	G
cold cereal[b] with sugar and milk	1, 3, 4	G
fried potatoes, dried	3	G
bacon bar[c]	3, 4	B
eggs, dried[d]	3, 4	B
pancakes[e] with brown sugar syrup	1, 3	G
cornbread or biscuits[f]	3	G
toast, dried	3	G

[a]In cool weather, this is an excellent picker-upper. Lime is our favorite. Just put 1/4–1/3 of a small package of Jello in a cup, add boiling water, stir, and drink. It may sound ghastly, but it tastes great when you're cold.

[b]A compact cereal like Grapenuts is most efficient. Cereals like Granola and Familia are compact and popular on these trips.

[c]Can be crumbled in eggs, or eaten straight. They are quite a concentrated food, and most people won't eat more than 1/3 of a bar.

[d]Are worth the expense; some brands are much better than others.

[e]Very time consuming for a large group.

[f]Can be baked the night before to save time.

Sample Breakfasts

A. oatmeal with raisins, brown sugar, and milk
scrambled eggs, dried
coffee or tea
orange juice, dried

B. bacon bar, 1/4 to 1/3 per person
Granola cold cereal with milk
coffee or tea
grapefruit juice

Lunch Foods

On boating trips we usually don't want to bother with a hot lunch. Heavy lunches make it difficult to get back in the boat and face that hairy rapids around the bend, so we settle for light, quick-energy nibblies.

Our lunches contain:

1. a quick energy source
2. a cold drink
3. a filler
4. a source of protein or fat

Specific items are selected from the following table:

Type of Food	*Provides components in the preceding list*	*Available from B, backpacking stores only; H, your home kitchen; and G, grocery stores*
Rye Crisp[a]	3	G
crackers	3	G
Logan bread[b]	1, 3, 4	H
"fodder"[c]	1, 3	H
cheese[d]	3, 4	G
dried cheese spread[e]	3, 4	B
peanut butter[f]	1, 3, 4	G
dried peanut butter	1, 3, 4	B
dried jelly[g]	1	B
jerky[h]	3, 4	H, G
honey[i]	1, 3	G
dried fruit	1, 3	G
candy or nuts[j]	1, 4	G
gorp[k]	1, 3, 4	H
dried lemonade, iced tea, etc.	1, 2	G

[a]One box/day/eight people.

[b]See recipes, Appendix B.

[c]See recipes, Appendix B.

[d]Heavy and will only keep for a few days in hot weather; keeps best if you buy the kind enclosed in wax.

[e]Good, lightweight, and not too expensive; just add water.

[f]Store it in plastic bottles.

[g]Reasonably priced; just add water.

[h]Can be made at home easily and very economically. See recipes, Appendix B.

[i]See discussion on packaging.

[j]Most adults seem to prefer nuts to candy. Individually wrapped candies are the easiest to handle.

[k]A popular mixture of two or more of the following: nuts, raisins, chopped dried fruit, semisweet chocolate bits, M & M's.

Sample Lunches

A. lemonade
   Rye Crisp with peanut butter and dried jelly
   dried apricots
   English toffee

B. iced tea
   jerky
   Logan bread

C. root beer, dried mix
   Triscuits with dried cheese spread
   raisins
   salted peanuts

Dinner Foods

Dinner is usually the only really leisurely meal on boating trips, and is often the highpoint of the day. It can be a relatively heavy meal, and should be filling. We usually have early dinners since people are hungry, and then have a hot drink around the campfire just before bed. At least a few dinners should be very quick and easy to prepare for late camping days, rainy weather, and other contingencies. Of course, if you are planning a leisurely trip, you can also have some fancier dinners with luxuries like cakes fresh baked by reflector oven.

Our dinners are planned to include each of the following:

1. soup, 1½ cups per person
2. "glop" (2–3 cups per person—a one pot meal containing:
   a. meat or cheese
   b. a filler (rice, macaroni, potatoes, etc.)
   c. a vegetable, unless the soup contains lots of vegetables

3. dessert
4. a beverage

Soups

A number of excellent dried soups are available in grocery stores. Some are quite filling. Use vegetable soups for nights when the glop doesn't have vegetables. Hot soup seems to be welcome at dinner, even on hot days.

Glops

These give a tremendous opportunity to be creative. They can be purchased at backpacking stores, or you can invent your own from supermarket makings. A nearly infinite number of combinations are possible. Just choose combinations that sound good to you from the following list:

a. MEAT OR CHEESE PART OF THE GLOP	*Available from B, backpacking stores only; H, your home kitchen; and G, grocery stores*
tuna or chicken, small cans	G
beef, dried or freeze-dried[a]	B
chicken, dried or freeze-dried	B
ham, freeze-dried	B
bacon bits, imitation[b]	G
fish, dried[c]	G

[a]Dried or freeze-dried meats are expensive. To cut costs, buy the dried diced or ground meat, and purchase the rest of the glop makings at the grocery store.

[b]These are relatively inexpensive, are good sources of soybean protein, and in our opinion, taste better than dried beef or chicken.

[c]Oriental grocery stores carry a selection of dried fish.

a. MEAT OR CHEESE PART OF THE GLOP	*Available from B, backpacking stores only; H, your home kitchen; and G, grocery stores*
parmesan cheese, dried	G
cheese	G
meat balls, freeze-dried	B
pork chops or patties, freeze-dried	B
beef steaks or patties, freeze-dried	B
jerky[d]	H, G
fish, fresh if you're lucky	

[d]A great way to save both weight and money is to make your own jerky (see recipes, Appendix B).

b. FILLER PART OF THE GLOP	*Available from B, backpacking stores only; H, your home kitchen; and G, grocery stores*
macaroni[e]	G
rice, white or brown[f]	G
noodles[g]	G
potatoes, dried[h]	G
chowder mix, corn or potato[i]	H, B
vegetable stew[j]	H, B

[e]The dried macaroni and cheese mix available in grocery stores is inexpensive and not bad.

[f]Allow 1/2–2/3 cups of uncooked rice per person. Minute rice is much quicker, but is relatively heavy and bulky.

[g]Allow about 3 oz. noodles per person.

[h]The scalloped potatoes with cheese mixes make an excellent glop base. Dried mashed potatoes and hashbrowns are also available at grocery stores.

[i]This makes an excellent base for a fish meal and if you don't catch any, it's still good. To make your own, see recipes, Appendix B.

[j]Add dumplings to make it more filling.

b. FILLER PART OF THE GLOP	*Available from B, backpacking stores only; H, your home kitchen; and G, grocery stores*
biscuits or cornbread[k]	G
dried dinners, Lipton's, etc.[l]	G
c. VEGETABLE PART OF THE GLOP	
vegetable flakes, dried	G
onion flakes, dried	G
Additional flavorings	
sauces and gravies, dried[m]	G
herbs[n]	G

[k]If you have a reflector oven.

[l]Allow two boxes for three people. Edible, especially if you spice it up.

[m]Mushroom and sour cream types seem especially good.

[n]A few herbs, such as thyme or rosemary, weigh almost nothing and can make the difference between a tasteless glop and something you might even eat at home.

Desserts

A reflector oven adds tremendous variety to the dessert possibilities.

a. NO-BAKE DESSERTS	*Available from B, backpacking stores only; H, your home kitchen; and G, grocery stores*
puddings, instant or cooked[a]	G
stewed dried fruit or applesauce	G, B
cooked mincemeat[b]	G

[a]Remember to bring enough dried milk for them. Mix up the milk first, then add the pudding.

[b]A dried variety is available in grocery stores. Adding a little water and cooking for a few minutes makes a surprisingly good and filling dessert.

a. NO-BAKE DESSERTS	*Available from B, backpacking stores only; H, your home kitchen; and G, grocery stores*
cheese cake, mix[c]	G
instant fudge, mix	G
ice cream, freeze-dried	B

b. DESSERTS BAKED BY REFLECTOR OVEN (Any mix will do as long as only water is required and the mix isn't too heavy.)	
date bar mix	G
brownie mix	G
cake mixes, the smaller ones	G
pudding cakes	G
gingerbread	G

[c]Has come on the market recently. Amazingly easy, and a real treat on camping trips.

Sample Dinners

A. split pea soup, the 3-minute variety

spinmac, an excellent combination of macaroni and cheese mix from the grocery store cooked with dried spinach from backpackaging stores

brownies, cooked in a reflector oven

iced tea

B. corn chowder (see Appendix B) with imitation bacon bits, freeze dried ham, or fish

Sierra salad (lime jello combined with the dried vegetable flakes available at grocery stores)

Cheese cake, instant, no-cook mix from grocery stores

lemonade

C. Vegetable-beef soup, dried

chicken schlock (chicken—dried or canned, dried vegetable flakes, rice, herbs, one or more of the following dried sauces from the grocery store: mushroom gravy, sour cream sauce or stroganoff sauce

chocolate pudding

root beer, dried

Staples

We find it convenient to carry the staple items that are usually needed at breakfast and dinner separately in their own bag, rather than to try to include just the right amount of salt, coffee, and sugar in each breakfast (which invariably results either in carrying unneeded food or scrounging through dozens of bags trying to find a breakfast that has coffee to spare). If the staples are carried separately, the staples bag is automatically unloaded for each meal, and you can gauge the amount of sugar you can put in your coffee by how much is left in the bag. This way, you don't run out although you usually don't have much left over. You may want to carry the following items for your staples bag:

coffee
tea
sugar, for coffee, tea, or cereal
salt
pepper
herbs (a mixture of thyme, marjoram, or whatever for glops)
dried milk, enough for emergency use. It is usually more con-

venient to include milk needed specifically for puddings, etc., in with the meals instead of having to gauge how much you can use from the staples supply.

dried onion soup for baking fish. See Appendix B.

dried onions

extra rice and package of soup to make an emergency dinner if needed

margarine or lard

EIGHT

Training for Wildwater Tours

Physical Conditioning

If you spend most of your time sitting behind a desk or doing housework and have begun to develop middle age spread, you may be a candidate for a bit of physical conditioning before a wildwater tour. Even if you are planning a leisurely, relaxed tour, you may have to portage loaded boats, you may want to hike, or you might even have to walk out of the canyon should catastrophe befall you. We do not believe that a person has to be in peak athletic form for most wildwater river tours, but you may find the trip far more enjoyable if you have made some effort to condition yourself beforehand.

At home we have used the Royal Canadian Air Force exercise manuals and have found them both realistic and useful. These exercises combined with a bit of hiking before the trip may enhance it. Some flat water paddling or rowing, mentioned below, is also very useful physical conditioning.

Psychological Conditioning

There are two principal questions about river touring that may give you psychological qualms before the trip ever starts:

1. What sort of hazards are on this river that we will run and how bad are they? Knowledge about the river is the best technique to allay these qualms. Find out all you can about the river. You have just read half a book telling you how to get this knowledge. Use it. If your party includes worry warts, give them as complete and accurate descriptions as you can without making the descriptions lurid.

2. Suppose we tip over or have to swim in turbulent water? This is a question that occurs to all boaters in paddle boats and should occur to even experienced drift boaters some of whom have never tipped over.

You can take care of the second question easily. First for safety make sure that the person is an adequate swimmer, e.g., by using the swimming test mentioned in Chapter 3. Then if you have a local river that has a small rapids on it, have the person swim through the rapids with a lifejacket on. The best way to learn about swimming in rapids is to do it. If you face downstream in a sitting position with your feet slightly lower than your bottom so that feet, not backbone, bounce off the rocks, you will be able to control your orientation at least part of the time. The main thing to learn is that you can't fight powerful currents—so don't try! Conserve your strength and avoid damage until you get to quieter water where you can swim. A session or two of rapids swimming can alleviate irrational fears about swimming after tip-overs. With this technique you may also find out about problem people before you take them on an isolated tour.

Boating Training

There are a number of reasons to practice in your boat before a wildwater tour. The most important is that you gain familiarity with your equipment and its failings before you go to an isolated area.

Training sessions on lakes or in swimming pools furnish opportunities to find out whether the spray skirt on a paddle boat is adjusted properly. Try tipping over a few times with the spray skirt on and see if you can get out of the boat easily. This technique is a great confidence builder. Be sure to have someone to help you if something goes wrong.

A local lake is also a fine place to assemble and try out raft frames, oars, paddles, etc. Don't be too gentle in your testing. If a piece of equipment is going to fail under reasonable stress, you want to find out about it at home, not in some isolated canyon. If your equipment is satisfactory and you are a novice, try paddling or rowing on the lake for a time, learning to control and maneuver your boat. This is also good exercise for the muscles you will be using most on the river. You might also try some rescue practice, dumping swamped boats, etc .

The next stage of training for river touring is to run some rivers. If you have several years of previous wildwater experience, run local rivers on one-day trips. Work up to rivers of difficulty and size similar to the river on which you wish to tour. If you plan to go on a river with overall Class III difficulty, develop your skill on local rivers until you are comfortable and in full control on local rivers of at least Class III difficulty. If there are no suitable rivers in your area, contact one of the whitewater groups listed in Appendix E for information about their areas, and try to run several of their rivers to polish your skills.

If you are a novice with less than 5–10 days of previous whitewater experience, it is best to consult the nearest organized whitewater group to find out about local rivers and their difficulty. If possible, boat with the group on some of their easier rivers. Be realistic about your experience when you discuss your river experience with members of organized groups. A novice boater with a bit of sales ability may be able to talk himself on to a Class III river with a group, but neither he nor the group is likely to be happy with the result.

Most of the organized whitewater groups we have heard about are very willing to train novices if the novice is willing to try new ideas and techniques. The know-it-all, the person who has become an expert because he ran a riffle once, often gets a cold reception, especially when a real lack of talent becomes obvious.

A novice living in an area which has no organized whitewater group will have to learn on his own. To begin the learning process, read one or several of the books in Appendix A.1, then rate one or more of your local rivers, preferably a river with some rapids, using Chapter 1. Novices using Table 1-1 almost invariably rate the following categories too high: obstacles, waves, turbulence, and water speed. You can avoid overestimating these phenomena by viewing them from river level, using your height as a measure of waves and measuring the rate of travel of a stick in the current (4.4 ft./sec. is 3 mi./hr.). Obstacles and turbulence require experience to evaluate, although usually you will be at most four to six points high for the combination of these two items. Rate the river by actual inspection using Table 1-1. A corollary to Murphy's Law* states: "The most difficult rapids cannot be seen from the road." A classic example of this, on the Skykomish River in Washington, has taken a number of lives. Your inspection should include a series of short hikes into the sections of the river which cannot be seen from the road.

Some of the following suggestions may be greeted with laughter by novice boaters. Try them anyway; they may help you learn to read water. These suggestions originated with an observation

*Murphy's Law, well known in the experimental sciences, says "Anything that can go wrong, will."

that we made some years ago: avid stream fishermen seem to acquire water reading skill far more rapidly than nonfishermen. Apparently the reason is practice. The avid stream fisherman has learned about currents and current differentials by wading in the river. He has learned about eddies and eddy lines as places where fish will feed. As a novice, you can use an adaptation of this technique. Go to a local creek or river which has rapids and study the river in several ways. First, wade in and use your body as a probe for the power of the current (you might want to wear a lifejacket and wetsuit). Then with your eyes near water level, study the riffles and rapids from upstream. Form a careful mental picture of the rapids from above, then go downstream and look at the rapids from the side and the bottom to determine the cause of the turbulence, waves, etc. The basic hydraulic phenomena that occur in creeks, small rivers, and large rivers are very similar. The only real difference between larger rivers and creeks is that the high volume of flow on a large river requires a much smaller gradient to produce hydraulics than the gradient required to produce them in a creek. The hydraulics in a large river have much more power than creek hydraulics and a greater effect on your boat. The reason for this effect is that the weight (really the momentum) of your boat is small compared to the weight of the moving water in a big river. In a small river or creek, your boat is heavy compared to the weight of moving water. If you go swimming in creeks or rivers and try to read the water in these ways each time you go, you'll be amazed at the ease with which you learn to read water.

To determine the effect of the water on a boat, however, you will need experience running rivers. You can get a crude idea of the effects of water by floating small sticks down a creek. Unfortunately the sticks rarely have the same shape and buoyancy as boats.

When you have found a section of river which seems to be Class I, or at most Class II–, try running it. Strive for control of your boat in the moving, perhaps turbulent water. To find out what degree of control is possible on whitewater, try to get one of the wildwater or slalom movies which can be rented for a nominal fee through some of the advertisers in *American Whitewater* (see Appendix A). These movies also are often very good technique illustrations for paddle boaters.

Once the novice has run one local II− river, is he ready for his tour? No. After he has run several II− to II rivers, he may be ready for a Class I+ or perhaps a Class II tour, but certainly not for a Class III tour.

If you are trying to boat safely, start slowly and work up. We have observed novice parties having serious trouble or have seen the wreckage of novices' boats on each of the five most difficult tours given in Section III of this book.

As a last item of boating practice before a trip, try a river trip, or even lake trip, which requires overnight camping. Be extravagant in your food and equipment: take steaks, wine, and other goodies to try to get a significant amount of weight and volume in the boat. This way you will discover the difficulties of packing gear in your boat and the changes in handling properties of a loaded boat compared to an empty boat, etc. You may find that your sleeping bag wasn't in a waterproof bag after all, or that you forgot to bring matches, or that your shelter really isn't very good. Be happy. One night's misery is bearable, if you learn from it. The overnight shakedown cruise may ensure you a far more pleasant extended tour.

These ideas may sound complicated and time-consuming to you. In fact, to do all the preparation that we have suggested will take at most six to eight days (say three or four weekends) before the trip. Hopefully you will find the preparative trips fun themselves.

Take tried and tested equipment and people on wildwater tours. If you want to try vital but untested equipment, take it along, but have another tested piece of equipment ready in case the new one fails.

NINE

The Art of the Shuttle

A necessary part of every wildwater tour is the car shuttle. One way or another, you have to get transportation to the put-in and from the take-out of your tour. The shuttle presents problems you should try to solve before you get to the river to avoid undue delays and frustration on your actual trip.

For getting to the general area within 50 or 100 miles of the tour, road atlases or state highway maps are usually adequate and may be obtained from state tourist bureaus or gasoline companies that serve the area. They will give you some idea about mileage and road conditions, so that you can estimate the number of hours or days of driving needed to get to the general area.

Shuttle Road Information

Your problems usually begin when you try to find roads from the town nearest to the specific put-in or take-out points. Sometimes, no road at all is shown on the state highway maps that will take you to the put-in or take-out. For example, most Idaho road maps show no road to Dagger Falls, the put-in for the Middle Fork of the Salmon (Tour 5).

To determine whether a road does exist you can use one or more additional maps. If the land in the area is managed by a government agency, such as the Forest Service, state, federal, or provincial Park Service, or Bureau of Land Management, a very large land holder in the western United States, the controlling agency probably has maps of the area. The maps may or may not be available for public distribution, but write to find out, explain why you need the map, and ask that the agency inform you immediately if there is a charge for the map. The combination of your explanation of why you desire the maps, and your apparent willingness to pay for them demonstrates your real need. Most of the time you will get a form letter with information about availability of maps, cost, etc., or perhaps the maps themselves. Occasionally you may get a letter from a person in the agency who is interested in your trip and information which he thinks might be useful to you. Your letter might be the most interesting one he has handled in months.

If no maps are available through government administrative agencies or if you want an additional check, U.S.G.S. 1:250,000 scale maps or the Canadian equivalents are usually very good for determining road access points. Check the date on the map. Pioneer wagon routes and passenger cars don't get along well together.

In addition to these map sources, you may be able to get maps of the counties in which your put-in and take-out points are located. These are sometimes available through State Highway Commissions, sometimes through County Planning Boards, and for some states, through commercial sources (see Appendix D.4.b).

Having determined that roads exist leading to the put-in and take-out, your next problem will be to determine the quality of these secondary roads. If the road surface is shown as anything but high quality pavement on your map, local inquiry is in order. Road surfaces change from long-term weathering, lack of maintenance, and wet weather. Local standards of passability may differ markedly from the standards with which you are familiar.

How do you inquire locally when you are planning a trip from your home 1,000 miles away from the locale of the river? The cheapest and the most satisfactory way to get information on the local road conditions is to write to local residents in the vicinity of the river or to the agency that maintains the road. Begin by writing to the owner of a resort or motel on or very near the river. Names and locations of resorts can be obtained through the state's tourist bureau in most states. These people have a vested interest in your trip to their area: you might find their accommodations convenient. The off-season is usually the best time to write. As with the government agencies, explain what you are planning and ask questions which are as specific as possible, such as: "Is the road from Nowhere to Deadend passable in an ordinary passenger car? Is a four-wheel-drive vehicle necessary at some seasons on this road?" You might also inquire whether your informant knows of other parties who have run this section of the river. An inquiry of this sort may produce some useful information or may just add to your stock of horror stories about the tour in question. If you can't get sufficient information from resort owners, you might try the county sheriff (or local RCMP office in Canada) or fuel oil distributors, both of whom have reason to be driving on the secondary roads and some familiarity with them.

When you write letters of this sort, requesting that someone take his time to answer them, keep your queries brief and to the point. Including a stamped, self-addressed envelope may help you get a reply. Once you have extracted information about the secondary roads on which you will have to shuttle, you will need to evaluate it. We have only one suggestion to offer. The locals will often drive their passenger cars over abominable roads which most outsiders would consider strictly four-wheel-drive roads. If the locals consider a road suitable only for four-wheel-drive vehicles, *believe them* and plan to bring such a vehicle or hire one locally for your shuttle.

Hiring Shuttles—Pro and Con

Having compiled information about the location and quality of the roads which you must travel on the shuttle for your tour, you must decide who will do the shuttle.

Figure 9-1 Shuttle car

If there are nonboaters traveling with you who are willing to go to the put-in with you and to meet you at the take-out, your problem is solved. If all the party members are boaters, you have the option of doing the shuttle yourself or hiring someone else to do it for you if possible. It is surprisingly easy to find shuttle drivers for hire, particularly in the isolated areas where river tours are made. Shuttle driving can add a substantial percentage to the often very low cash income of the local residents. Housewives, ranch wives, local high school students out of school for the summer, and in desperation, local barflies (preferably sober) may serve as shuttle drivers.

To decide whether to hire someone or to do it yourself you will want to examine a number of factors.

Cost

Suppose you have two cars A and B and both have to go to the put-in to deliver all the people and gear. Then consider the following possible shuttles:

1. Do-it-yourself. Drive cars A and B to the take-out after unloading at put-in; leave car B; return in A to the put-in with your boating drivers. At the end of the trip drive car B back to the put-in and pick up car A; then return both to take-out for the rest of the passengers and gear. Cars A and B do one and one-half round trips from put-in to take-out.
2. Hired Drivers. Drivers are picked up and taken to put-in. After gear and people are unloaded, drivers take cars and either meet you at the take-out at a specified time, or leave your cars at the take-out and return to their homes in their own vehicle. Total mileage on A and B is now one-half a round trip.

How much does it cost you to operate a car, including wear and tear: 5¢/mile, 10¢/mile, 15¢/mile? What is the cost of those extra round trips in A and B when you do it yourself? Besides extra cost, if the roads are poor on the shuttle, you will avoid some of the excessive wear by avoiding an extra round trip. You may find that hiring shuttle drivers isn't really as expensive as it sounds initially. For example, suppose it will cost you $20 in extra mileage to shuttle your own car and $40 to hire a driver to do it for you. For $20 extra you can avoid extra wear and tear on the car and yourself; if divided among three or four passengers in the car, this cost is negligible. Although oversimplified, this is the kind of mental calculation you can make to decide whether to hire a shuttle.

Safety of Vehicles

A factor that must be considered in establishing your shuttle technique is the safety of your car from vandalism and theft if it is left at isolated put-in or take-out points. You may not always be able to get permission to park at a house or gas station near the put-in or take-out. For example, at the put-in points for Tours 5 and 8 and the take-out points for Tours 5 and 9, there is no habitation within several miles. If you do your own shuttle, you may be forced to leave your car in such isolated places for several days, ample time for mischief. (We have had very few problems with vandalism or theft, except at the mouth of the Grande Ronde River—see Tour 7, the Lower Salmon.) Hiring a shuttle driver may be safer. He may be willing to park your car in his own yard while you are on the river, then drive to meet you at the take-out at a prearranged time.

Convenience

Obviously you will find it far more convenient and less time-consuming to have all your cars at the take-out. You simply load gear and people and go home with no worry about a post-trip shuttle. This convenience is especially significant to people who wish to make long tours during short vacations.

Reliability of Hired Drivers

We have had excellent service from experienced old hands at shuttle driving. They know how important it is to have a car at the take-out at the proper time.

With inexperienced hired drivers you are never certain what kind of service you are going to get. We can make two suggestions. First, get "eyeball-to-eyeball" contact with the person who will be driving your shuttle. Does he seem trustworthy? Do you trust the person to drive your car over poor shuttle roads? Second, if possible, arrange to pay the person when the car is safely delivered.

Another Do-It-Yourself Possibility

Another way to shuttle for yourself, either to minimize cost or because you can't hire a shuttle, is to use a bicycle or trail bike (although the latter may be repugnant to some). This solution also enables a group with only one car to do their own shuttle. A 10-speed racing bike can be mounted on the outside of a vehicle; either racing bikes or trail bikes can be put inside pickup trucks or vans. If you must leave your bike in an isolated place, hide it, if possible, and chain it to a large tree with heavy chain. Racing and trail bikes are both high on the list of things that get stolen. Although bikes can furnish very cheap transportation, clearly most people won't wish to use them on 200-mile shuttles.

PART TWO

ON THE RIVER

TEN

River Running

In many respects, the most difficult parts of a trip—evaluation of river and party, food and equipment planning, various preparative steps, and that horrible shuttle—are over when you finally get into your boat at the river. Now you can enjoy the trip!

Loading Boats

Before you can proceed, of course, you must get that mountainous pile of gear into your boat. Assuming it is physically possible to get it all in, you will have to decide where to put each item. Three needs should guide you: turning ability, trim, and convenience. Also, the boat should be packed so that it doesn't list heavily to one side or the other.

Turning ability, measured by the amount of effort you will have to use to turn the boat, depends on the moment of inertia of the loaded boat. The larger the moment of inertia, the more difficult to turn. The moment of inertia is determined by the dis-

Figure 10-1 Pushing off! Owyhee River (Tour 9)

tribution of weight about the pivot point of the loaded boat. If a weight of w lbs. is located d ft. from the pivot point of the boat, the weight will contribute:

$$w \times d \times d = wd^2$$

to the moment of inertia of the boat. Thus, a weight of 10 lbs. at $d = 2$ ft. would contribute $10 \times 2 \times 2 = 40$ units of moment of inertia to the boat. But if this same weight were located at $d = 4$ ft., it would contribute $10 \times 4 \times 4 = 160$ units to the moment of inertia. From this comparison, we conclude that heavy objects should be close to the pivot point. If heavy objects are way up in the bow or stern, the boat will turn very poorly. For this reason we usually load sleeping bags and other lightweight gear, rather than food in the extreme ends of the boat.

Trim, that is, whether the boat is bow heavy or stern heavy, affects the behavior of the boat in waves. A boat that is bow heavy will normally rise more slowly in waves than a boat which has even trim. With both rubber and wooden drift boats, slightly bow-heavy loading is sometimes practiced to help keep the boat from flipping end-over-end backwards in large curling waves. With paddle boats, however, bow-heavy trim is prone to make the boat behave like a submarine in big waves. Thus, paddle boats are usually loaded slightly stern-heavy.

Convenience is often a dominant consideration in loading boats, particularly paddle boats. It is disconcerting to have your lunch or camera buried deeply when you want them. Small wetpacks for such items are helpful in solving this problem. Try to guess which items you will need during the day and locate them as conveniently as possible when you load the boat.

Party Organization

Once the boats are loaded and the party is ready to put in, in what order will you boat? Who should be the first person in the party when an unexpected obstacle appears? Clearly not the weakest boater. The order of boats, at least the first, second, and last, is important on an unknown river. Normally the person in the lead boat should be one of the two most skilled boaters in the party and should have careful, conservative judgment. The lead boater must be able to evaluate river dangers far enough in advance to decide whether scouting or other measures are in order, not only for himself, but also for the rest of the party.

What are the functions of the second and last boaters? The second boater, if possible also skilled, provides communication between the lead boater and the rest of the party. He tries to keep the lead boater in sight and yet he remains far enough behind so that he can direct the rest of the party to shore if the leader has difficulty. The second boater's task is difficult at times; he has nearly as much exposure to dangerous situations as the leader, with immediate responsibility for the safety of the less skilled boaters behind him.

The last, or sweep, boater also has responsibilities for party safety; if the party becomes dispersed, he may be the only person available to help should a boat be damaged or should first aid be needed. The last boater should be a thoroughly reliable boater, although not necessarily the most skilled. The desirable attributes for a sweep man or woman are a high survival quotient and talent as a jack-of-all-trades. The sweep boat carries a rescue rope, the main first aid kit, a fairly complete boat repair kit, a spare paddle and emergency food.

Finally, concerning party organization, the following safety guidelines are intended to make sure that a boater who is in trouble will have someone to help him:

1. The minimum party size on a river should be two boats, or better, three.
2. Each boater is responsible for the boat *behind* him.
3. The sweep boat should never pass the other boats.

An Attitude About "Unknown" Rivers

Our attitude toward rivers we have never run before or toward rivers we haven't run since the last high water period can be summarized in this advice: *Know what you are going into before you enter, or stop while you can still get to shore.*

This attitude, subscribed to by many other river tourists, is highly conservative. Why? Here are two examples to illustrate our reasons for conservatism and we are aware of many more.

Example 1

Some years ago, several members of our rather inexperienced boating group were investigating the Sturgeon River in Michigan as a possible whitewater run. Much of the river has a road along it, and the sections along the road seemed to have pleasant whitewater. In the middle of the best-looking whitewater run, however, the river dropped into a small canyon and was no longer visible from the road. Aware of the adage that the most difficult rapids cannot be seen from the road, we hiked down into the canyon. As we approached river level we could hear a rapids, and we soon found a 2-ft.-high ledge with several runnable chutes. Just below the ledge, the river turned left; about 20 yds. down, it turned right, flowing swiftly over a smooth, sloping granite shelf, after which it disappeared from sight behind boulders on the shore.

As we were about to hike back to the car, one of the people in the group decided to look downstream from the boulders that blocked the downstream view. He was visibly shaken as he motioned to us to join him. Just below the point where the river had disappeared from sight was a 15-ft. waterfall, studded with sharp rocks. The bend in the river and boulders on shore would have prevented us from seeing the falls until we got to the lip, and the noise from the ledge would have prevented us from hearing the falls in advance. At that point we would have trouble getting ourselves out on the sloping shelf, much less our boats. In short, this was like a fiendishly constructed trap for unwary boaters. Cautious boaters would not go below the ledge without first getting out to look downstream.

Example 2

The Metolius River in Oregon is a beautiful, cold mountain river, flowing through a heavily forested area. The river has a large gradient creating some Class IV rapids and a very fast current of 5–6 mi./hr. even in the areas where there are no rapids. A group of us were running the river one July, having run it in previous years. We were descending a delightful section of very fast, Class II rapids which seemed to end in swift water just above a bend to the right. Suddenly the lead boater paddled his kayak furiously toward shore, and lacking an eddy, drove his boat directly up onto the small rocks on the bank. After contemplating his eccentric behavior for an instant, the rest of us realized that something more urgent than a call of nature had prompted his anxiety and we followed his lead. Having seen several logs piled against the bank just below the curve, he had decided to get out above the corner to see if more logs were just below, as there was no way to get to shore at the corner. His suspicion was justified by a large log jam completely blocking the river just around the corner. Many of the individual logs in the jam had sharp broken branches immersed which could snag or impale an unfortunate boater swept under the jam. This log jam had not been present in previous years but had formed during the spring runoff. Because the lead boater was cautious and suspicious, the party was spared at best some very tense moments, at worst, a fatality.

These case histories illustrate the reason for our cautious attitude. Of course, another factor contributes to our caution. We run rivers for pleasure, not to fulfill a suicide wish.

The Look from Above

With every rapids you encounter on a whitewater tour, you will have a decision to make. Do you run the rapids, scout it, or line or portage it? With the easy rapids (remember that easy is a relative term—Class III might be easy for a Class V boater and Class II terrifying to a novice), you will run after inspection of the rapids from your boat. With the harder rapids, you will need some basis for your decision to run, scout, or line. What sort of danger signals do you look for?

Suppose you are approaching a drop in the river which is steep enough to preclude seeing all or perhaps any of the drop from well upstream. There are three danger signals that may warn you of the drop. First, there will be a discontinuity in the river; the river before the drop and after the drop will not seem to have a continuous single flow pattern. In addition, there may be a visible elevation difference between the river nearby and in the distance. Second, the rapids may be audible. But don't depend on hearing this danger signal! Not only is the roar of a rapids or falls sometimes masked by either upstream rapids or heavy wind, but in a few cases rapids, even large rapids, are completely inaudible from upstream. This phenomenon is apparently caused by unusual acoustical shapes in the region near the rapids. Velvet Falls on Tour 5, for example, is notorious for its near absence of sound, a phenomenon which has led to a number of disasters at this rapids. The third and very obvious danger signal is the presence of whitewater, either continuously visible or in the form of spray.

The next question is "What do we do now?" Our usual approach is to look at the runout, the section of river immediately below the sharp drop, which may determine our fate and that of our boat as well as the possibility of rescue should we have trouble in the sharp drop. If we think that the drop is probably runnable, we will approach it much more closely for confirmation if it has a good runout such as a pool than if it has a bad runout such as a half mile of Class III–IV water. Needless to say, a large falls should not be approached closely just because it has a good runout.

Having decided how closely we will approach the drop, on the basis of the runout and the availability of usable eddies or other stopping places, we can sneak up to that point and peek at the drop. From this close approach, we may or may not be able to see all of the rapids. If we can't see whether all of the rapids is runnable from this close view, we get out and scout from shore. Remember: *If in doubt, scout.* If the whole rapids is visible, what do you look for? In brief, look to see whether there is a clear-cut path through the rapids which is free of obstructions such as logs, rocks, and souse holes (see Glossary). *Be particularly wary of logs and log jams* either in the rapids or in the runout. They pose one of the most serious river hazards to boaters because the water often flows directly under the log jam and can take boat and boater with it. If possible, study the rapids from your boat for a few seconds or more to detect changes in the patterns of water motion. Such changes may allow you, for example, to distinguish between souse holes, which are usually fixed in position, and waves which often change position. If you can't tell what is causing a water pattern in your chosen path, the safest thing to do is to scout. Scouting *is* a nuisance. Scouting *is* time-consuming. Scouting, at times, *is* dangerous since rattlesnakes or loose boulders often add sport to a scouting walk. But scouting is preferable to rebuilding broken boats or searching for bodies.

Even though you may have done a meticulous planning job for your river tour, trust your eyes and ears, using your homework as a guide, not as an explicit cookbook description about the river and the rapids on it.

Lining and Portaging

So you decide that the rapids is too difficult or dangerous for you or part or all of your party to run. What next? Lining, letting the boat down the rapids with a rope, and portaging, carrying boat and gear around the rapids, used separately or together, will solve your problem.

Lining boats through the shallow water alongside rapids to bypass a difficult or dangerous section of the river is in principle a very simple operation, and yet in practice is extremely hazardous to boats. Many disasters and near disasters occur during lining. The basic rule of lining is to let the boat float as much as possible, and never let it fill with water.

Three precautions are useful to prevent the boat from filling. First, try to keep the boat from getting into a position broadside to the current. If a boat hits a rock while it is broadside to the current, the downstream edge of the boat will ride up onto the rock, the upstream side will dip under water, and the boat may wrap around the rock as it fills. Even if the filled boat doesn't find an affectionate rock, it will probably be uncontrollable in the current because of its weight. Second, make sure that you have enough rope to avoid the possibility of holding the boat in a souse hole. The boat may fill or flip if it remains in a souse hole for even a few seconds. If you must line through a hole make sure that the boat has momentum when it reaches the hole, pulling it downstream if necessary, and that you have enough rope to bring the boat below the hole. Third, if you are lining a paddle boat, use a lining cover, a nylon cover which can be tied securely over the cockpit, to keep out deluges of water. A spray skirt will help, but you could lose it if the boat tipped over.

Long ropes are useful for lining (20–30 ft. for paddle boats and 100 ft. for drift boats). When not being used for lining these ropes, of course, should be carried in a secure place in the boat, to preclude your getting tangled in them in a tipover.

Portaging boats alongside a rapids would seem to be a safe and conservative technique for bypassing rapids. But a great deal of damage can be done to boats that are portaged. Unhappily many portage routes are over boulders or through brush. If loaded boats are carried, boat damage is probable should a boat be dropped on rocks. This is one reason for avoiding ultralight "competition" construction in paddle boats which you plan to use for touring. If you decide to carry the empty boat and the gear separately, you will have to make several trips; on a long or difficult portage, this may require so much additional time that your margin of safety is diminished. A good example of this time shortage occurred in Spring of 1972 when an Oregon group spent over eight hours carrying boats and gear separately around a rapids which was too low to run. The group then had to use forced marches to finish their trip on schedule.

One of the greatest delights to river touring without an outfitter is making your own decisions about what to run, how to run, and when not to run on a wildwater tour. We always have a sense of accomplishment after we run a river, even an easy river. We did it ourselves and we did it *safely*.

ELEVEN

River Safety

This chapter will attempt to fill a gaping void in the backgrounds of many wildwater boaters. We have been appalled at the ignorance exhibited by many boaters of the effects of exposure and inadequate or unused lifejackets or helmets. We have also been dismayed by bumbling rescue attempts sometimes performed by even experienced boaters. Although we make no pretense that our answers to these problems are the only or the best solutions, they do work. Let's look at each of these problems, their severity, and some solutions. Then we will go on to consider some of the miscellaneous land-based safety problems in wildwater touring.

Exposure

Exposure to cold water, cold air, or both, is potentially the most serious danger in wildwater boating for two reasons. First, exposure can be fatal when it produces hypothermia, second, exposure effects, unlike those of Class VI rapids, are subtle. The effects of exposure can sneak up on an unwary boater with fatal result. Severe hypothermia, the end result of over-exposure, is a loss of the body's thermal regulation ability. The hypothermic body loses its ability to produce heat rapidly enough to offset the losses of heat by conduction, convection, and radiation. The result of this loss of control is a rapidly decreasing body core temperature, loss of ability to function in coordination and analytical ability, and finally death.

The basic physical conditions under which hypothermia develops are conditions during which there is an extremely high rate of heat loss from the body. Being immersed in cold water, wearing wet clothing in a cold wind, or even having a cold wind impinge on your bare skin or dry but inadequate clothing can cause extremely rapid heat loss from your body. The effects of wind chill are mentioned in Chapter 6 and are discussed in *Outdoor Living* (Appendix D.2), so will not be considered further here. We will discuss immersion in cold water, usually a far more important problem to boaters.

A nude or lightly clothed person when immersed in cold water has a very brief period in which to rescue himself before exhaustion or unconsciousness overtakes him. Some approximate figures given by A. F. Davidson, Surgeon General, British Royal Navy, are shown in Table 11-1 for illustration. Note that these are the

Table 11-1 *The Effect of Cold Water*

Water temperature, °F.	*Time immersed before exhaustion or unconsciousness*
32.5	less than 15 min.
32.5–40	15–30 min.
40 –50	30–60 min.
50 –60	1–2 hr.

Source: American Whitewater, XII, No. 1 (1966).

maximum lengths of time during which you could help yourself. Our own observations during winter boating and steelhead fishing trips suggest that even 2–3 minutes in freezing water may severely affect your capacity for self-rescue.

Be particularly careful about cold water if you are a he-man type. He-men are short of subcutaneous fat to serve as insulation. Since women's bodies, even thin ones, have a layer of such fat, your wife probably has a higher survival quotient in very cold water than you do.

The mechanisms of heat loss which are probably most important in immersion are conduction and convection. A means of minimizing these mechanisms is to use a wetsuit. The neoprene foam suits commonly used by scuba divers are widely available from diving shops and a few mail-order companies whose ads you will find in *Skin Diver* magazine.

If you wish to purchase a wetsuit for boating, a few suggestions might be helpful. For boating, a 1/8- or 3/16-in. thick, nylon-lined suit is usually adequate (see Table 11-2). We like the nylon-lined suits because they are durable and easy to put on. As for fit, you may buy a custom-fitted suit if you wish, but the off-the-shelf sizes are much cheaper and seem to be adequate for boating. The custom-fitted suits give better protection for long immersions of a half hour or more, but as a boater you probably won't have to spend extended periods immersed. You should be interested in shock protection more than comfort. Table 11-2 gives a series of recommendations based on our own experience of the type and thickness of wetsuits which you will want for various conditions.

The air temperature to which you will be exposed after immersion should also be considered when you are choosing your outfit from Table 11-2. We generally use an outfit which is suitable for the next higher water temperature range if we expect hot, sunny weather. Similarly, the suitable outfit for the next lower water temperature range is chosen if cold or windy weather is anticipated. We have found that owning a full 3/16-in. suit and a short-

Table 11-2 *Wetsuits for Boating*

Water temperature, °F.	*Wear*	*Reason for wearing*
60 and above	1/8-in. jacket or no suit (paddling jacket for wind)	comfort
50–60	1/8-in. jacket or 3/16-in. jacket	comfort; safety in case of long immersion
40–50	3/16-in. jacket 3/16-in. pants	jacket minimum for safety; pants give comfort and additional safety
32–40	3/16-in. jacket and pants	minimum for safety
	neoprene foam socks and gloves	comfort
	light wool sweater and paddling jacket, particularly if windy	comfort

sleeved, 1/8-in. jacket covers all our boating needs quite adequately from midsummer (water 60°F, air 80°F) to midwinter (water 32–36°F, air 45°F).

We'll add a comment about wetsuits or exposure protection in connection with the attitude evinced by a number of boaters, notably those in wooden drift boats, "If we might tip over in the rapids, we don't run it." If your judgment is infallibly correct, you won't have to swim, and a wetsuit probably won't be necessary. But will you be infallibly correct?

Lifejackets

Personal flotation, in the form of a lifejacket and/or wetsuit, is both physically helpful and psychologically gratifying to most boaters who have gone for an unexpected swim. People seem to vary, if unclothed and in still water from a few pounds buoyant tendency to a few pounds sinking tendency. The exact amount of buoyancy will depend on the relative amount of fat the person possesses, the amount of air held in his lungs, and several other variables.

Although even a few pounds of buoyancy may allow a conscious person to breathe and survive for a long period in completely calm water, substantially more buoyancy will be required to keep him afloat and breathing easily in turbulent water. The turbulence of the water itself will determine your buoyancy. As the turbulence increases, more air is mixed with the water, lowering its density and thus your buoyancy. The general rule for lifejackets is therefore: the more turbulent the water you expect, the more buoyant the lifejacket you should wear.

How much flotation should be worn for turbulent water survival? To answer this question, we must face a conflict between the adequacy and the size of the flotation. The amount of buoyancy produced by a lifejacket depends on the weight of the volume of water displaced by the lifejacket less the actual weight of the materials of which it is constructed. One cubic foot of water weighs about 62 lbs., which would mean, with typical foam lifejacket materials, a net flotation of 55–60 lbs./cu. ft. For a fairly typical set of lifejacket dimensions (front panels $1\frac{1}{2}$ ft. × $1\frac{1}{2}$ ft. and back panels 1 ft. × $1\frac{1}{2}$ ft.) there is about 13 lbs. of flotation for each inch of thickness. Thus, to get 60 lbs. of net flotation, we must have over 4-in. of thickness. Most people find this thickness extremely cumbersome and constricting to the normal movements they must make to operate their boats. This leads to a requirement that establishes the maximum amount of flotation desirable. The lifejacket must be sufficiently compact to be usable in boating, and thus probably well under 60 lbs. net flotation. (More commonly about 40 lbs. is the maximum buoyancy that boaters find tolerable). As for a minimum amount of flotation, a reasonable guide would be that the jacket should keep your head out of water most of the time, implying a net flotation of about 10 percent of your body weight as a minimum. This minimum, in our experience, has been adequate to keep heads above water enough of the time in Class I to III− whitewater. We would recommend this 10 percent as a *bare minimum* on the rivers in the guide section at the suggested running levels. As the water becomes more turbulent, a lifejacket with a net flotation of as much as 20 percent of your body weight becomes nearly essential if you prefer to breathe air rather than water. For example, a 170 lbs. person would want at least 17 lbs. of net flotation; for more turbulent rivers, up to 34 lbs. of net flotation or even more if bearable.

In addition to flotation, several other features of lifejackets merit consideration:

1. Does the jacket float the victim face up or face down if he is unconscious?
2. Is the jacket "idiot-proof"?
3. Are the materials durable enough to hold up on long trips?

The answer to the first question depends on several things, the most important being the relative amounts of flotation in the front and back sections of the jacket. Look for jackets that have at least 20 percent more flotation in front than in back. If possible, try the jacket in a swimming pool before buying it. Several categories of jackets approved by the U.S. Coast Guard are supposed to float the victim face up. In fact, for a few specific individuals, some of these jackets don't float the person face up at all. An excellent and rather extensive article on lifejackets by Carl Trost appeared in *American Whitewater, XVII,* No. 1 (1972). The article includes measured buoyancies for most of the jackets commonly in use by whitewater boaters. The article has, among other things, photos of face-down victims using face-up life jackets.

The second question is often overlooked by people buying a lifejacket for whitewater use. In particular, does the jacket have so many straps, buckles, or other devices that it would be impossible to remove if you were caught underwater by brush or a log jam? Does the jacket require that you find and manipulate a trigger to inflate it? If so, will you remember to operate it in the state of minor panic to which most unexpected swimmers are subject?

The third criterion, material durability, is rather crucial on an extended trip. We have had or observed deficiencies with several types of lifejackets. Jackets with kapok-filled plastic bags or inflatable air chambers eventually seem to leak, making the jacket first less valuable and later unsafe. Also, jackets made from cotton cloth materials seem to slowly, subtly rot, eventually tearing under the slightest stress.

To summarize this section, we can make the following recommendations of what to buy in a lifejacket:

1. Flotation. 10 percent (minimum) to 20 percent of your body weight and at least 20 percent more flotation in front than in back.

2. Fastening. snaps; zippers or ties as second choice.

3. Materials. polyethylene or polyvinyl chloride (PVC) foam, properly treated to make it impervious to water. Nylon or other synthetic cloth which is durable with repeated wetting and moderately durable in sunlight. (Nylon, though affected by the sun, has worked well for us.) Unfortunately, most of the high-flotation jackets are available only with kapok-filled bags and cotton cloth material.

Our own particular compromises are Stearn's San Souci lifejacket for small water and the 160.002, Type 3 (Coast Guard designation) for big water. The Stearn's jackets range from 17 to 25 lbs. net buoyancy depending on size and are widely available through sporting goods stores. The 160.002 is available in many marine supply stores and has about 33 lbs. of net buoyancy when new. Both of these jackets happen to be Coast Guard approved, although this was not our reason for choosing them. We have found that both jackets are reasonable for boating even in kayaks.

About some of the popular jackets used by paddle boaters: try swimming in rapids with one! We have seen many boaters swimming through rapids in these jackets, mostly under water. Flotherchoc (TM) and a number of other jackets in the 13–16 lbs. buoyancy category seem to be marginal in turbulent water for most people. If these jackets are worn in addition to a full 3/16-in. wetsuit which gives about 10 lbs. of buoyancy itself, they will serve. Without a wetsuit, plan to spend some time under water if you swim in turbulent water with these jackets.

One obvious comment is in order about lifejackets and buoyancy. A lifejacket doesn't help your buoyancy much unless you have it *on*!

Head Protection

All boaters should wear some form of head protection for safety on any whitewater of Class IV or greater difficulty. A swimmer in such water is likely to spend some time submerged in the turbulence. During this time his head may collide with a rock which, of course, may lead to unconsciousness or drowning.

For kayakists and canoeists, head protection is needed on whitewater of any difficulty. After an upset they will spend some time upside down under water before they can emerge from the boat or roll.

Helmets worn on whitewater include climbing, hockey, and motorcycle helmets. Not all of these seem to provide the desired protection; an article by Dr. Donald H. Wilson* cites a problem

**American Whitewater*, Vol. XVIII, No. 1, p. 14.

with the inadequacy of hockey helmets for whitewater. In choosing a helmet the boater must compromise among degree of head protection, comfort, and cost. We don't worry about cost; money is replaceable, heads are not. A helmet for boating must provide adequate impact protection without hampering vision or hearing and should be light enough to be comfortable. The materials must not deteriorate after being wet.

The helmets which seem to meet these specifications most closely are designed for rock climbing, surfing, or specifically for boating. One basic design uses an internal suspension to absorb shock; the other uses a crushable foam which yields under heavy impact. Our own experience suggests that the designs using crushable foam are more comfortable and are adequate for safety. We have used Bell-Toptex "Malibu" helmets with complete satisfaction. There are several other helmets of similar design on the market now. These helmets contain a crushable foam liner over most of the helmet inside a strong fiberglass shell, and a forehead band which keeps water from entering while upside down. The helmet is secured by a sturdy nylon strap riveted to the helmet.

Rescue

Survival

The first, most important, but often forgotten question in a rescue operation is very simple: "What comes first?" The answer is simple too: "People." When a boat, boaters, and perhaps equipment are floating along in the water, *first make sure that the people are not in danger.* Our usual order of rescue in either cold water or very turbulent water is to get the people who are in the worst situation to safety first, then worry about the other people, and finally the boats and equipment. There are at least three major dangers to the victims, assuming that they have proper lifejackets. The first danger, exposure to cold water, was discussed at the beginning of this chapter. The second danger to the victims, the possibility of being pinned against a rock by a boat which is filled with water, must be avoided by the victims themselves. A kayak, the smallest boat we are discussing in this book, contains more than half a ton of water when it is filled. To be pinned against a rock by even a small boat is a frightening experience, and to be pinned by a filled wooden drift boat is likely to be a terminal experience. The means to avoid this potential problem lies with the victim. He must get on the upstream side of the overturned boat. Grace and dignity in getting to the upstream side are not essential—crawl over the boat, swim around or under the boat—but get to the upstream side and stay there! The third danger to the victim is himself. Many people, even strong swimmers, have a tendency to panic when dumped unexpectedly into the river. Often the presence of a boat to which they can attach themselves is sufficient to allay their fears, whether their own overturned boat or a rescuer's boat. Hanging on to an overturned boat has much to commend it. If often makes it possible for the rescuer to rescue both the victim and his craft at once, and for the swimmer to guide the boat to prevent damage. Finally, the boat supplies welcome additional flotation for the victim. To repeat an earlier warning: as a victim you would want to be voluntarily attached to your overturned boat; to be attached to a boat by a rope tangled about one's feet is an unforgettable experience. The victim may want to part company with his boat either if the water is cold enough to put him in immediate danger or if the boat has become uncontrollable.

Let's summarize the comments we have already made and add a few more comments to make possible rescue formats for both the rescuer and the victim. Once the boat is over and people are in the water, remember the following:

1. *Rescuer:* a) Are the people in danger? b) Can I participate in the rescue without becoming another victim? (This is often a problem, particularly when one spouse is the victim

and the other spouse a potential rescuer.) c) If the people aren't in danger, what things should be rescued first? The answer to this question will be dictated by a further question about what items you can least afford to lose. d) Communicate with both victims and their rescuers to make sure that victims are not in trouble and that you are not simply duplicating effort with another rescuer.

2. *Victim:* a) If possible hang on to your paddle or other loose vital equipment. b) Are you free of all ropes, all involuntary attachment to the boat? c) Get to the upstream side of the boat. d) If the boat is controllable and the water is not numbingly cold, use the boat for flotation and enjoy the ride. Leave the boat upside down and the air trapped inside will act as flotation. You may be able to work the boat to shore yourself. e) While in the rapids, take a sitting position, facing downstream with your feet below your body to fend off rocks. In turbulent water, conventional swimming is usually a waste of effort. Wait for the quieter sections before you try to swim, then swim directly toward shore, not upstream. Upstream swimming is a fine way to train for the English Channel, but not a good way to get out of a river. Sidestroke is usually the most feasible way to swim with a lifejacket on. Plan your swimming route, if possible, so that currents help you to get to shore. Obviously, if there is something downstream that you don't want to go over, like a waterfall, sacrifice the boat and head for shore at once.

Practical Hints

Next we'll list some helpful hints for the rescuer about how to rescue effectively once he has decided what to rescue. If your boat is a raft, you usually can just drag a swimmer aboard. Otherwise, to rescue a swimmer, have him hang on to the stern of your boat or the stern grab loop in paddle boats, then paddle straight across to the nearest usable shore. Don't waste time trying to fight the current by paddling upstream. Use exactly the same technique if the swimmer is holding on to his boat. The victim can help here either by floating on the surface to minimize drag or by helping to swim his boat to shore.

To rescue the boat without the swimmer attached two techniques are possible. The most effective unless the boat is very heavy is to attach the stern line of the boat to your paddle, or for drift boats, to the boat. Of course you should only attach the boat to you if there are no difficult rapids immediately below you, and you should attach it in such a way so that you can release it quickly and easily. The other technique is to nudge the boat to shore with your boat, although this requires a number of nudges to be effective.

Particularly on small rivers, a rescue rope may be useful. A person with the rope, say a 3/8-in. nylon rope about 60–100 ft. long, can be posted alongside the most likely trouble spot in the rapids to throw the rope to the unfortunate boaters. Nylon rope is recommended here, rather than polyethylene or floating ropes, because it is easier to grip. Don't expect too much from rescue rope techniques; even with practice you can throw a rope accurately only about 30–50 ft.

Even with adequate flotation in a boat, some water must be removed after a capsize. The two most common ways to empty a boat are bailing it and inverting it. Bailing requires no explanation, only a container and labor. Inverting a boat, though seemingly a trivial operation, does require care. Even well-made rigid boats can be broken badly by inverting or attempting to invert them when filled. Try instead to empty most of the water by rolling the boat gently onto its side while it is still in the water, or by bailing before you attempt to pick it up and invert it.

In all rescue operations, don't start the rescue proceedings unless they will help. We have seen a number of rescues started at the brink of a rapids that succeeded only in putting the rescuer and the swimmer or boat in the worst possible place to run the rapids. If there is a rapids immediately below you, just try to aid the swimmer and boat into the easiest chute, and then rescue them in the first available pool below. Although one might write a whole book on various rescue techniques, it is probably more valuable to stress heavily the few really important points as we have tried to do here and hope that these *will* be remembered and used.

Nonwhitewater Hazards

Natural Dangers

Sun can be a serious problem on river tours, particularly on desert rivers. People who are unusually sensitive to sun should consider carefully whether to run desert tours or not. We would suggest several preventatives for sun hazards. For sunburn protection use any of the gunks that you have used successfully before, but apply them frequently since most of them are water soluble, or use zinc oxide cream, which although messy is very effective. A wide-brimmed hat, at least off the river, and a long-sleeved shirt on or off the river are excellent protection. Judicious use of salt tablets helps prevent heat exhaustion on desert rivers.

Poison oak or poison ivy are common on most western and many other rivers. Poison ivy is fairly easily recognized during much of the boating season by its pretty leaves, which stay a shiny, lush green until early fall and occur in threes. Poison oak leaves also occur in groups of three, but it is much less conspicuous than poison ivy; study pictures of it in a plant book if you are not familiar with it. The best approach to these plants is a distant one. If you think you have come in contact with them, wash immediately and thoroughly with cold water and strong soap; hopefully this treatment will remove the oils quickly enough to prevent poisoning.

Varmints are at times a nuisance on rivers. Probably the only mammal in North America which is dangerous with little or no provocation is the grizzly bear. We have had no reason to worry about personal safety from mammals in over twenty years of river and mountain experience in the United States. The only animals we have found dangerous are snakes.

These physical dangers aside for the moment, consider the real hazard of varmints. A large number of species just love a free meal and are rather callous about opening the lunch bucket, sometimes badly damaging food containers. Squirrels, rats, raccoons, bears, and others will take any opportunity that arises to help themselves to your food supply. To prevent such thefts hang your food supply from a high limb at night or when you are away from camp or use animal-repellent containers such as rubber wet-packs. We suspect that the smell of such bags is repulsive to animals; also the bags are airtight, preventing those nice food aromas from circulating.

Snakes, the only dangerous residents of most of the areas we visit, can be a hazard. Avoiding snakes simply requires caution. Look before you put down your hands or feet in snake country. Contrary to much popular opinion, a rattlesnake does not always rattle before it strikes, especially in the morning or evening when the snake is hunting. We generally kill rattlesnakes only if they are in the camping area or on the only portage route; in a place where they will constitute a substantial danger to the party.

If you do get bitten, the agent most likely to kill you is panic, not poison. Both rubber suction cup kits and antivenin kits are available in drugstores in snake areas. Based on discussions with a number of physicians, our own opinion is that the suction cup kits may do some good, whereas if used improperly the antivenin kits may do substantial harm to the patient. We suggest that you keep the patient as quiet as possible and use the suction cup kit according to directions. If you are not too far from civilization, try to get medical help. Although we carry an antivenin kit, we plan to use it only for dire emergencies. The documented mortality from snakebite among healthy adults seems to be very low in the western states. Don't let these comments on snakes prevent you from making a tour! We have seen only a few snakes on the rivers in the guide section, and have never had a tour member bitten by a snake.*

No discussion of varmints would be complete without a few comments about insects. The principal insects which give trouble on western rivers are mosquitos, yellow jackets, and various flies. No-see-ums are occasionally troublesome in grassy areas. Mosquitos and No-see-ums are repelled quite effectively by N,N-Diethyl-meta-toluamide, the active ingredient of a number of commercial insect repellents. Use the preparation with the highest percentage of active ingredients that you can buy so you don't have to carry as much, but check first at home to make sure that you don't have an allergy to it. We have found 71 percent material obtained from a surplus store effective.

Biting flies and yellow jackets seem only slightly deterred by this repellent; if these flies are really bad, covering up skin and perhaps even wearing a headnet will be essential. Note that such drastic measures are not necessary for the rivers discussed in the guide. Compared to the East, the Midwest, and Canada, the Northwest is a bug-hater's paradise!

Equipment Loss

Another hazard is the loss or misplacement of essential boating or camping equipment. Among the various causes of equipment loss, tipovers seem to rank first, with individual carelessness a close second. Many people on river tours, beginners in particular, are not fully aware of the seriousness of losing an irreplaceable oar for a drift boat or the only spray skirt for their kayak. They become aware after losing the item when their pleasant river tour suddenly becomes an unpleasant bushwack to civilization or the party is delayed for hours or days while they manufacture a replacement part so that the trip can continue. A delay of several

*For comprehensive discussion of the proper treatment, see *What to Do About Bites and Stings of Venomous Animals* by Robert E. Arnold, M.D. (Collier Books, 1973). It covers all dangerous snakes, lizards, spiders, insects, and marine animals of North America.

days can turn a well-planned trip into a series of forced marches against a short supply of food.

To prevent losses in tipovers, make sure that all gear is securely fastened into the boat. To prevent misplacement and subsequent loss of equipment, eternal vigilance is necessary. The trip leader has a very important function to perform in this respect. He must either himself or by delegation to another responsible person, ask such things as:

1. Are the boats adequately secured to prevent loss or damage by wind or a rising river during the night?
2. Are all small items weighted with rocks or otherwise adequately secured to prevent loss by wind or animals during the night?
3. Is equipment being dried too close to the fire?
4. Has the campsite, lunch spot, or rest stop area been checked before leaving by several people for forgotten items?
5. Do the particularly careless people in the party have one or more "keepers" to prod them to remember their equipment? This can be a rather sensitive matter, but the negligence of even one very careless person can endanger the safety of the party.

A trip leader should also take the responsibility of ensuring that some spare items are available to replace commonly lost items. There is a limit, however, to the number of spare items you can carry. The suggestions about spare equipment in Chapter 6 may be useful to you until you have experience on your own trips to guide you.

Summarizing this chapter on safety in whitewater touring, we must stress again that the most effective safety techniques are the preventative measures. Worry in advance, not neurotically, but constructively.

TWELVE

Living on the River—Camping Techniques

Camping is an integral part of whitewater touring, and the success of the trip as a whole is partly dependent upon the success of the camping experience. Some members of the group should be experienced campers, and all members should be camping types, defined as workers not whiners when setting up camp at dusk in an icy downpour.

Choosing a campsite

When should you start looking for a campsite? A certain amount of luck is involved in finding one, and no matter when you start looking, that last campsite you passed before you began looking will seem better than what you actually select. But you can do something to increase your chances of success. Start looking for

Figure 12-1 Beach camping on the Snake River (Tour 7)

a campsite a little before you actually wish to camp, and if you find a really good one, grab it. Sometimes you will have to travel a good many miles through difficult rapids before finding another campsite. Second, if the river is crowded with boaters, plan to break camp early in the morning, and make camp by four in the afternoon.

Next, what should you look for? Any functional campsite needs six basic prerequisites: a suitable landing spot, water supply, firewood supply, cooking area, sleeping area, and bushes area. Finding a suitable landing spot doesn't pose much of a problem for kayaks as they can dart quickly into small eddies and thus camp along shore in the middle of rapids (In fact, this is an excellent place for them to camp if the river is heavily traveled). Less agile rafts and rigid drift boats are more restricted, requiring more advance notice of an approaching campsite. On one mixed kayak and raft tour frustration reigned as the rafter valiantly struggled to make our little eddies. We soon learned to choose larger eddies and to have the raft follow well behind, so he had plenty of time to maneuver into our eddies. Small, bouldery landing spots will do for kayaks and small rafts which are light enough to be readily moved; but heavier boats will need campsites with some form of beach where they can be left.

Suitable landing spots are far more likely to be found in areas where a river meanders through a series of gravel bars than where it enters rock gorges. On rivers with few gravel bars or sand bars, flat benches above the river make good campsites. At higher water levels, these benches are often the only campsites, as the bars are under water. Rafts have a difficult time landing at high water. Several times we have watched a raftsman make a dramatic leap for shore with rope in hand only to be dragged on down the river after the raft, still doggedly grasping the rope.

The next feature to look for in a campsite is a drinking water supply. On some rivers, the river water itself is safe to drink. Few experiences are more delightful than drifting a river on a hot day and bending over for a cool draught whenever you feel the urge.

But frequently river water is not safe to drink without treatment. If the river is your only source of water, and you suspect that it is not safe to drink, boil it for twenty minutes or add Halazone tablets to it. When we are really dubious about a river, we use the Halazone according to directions, and then boil the water too. This treatment removes most of the contaminants.

Although it is preferable to avoid the need of such measures by locating and using a pure water supply, on some rivers (such as the Grande Ronde, Tour 2) the sources of pure water do not coincide well with the campsites. On such rivers your equipment should include sufficient water containers to transport water from the water supply to the nearest attractive campsite.

One source of drinking water is sidestreams entering the river; they are usually indicated on river maps. On many of the wilderness rivers, the headwaters of the sidestreams are in the mountains or other remote areas, and the streams continue to flow through fairly remote areas before joining the river. Even so, they are not necessarily safe to drink. On the lower Salmon Canyon, for example, we drink water from the main river in preference to the few sidestreams, which are small and heavily used in their upper reaches by cattle. Grazing animals can be a serious source of pollution on small sidestreams, particularly in ranch country. In high forest areas grazing is much less prevalent, and sidestreams are less likely to be polluted by cattle or sheep. National forest maps and U.S.G.S. topographic maps often can give you some idea of the sidestream's environment.

Springs are another excellent source of water, but sharp eyes are often needed to spot them. Watch for spots that look green and damp compared to the surrounding area, and then investigate closely. Water may be springing out of the rocks there, or may be just under the surface. We find that a short piece of flexible tubing is often useful in directing the flow of tiny springs into water bottles.

Unless you are carrying a small stove, you will need a source of firewood near your campsite. On most of the western rivers there is an ample natural supply of firewood. Even in treeless desert areas, driftwood has always given us an adequate firewood supply. But other campers use firewood too, and if you camp at a popular campsite on a heavily used river such as the John Day (Tours 3, 4) you may have to really scrounge for wood. If firewood hikes don't appeal to you, avoid the more heavily used campsites.

The campsite should have a suitable cooking area, where the fire can be built on gravel, rock, or bare earth, and where there is no chance of sparks igniting surrounding vegetation. Because fire danger is often quite high along western rivers in the summer, caution should be exercised in choosing a suitable spot for the fire. Although sand does offer some advantages for the "kitchen," you may wish to avoid it if there is a wind unless you *like* extra crunchies in your food.

Finally, your campsite will need a flat area to provide comfortable sleeping that has some protection from the wind, and an area where trees, bushes, or rocks provide some privacy for answering nature's call. If you are in an area where insects are a serious problem, you will want to seek out breezy areas and avoid swampy spots, grassy meadows, and heavy timber.

Organization in camp

The most immediate task after selecting a camp is to put boats and boating gear in a safe place. It is easier to be careless and ignore them while you do something more inviting. We have, but we've been sorry. The afternoon winds on rivers can be quite powerful. On one tour, a member of our group neglected to stash his spray skirt in a windproof place, and it disappeared (we had a spare, a *must* on a river tour). On another trip, a kayak was tumbled over and over down the beach and finally back into the river by the wind. Fortunately someone noticed and rescued it. And there have been close calls with windborn wetsuit parts and lifejackets. Since losing boating equipment on a river tour can put you in a very serious predicament, being careful with it is mandatory. Boats should be drawn well up away from the water, and kayaks and light rafts should be tied to trees if strong winds are expected. All other boating gear should be stashed in some windproof place, inside kayaks, underneath overturned boats, etc. (Since mice love inverted kayaks, you might want to look inside before crawling in the next morning.)

As far as campsite chores are concerned, you will have to decide whether organization or lack of it is preferable for your group. For a small, experienced group, lack of organization is often more enjoyable, with people spontaneously sharing the work. But, if a group includes inexperienced campers, the old hands may find themselves doing almost everything, while the newcomers helplessly look on. In such situations, it is often to your advantage to organize teams, so the inexperienced campers can be trained while they help. And, of course, in large groups, some organization into smaller work teams is needed to avoid chaos.

Chores in camp

Shelter

On many rivers in the summer you will never need a shelter, but will stretch out every night under the stars. Nevertheless you had better carry some form of shelter, because one of the unwritten rules of camping is "If you don't bring shelter, you're sure to need it." The type of shelter needed depends on the climate. The rivers described in the guides have fairly dry, relatively insect-free summer climates. This means that tarps and an ample supply of insect repellent will usually provide adequate protection. We always pick out the spots where we plan to pitch tarps before going to bed, and have the ropes and tarps handy if needed. If the weather looks threatening or we expect heavy dew, we pitch the tarp before going to bed. A few pointers on pitching a tarp:

1. Pitch it so that the high end does not face into the wind.
2. Avoid sags, they lead to pools which cause leaks.
3. Keep it low, but high enough so it is not in contact with your sleeping bag at any point.
4. Dig a shallow trench around the edges for drainage.

If you anticipate wet or cold weather or insects carry a tent equipped with a rainfly and mosquito netting for shelter. Beware of the so-called waterproof tents—the ones we have seen get so much condensation on the inside that the occupant gets soaking wet, rain or no rain.

Firewood and Fire Building

Anyone can pick up wood, but finding good firewood is almost an art. Most people think of good wood as dry wood, but there's more to it than that. Sometimes you will need wood that provides a quick hot fire; sometimes you will need wood that gives a long-lasting fire or a good bed of coals. If fire danger is great or the wind is up you will want to avoid wood that produces many sparks.

First you will need tinder to start the fire; tiny dead twigs, dry pine needles, dead grass or leaves, and paper all make good tinder. If rain has soaked everything, firemaking becomes more challenging, and you may have to resort to cheating, such as using Hexamine firestarters or candles to give you a longer-lasting starter flame. We always carry them, along with a supply of waxed paper and matches, in a special fire starter kit. Often tiny dead twigs on trees near the trunk are sufficiently protected from the rain by upper branches that they remain dry. If not, splinter out some pieces from the inside of a piece of wood. An ax or

Figure 12-2 Tarp tent before a storm (Tour 7)

hatchet will make this easy, but a strong sheath knife will do if you don't want to bother to carry an ax. We have found little necessity for an ax on any of the tours in Part III.

Next you will need small kindling to place on the tinder. Small dry twigs do well here. "Standing dead wood," dead wood taken from standing trees, is usually the best bet. And finally, you will need the bigger pieces of firewood. Wood in direct contact with the ground tends to rot rapidly; so check it before carrying it back to camp. You can usually find enough reasonably sized pieces so that an ax is not really necessary. Don't neglect sagebrush on desert rivers; it gives a very quick, very hot, though smoky fire. Driftwood is often one of your chief sources of wood, but use it as a last resort as it has a tendency to smolder rather than burn. Driftwood and river rocks that still contain water pockets inside can explode violently when heated, making the campfire a dangerous place. If you do use driftwood, gather it from near the high water line, where it may have had time to dry.

As you may know, hardwoods provide long-lasting fires and good coals, while conifers give quick, hot fires. On most western rivers, you don't have much choice—it's nearly all conifers. Occasionally you can find alder, maple, or apple trees, and in Southern Oregon and California you will find many oak trees as hardwood. Avoid cedar and hemlock if sparks will be dangerous.

Cooking

The first task associated with cooking on the river is finding the food. Unless you want to waste valuable time with your head buried in a wetpack groping around for pudding, salt, or what-have-you, spend a little time packaging and labeling food in advance as already suggested in Chapter 7. The most useful system for us has been to carry a dinner and the next morning's breakfast together in the same wetpack, labeled on the outside. The staples, including coffee, tea, salt, and sugar, are carried in their own special wetpack as is the lunch of the day. Thus, each night we just have to find two wetpacks, the dinner-breakfast, and the staples, then pull out the dinner package, and cook away.

Foods were discussed more completely in Chapter 7, where the use of baked goods was suggested to add variety to the menu. For baking, a folding reflector oven is light, compact, inexpensive, easy to use, and really works. The only trick is building the proper fire. You want the heat distributed fairly evenly throughout the oven, which requires a fire as high and as wide as the reflector oven for the entire cooking period. Oven temperature can be varied by moving the oven toward or away from the fire. Most difficulty with reflector ovens arises when the cook neglects the fire, which dies down and provides more heat at the bottom of the oven than the top, burning the bottom of the goodies. Reflector ovens usually are quicker than home ovens, so keep a close eye on your masterpiece. Of course, there isn't much point in taking a reflector oven on rivers where firewood is scarce.

Latrines

Large parties or parties on heavily used rivers should dig latrines in an appropriate spot. Carry a small folding shovel. The task is pretty simple, digging the appropriate sized hole. Be sure, of course, that it is a reasonable distance from the river and that you fill it in before you leave.

Bedtime

Before going to bed be sure that all food is placed in waterproof, animal-proof containers such as fastened wetpacks. Hang fish on high tree branches. Also check the boats and boating gear to be sure that they are safe from wind and rising water.

Breaking Camp

Burn all burnable garbage and pack the unburnables like foil, cans out with you. Remember, these objects are a lot lighter now than when they were full of food. Burying them doesn't work, animals dig them up and make a terrible mess. Be sure that the fire is thoroughly out. This doesn't mean just dumping a little water on it. The coals underneath the surface may still be burning; the water must be thoroughly stirred in so that all coals are dead. Fill in the latrine.

Always have at least one person make a careful check of the entire camp area just before casting off. This often results in finding an item that would otherwise be irretrievable.

THIRTEEN

Notes on Photography and Fishing

To bring film or fishing tackle that are wrong for the river you are touring, is a thoroughly frustrating experience. The following notes, aimed purely at the novice photographer or fisherman, are designed to give you some idea about usable equipment to bring on a river tour. The expert photographer or fisherman will have his own ideas and probably a good bag of tricks to allow him to improvise.

Photography

Camera

A camera for use on whitewater tours is difficult to choose. Because nearly all ordinary cameras become terminally ill if they are soaked in water for a few minutes, the first question to ask is whether you wish to shoot pictures from the boat while in rapids. If you wish to shoot on the run, you have one of two choices, a camera and accessories suitable for underwater use or a camera inexpensive enough to be considered expendable. If you have a camera for which an underwater housing is available you may wish to use your usual camera with a housing. Such housings can be purchased for many expensive cameras and even for some low-priced cameras such as the Instamatic, but are bulky and awkward to use. Another possible way to shoot from the boat is to use a scuba diver's camera. We have used a Nikonos II for some time now with complete satisfaction. This camera is small, light, of high quality, but expensive. One of us carries this camera strapped to his chest while we kayak and shoots pictures at nearly any time.

Should you elect to shoot pictures only from shore or from very quiet sections of the river, then you have a nearly unlimited choice of equipment. We have found that medium-priced Super 8-mm. movie cameras and medium-priced 35-mm. still cameras seem to have versatility and the ability to handle photography on whitewater tours. Single lens reflex cameras are very convenient for close-up work on flowers, Indian paintings, etc., as well as for use with a polarizing filter. For rapids photography, a telephoto lens is sometimes convenient. For canyon photography, a wide-angle lens can be useful. For a 35-mm. camera, a 35-mm. focal length wide-angle and a 105-mm. telephoto are usually adequate. A wide-angle lens also gives apparent depth to a scene. (See Figure 2-1, for example).

If your camera has an adjustable lens opening and shutter speed, a light meter is nearly a must. Lighting in river canyons is often very deceptive. You may find the excellent and inexpensive book by Minor White, *Zone System Manual* (Morgan and Morgan, Inc., N.Y.), 1968, a very useful guide to use of a light meter under difficult lighting situations.

Film

Film choice for whitewater touring is relatively simple. Get enough speed. You need a moderate speed film (ASA 64 minimum; ASA 100 or so is better) for two reasons. First, you will want to shoot action shots such as running rapids at shutter speeds of 1/250 second or faster to help freeze the action. Because you often can't refocus easily as your subject comes racing down a rapids toward you, you will probably wish to shoot at a small lens opening, say f/8 or f/11, to get as much depth of field as possible. But 1/250 second at f/11 is the proper recommended exposure for an ASA 125 film on a bright, sunny day. If you are shooting on a dark day, a higher speed film would be useful. Films faster than ASA 400 are rarely needed except for special effects and aside from yielding poorer-quality slides or enlargements than slower films, may give very awkward shooting conditions, e.g., 1/1,000 second at f/32 in bright lighting. If you plan to do much shooting in the early morning or late evening, you might try a lightweight screw-in or clamp-on tripod to allow you to use longer exposures for scenery.

One warning on film is in order. Particularly if you keep your film in a wetpack: keep the pack out of the sun. We have placed fever thermometers in a wetpack on an 80° day and found a reading of 104° in the pack. Films can give very strange results when they are overheated.

Filters

Filters can be very useful in helping you alleviate two problems when you are shooting into a glaring white rapids or including some sky in your pictures. The light from the sky has a great deal of ultraviolet in it, a wavelength region in which film is most sensitive. The effect of ultraviolet is to give the sky a washed out appearance. The light from both the glaring whitewater and the sky are also partly polarized.

For color film, a polarizing filter, adjusted for minimum glare or minimum sky intensity, i.e., a dark sky, will help. A U.V. filter will help the sky problem, but not the glare. The U.V. filter simply cuts out part of the most effective light reaching the film from the sky, the ultraviolet.

For black-and-white film, polarizing and U.V. filters will have the same effect as they do with color film. With black-and-white, we also use a K-1 or K-2 filter, light yellow and medium yellow, respectively, to darken skies and accentuate clouds. See Figure T 7-1 for an example of the effect of a K-2 filter.

Take plenty of film. It's almost as much fun to "lie" about the trip with pictures as it is to go on it!

Fishing

This short section is designed for the Undedicated fisherman who has heard that there are fish in the river he is going to tour and might want to fish once or twice on his trip. Our only intent here is to give him some idea of what kind of tackle to take along with a few suggestions about lures, etc., that we have used successfully on a large number of rivers.

Trout or Bass (fish up to 4 lbs.)

5–6½ ft., 2½–3½ oz. spinning rod with either an open- or closed-faced spinning reel loaded with about 100–150 yd. of 3–4 lbs. test monofilament.

Or

7–7½ ft., 3–3½ oz. (6–7 weight) fly rod with a reel carrying a 30–35 yd. fly line. Use tapered leaders with about a 3 lbs. tippet.

Steelhead, Salmon, Large Trout (up to 15 lbs.)

8–9 ft., 6–8 oz. spinning rod, open-face spinning reel with a good drag and capacity for at least 150 yd. of suitable weight monofilament (6–10 lbs. test for steelhead, 12–15 lbs. test for salmon).

Or

$7\frac{1}{2}$–$8\frac{1}{2}$ ft., 4–$4\frac{1}{2}$ oz. (7–8 weight) fly rod, fly reel with a drag and with capacity for 30 yd. fly line plus at least 100 yd. of 12–18 lbs. test backing. Use 4–10 lbs. test tippets on a tapered leader.

These specifications will not give you the perfect outfit for the river you are on, but may keep you from taking a rod suitable for 600 lb. tuna on streams where there are only 9-in. trout. As for lures, a selection that we usually carry for trout has several Mepps-type spinners, red-and-white and hammered brass spoons (1/8–1/4 oz.) and the following flies: Royal Coachman, Black Gnat, and Brown Hackle in sizes #8 and #12. We usually carry some #10 hooks and split shot to use if grasshoppers, hellgramites, or other natural bait are found. For steelhead and salmon, the same types of spinners and spoons in 1/4–5/8 oz. weights have proved productive. Mature salmon seem to take flies only rarely in most streams, but steelhead in some rivers, especially the Rogue, takes flies well in the late summer. The flies which are productive for steelhead are apparently highly specific to each river. Sizes #4 to #8 are generally adequate for summer steelhead. If you are at all seriously interested in fishing, talk to owners of sporting goods stores in the area around the river to get their recommendations of the most effective lures and techniques for their area.

PART THREE

RIVER TOUR GUIDES

Introduction to Guides

These guides were written to allow you to make whitewater tours with ease, without the expense of hiring a human guide, but must be used only with the following reservations:

1. The difficulty classification listed for each rapids is for the *easiest* route through the rapids, and in most cases you will have to find that easiest route.
2. The difficulty ratings for the individual rapids on these tours rate the whitewater difficulty of the particular rapids exclusive of the isolation factor. If, for example, a tour has a large number of Class III rapids, it might be suitable for a group of Class III boaters if civilization could be reached in a few hours. On the other hand, this same type of river might require a predominantly Class IV party if the river is very isolated, several days' walk to civilization. You increase your safety margin on the tour if you have "too good" boat-

ers, people who are boating below their ultimate ability. This increase in safety margin is essential on rivers from which a walk out would be difficult and dangerous. On isolated rivers you try to avoid trouble.

3. The difficulty and location of rapids may change from year to year because of floods, erosion, or landslides. So if you see something that looks bad where the guide claims it should be easy: stop and look!

4. The guides only hold at recommended water levels. At higher water than recommended, the river is usually much more dangerous, and at much lower water, you may do more hiking than boating.

5. We consider listing every rock and every rapids on the tours both undesirable and impractical. Undesirable because part of the fun of wildwater touring is designing a strategy to run an unfamiliar rapids. Impractical because many rivers have sections that are too continuous to allow one drop to be distinguished from the next. What we have done is to list the rapids that are of the difficulty stated for the tour if we believe that they will present problems to boaters of appropriate skill level for the tour, those of greater difficulty, or *any* rapids that we believe present serious danger, even if the latter are easier than the tour difficulty.

6. Having the guide does not guarantee a safe trip. If you fancy yourself an expert but in reality are a Class II boater, you will probably have a disaster on a Class IV tour, guide or no guide. Don't be misled into believing that you can handle Class III whitewater because you are a fantastic lake canoeist who once made a 200-mile wilderness trip in Canada that even had a few riffles on it. Real whitewater is something else, and it requires many days of whitewater practice to handle it competently. Blundering down a Class III rapids once without upsetting does not mean that you are ready for

a Class III tour. Rather, you should try for complete control of your boat in Class III or harder rapids before attempting a Class III tour. If you then use these guides carefully, and your own common sense as well, you will be able to make tours with reasonable safety.

7. A last comment here is addressed to fortunately only a small number of people we have seen in our boating experience. At least a few people have no interest in learning river skills but take a dumb-luck-and-lots-of-thrills approach to survival on whitewater. To these mindless, hardcore thrill-seekers, whose interest is merely inflamed by serious warnings about river difficulty, we can offer one suggestion. Run local waterfalls. Then when your luck runs out, your body will be more easily and cheaply rescued than it will be on the tours we have listed here.

These guides are designed to be used on the river. In most cases, there is just too much to remember accurately. We suggest that you make two copies of the relevant material; one to carry in your gear, and one to carry in a transparent plastic bag in your lifejacket pocket or some other accessible spot. Keep track of each landmark as you pass it and remember that the guide doesn't help much if you don't know where you are.

In preparation of the guides we ran all the rivers in the guides at least three times and at different water levels. On all tours we kept a running record on the river, making notes with crayon or waxed pencil on freezer paper taped to the decks of our kayaks. We ran slalom kayaks on all the tours, but in many cases were accompanied by slalom canoes, rubber rafts, or wooden drift boats.* On each tour we have carried all our food and gear in the kayaks and found the loads quite bearable.

*The recommendations of boat types for each tour do not mention C-1's and C-2's. Any tour listed as suitable for kayaks is also suitable for C-1's and C-2's. We did not list them in the tables to avoid confusion with open canoes, which are not suitable for most of the tours.

Table TI-1 *Rivers in Order of Difficulty*

River	*Tour no.*	*Normal season*	*Length of trip*	*Difficulty*[a]	*Recommended flow, c.f.s.*
John Day	3	March–June	44 mi., 2½–4 days	I_2	1,500– 4,000
John Day	4	March–June	70 mi., 3–5 days	I_3	1,500– 4,000
Grande Ronde	2	June–July	44 mi., 3 days	II_{3-}	1,500– 4,000
Owyhee	9	April–May	38–63 mi., 3–5 days	$II+_{4-}$	900– 3,000
Rogue	1	June–Sept.	35–45 mi., 3–4 days	$III_{4-,6}$	800– 2,500
Salmon	7	Aug.–Sept.	70 mi., 4–5 days	III_{4-}	5,000–10,000
Salmon	6	July–Sept.	79–153 mi., 4–8 days	III_{4-}	3,000–10,000
Salmon	5	July–Aug.	96 mi., 6 days	$III+_4$	900– 3,000[b]
Owyhee	8	May	35 mi., 3 days	$IV_{5,6}$	1,000– 3,000

[a] I_{2+} means mostly Class I with one or more rapids up to Class II+.
[b] Very approximate.

Table TI-2 *Rivers in Order of Season*

River	*Tour no.*	*Normal season*	*Length of trip*	*Difficulty*	*Recommended flow, c.f.s.*
John Day	3	March–June	44 mi., 2½–4 days	I_2	1,500– 4,000
John Day	4	March–June	70 mi., 3–5 days	I_3	1,500– 4,000
Owyhee	9	April–May	38–63 mi., 3–5 days	$II+_4$	900– 3,000
Owyhee	8	May	35 mi., 3 days	$IV_{5,6}$	1,000– 3,000
Grande Ronde	2	June–July	44 mi., 3 days	II_{3-}	1,500– 4,000
Rogue	1	June–Sept.	35–45 mi., 3–4 days	$III_{4-,6}$	800– 2,500
Salmon	5	July–Aug.	96 mi., 6 days	$III+_4$	900– 3,000[a]
Salmon	6	July–Sept.	79–153 mi., 4–8 days	III_{4-}	3,000–10,000
Salmon	7	Aug.–Sept.	70 mi., 4–5 days	III_{4-}	5,000–10,000

[a] Very approximate.

All the rivers chosen are in wilderness or semiwilderness and offer tours of at least three days. We selected several rivers suitable for novice boaters and several suitable for intermediate boaters, as well as a few for experts only. We also chose some rivers that are runnable in late summer in addition to rivers for the spring and early summer. The location of the rivers is limited to Idaho and Oregon because Washington and California, the other states which border on Oregon, where we live, have little to offer in the way of long wilderness tours. The Northwest is one of the few regions in the United States offering good summer whitewater boating.

TOUR ONE

Rogue River

RECOMMENDED BOAT TYPES: *kayaks, rubber rafts, drift boats, inflatable kayaks (below 2,000 c.f.s.).*

DIFFICULTY OF RAPIDS: *Class II–III, with a little IV−.*

AVERAGE GRADIENT: *13 ft./mi.*

WHEN TO RUN: *June–September.*

LENGTH IN MILES: *35–45 depending on put-ins and take-outs.*

LENGTH IN DAYS: *2½–5.*

Description

Southern Oregon's Rogue River is justly famous as a white-water run in the summer and as a fisherman's river in the spring

Figure T1-1 Entrance to Mule Creek Canyon

and fall. It combines outstanding scenery with magnificent whitewater of intermediate difficulty and appeals to boaters of a wide range of skill. The Rogue is one of the national Wild Rivers, and its scenery is unique. The banks are heavily forested, predominantly with hardwoods. The trees include a variety of oaks (Oregon white oak, California black oak), as well as Pacific madrone with orange bark, cottonwood, and alder. Many conifers are also present, including cedar, Douglas fir, and Ponderosa pine. Shrubs include Oregon grape, rhododendron, and azalea. Large grassy meadows break the monotony of the forested hills, and crystal clear sidestreams form lovely dells of ferns and flowers. The river water itself is a disappointment; pollutants from upstream towns like Grant's Pass and algae growths due to its warm temperature often make it a turbid and unappetizing sight. But it is clean enough to swim in, and the warm water makes boating a delight. Throughout much of this section, the river flows through low rock-walled gorges, with occasional pot holes and small caves.

Our run includes 10 mi. along the road, but the remaining section of 35 mi. is roadless and wild except for the occupants of a few lodges and cabins. A completely roadless shorter run that misses a few rapids can be made by starting at the end of the road at Grave Creek and taking out at Foster Creek.

The Rogue has an interesting assortment of campsites including sand beaches, meadows, oak groves, and some strange wild rocky spots. Some travelers prefer to make reservations at the lodges offering room and board that are spaced along the river. In midsummer the travelers include a fair number of backpackers on the trail that parallels the river, a few fishermen in drift boats, and whitewater boaters, including some commercially guided raft parties. Increased use by boaters had led to restrictions starting in 1974 similar to those on the Middle Fork of the Salmon. Information on these can be obtained from the addresses listed in the Specific Information section of this tour. Below the Blossom Bar area, there is an occasional jet boat, particularly on weekends. Listen for them before descending a rapid.

Camping problems include poison oak, which is abundant but avoidable, rattlesnakes, and drinking water. The last is not really much of a problem since there are a large number of clear, cool sidestreams and springs. The Forest Service suggests that, although some sidestreams are considered safe, it is wisest to boil the water or use Halazone before drinking it.

Rogue wildlife includes a large number of Columbian black-tailed deer, some black bears, herons, hawks, vultures, and otters, which you can watch for in the late evening and early morning. The river is famous for its salmon run in May and early June and the so-called summer steelhead run in September and October. Steelhead are rainbow trout that go out to sea and return to their native stream to spawn as huge as 5–20 lb. fish. At any time in the summer you can watch the salmon and steelhead trying to jump Rainie Falls. Fishing in July and August is generally poor due to the warm water.

One of the joys of the Rogue is the range of activities it offers. Besides boating and fishing, hiking and swimming there are excellent. The hiking trail along the river gives a welcome change from boating, and the warm water makes for pleasant swimming.

The weather in June and September is variable; prepare for rain, especially in September. In July and August the weather is generally hot and sunny with warm nights, but be prepared for a shower, just in case. Despite warm temperatures, in the 60's in June and 70's in July–August, a lightweight wetsuit top or a wool sweater and waterproof jacket make life much more comfortable if it rains. Mosquitoes are few, but flies and yellow jackets can be annoying.

The early history of the Rogue, like that of many other western rivers, is connected with mining. Gold was discovered there in 1859, and gold has been mined to a varying degree ever since. At least one old-time gold miner still lives and mines on one of the sidestreams. Occasional deserted cabins remain as relics of the gold rush and fur-trapping days.

The Rogue's main fame is probably its reputation for fishing.

In the first half of the century, it was a magnificent fly-fishing stream for summer steelhead, attracting fishermen from all over the country. One of them was Zane Grey. This author of western novels spent many summers on the Rogue. His cabin still stands, and, although it is located on private property, the owner maintains the cabin and in the past has allowed public access.

Nature of rapids

Most of the whitewater on the Rogue is easy enough for the intermediate boater yet interesting enough for the expert. The rapids are Class II to III, with two that approach Class IV (see Guide). The small gradient of the river (13 ft./mi.) is deceptive, as the rapids are of the pool and drop variety, with some very flat pools and some very steep drops. There are several rapids of the long rock-garden type, but the typical Rogue rapids is a short, steep (2–3 ft.), narrow drop with a fairly clean tongue. Because much of the river flows through a rock gorge it has very interesting but comfortably small hydraulics such as surging boils, even at lower water levels. The Rogue has a large number of interesting play spots for kayaks. In most sections, the stretches of flat water are short enough not to become tedious and provide excellent runouts for most of the rapids. There is one short and easy portage or line around Rainie Falls, and only one spot where scouting is mandatory (see Guide).

We have run the Rogue at a range of water levels from 800 to 2,200 c.f.s. At 800 c.f.s. it is marginally low especially for drift boats, but everything is runnable. At 1,500 c.f.s. it is at an ideal moderate level, and at 2,200 c.f.s. it is fairly high but quite manageable. Our recommended range of water levels is 800–2,500 c.f.s. As usual, rocks are more of a problem at lower water levels, and hydraulics are worse at higher levels.

The Rogue is best suited to Class III or better boaters, but a small percentage of the party can be Class II boaters who have had considerable experience on Class II water and who may wish to have a more experienced boater run their boats through the most difficult rapids. Rescue possibilities in case of an emergency are good, as the hiking trail running the length of the river is usually easily accessible and some of the lodges have airstrips.

Specific information

Location: S.W. Oregon, Northwest of Grant's Pass

Put-in

Almeda Bar Recreation Site about 2 mi. northwest of the town, i.e., the store, of Galice. Almeda Bar has a fairly nice campground and an excellent boat launching ramp. We experienced no vandalism of cars left there, but the ranger station within walking distance is probably safer. Some parties prefer to put in at the end of the road, at Grave Creek (see Guide).

Take-out

Agness. We have taken out at the bridge crossing the Rogue a few miles above Agness, a steep carry, and at a beach across from the jet boat landing in Agness. This beach has road access, but may be private property. If it is posted, be sure to obtain permission to use it. The ranger station at Agness provides a safe place to leave cars. Many parties prefer to take out at the boat landing at Foster Bar, a few miles upstream of Agness.

Shuttle

The drive from Almeda Bar to Agness is unusually direct. The road to Agness is well-marked, and turns west off the main road from Almeda Bar to Galice about 1/2 mi. southeast of Galice.

It is 41 mi. from this turn-off to Agness over rather slow, sometimes rough, but basically good logging road which is partly paved, partly oiled gravel. Allow 3–4 hrs. for the round trip. Note that in early summer, the road may be in poor condition. Check in Galice before driving it.

Maps

The Bureau of Land Management and the Forest Service jointly distribute a map showing major rapids, creeks, and campsites. Obtain these at the Rand Ranger Station, Galice, or write to:

Figure T1-2 Typical Rogue rapids

Bureau of Land Management
310 W. 6th St.
Medford, Ore. 97501

Water Level Information

The recommended water level is 800–2,500 c.f.s. Ask for the flow in cubic feet per second on the Rogue at Raygold from:

River Forecast Center
National Weather Service
320 Customhouse
Portland, Ore. 97209
(phone: 503-221-3811)

ROGUE RIVER

TOUR I

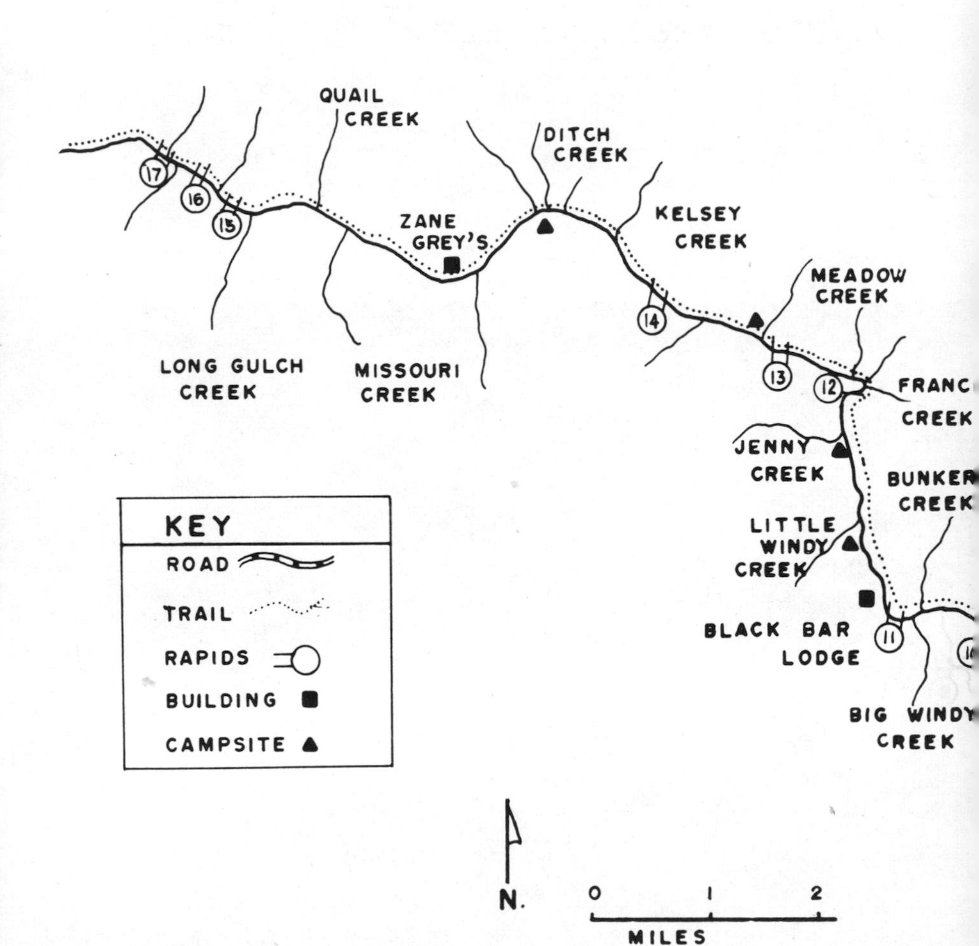

RAPIDS

1. GRAVE CREEK RIFFLE, III− TO III.
2. GRAVE CREEK FALLS, III−.
3. RAINIE FALLS, <u>PORTAGE</u>
4. TYEE RAPIDS, III.
5. WILDCAT RAPIDS, III.
6. RUSSIAN RAPIDS, II+.
7. MONTGOMERY RAPIDS, II+.
8. SLIM PICKINGS RAPIDS, II.
9. WASHBOARD RAPIDS, II.

   PLOWSHARE RAPIDS, II TO III.

10. WINDYCREEK CHUTE, II+.
11. BLACK BAR RAPIDS, III <u>SCOUT</u>.

    BLACK BAR FALLS, II +.

12. HORSESHOE BEND RAPIDS, III−.
13. DULOG RAPIDS, II.
14. KELSEY FALLS, SIX II TO II+ DROPS.
15. LONG GULCH RIFFLE, II+.
16. CLASS II.
17. JOHN'S RAPIDS, II +.

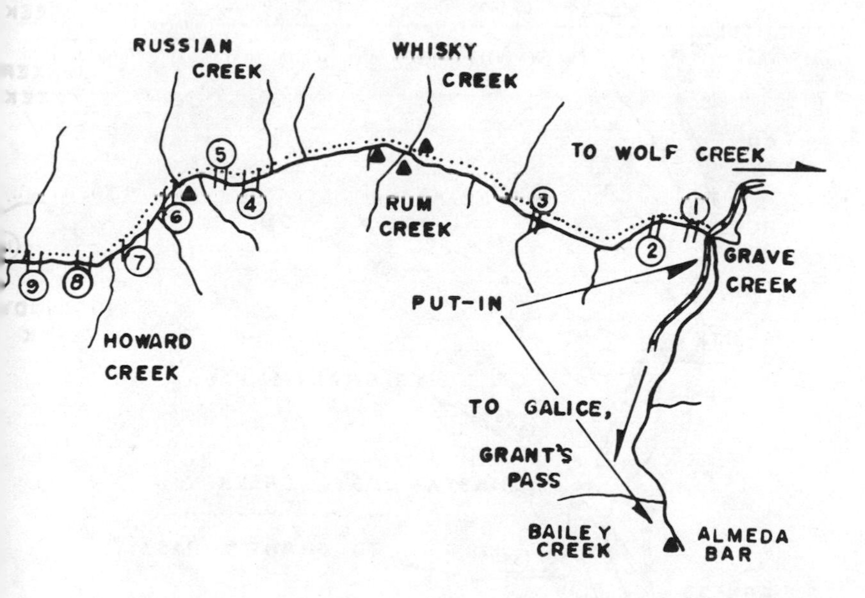

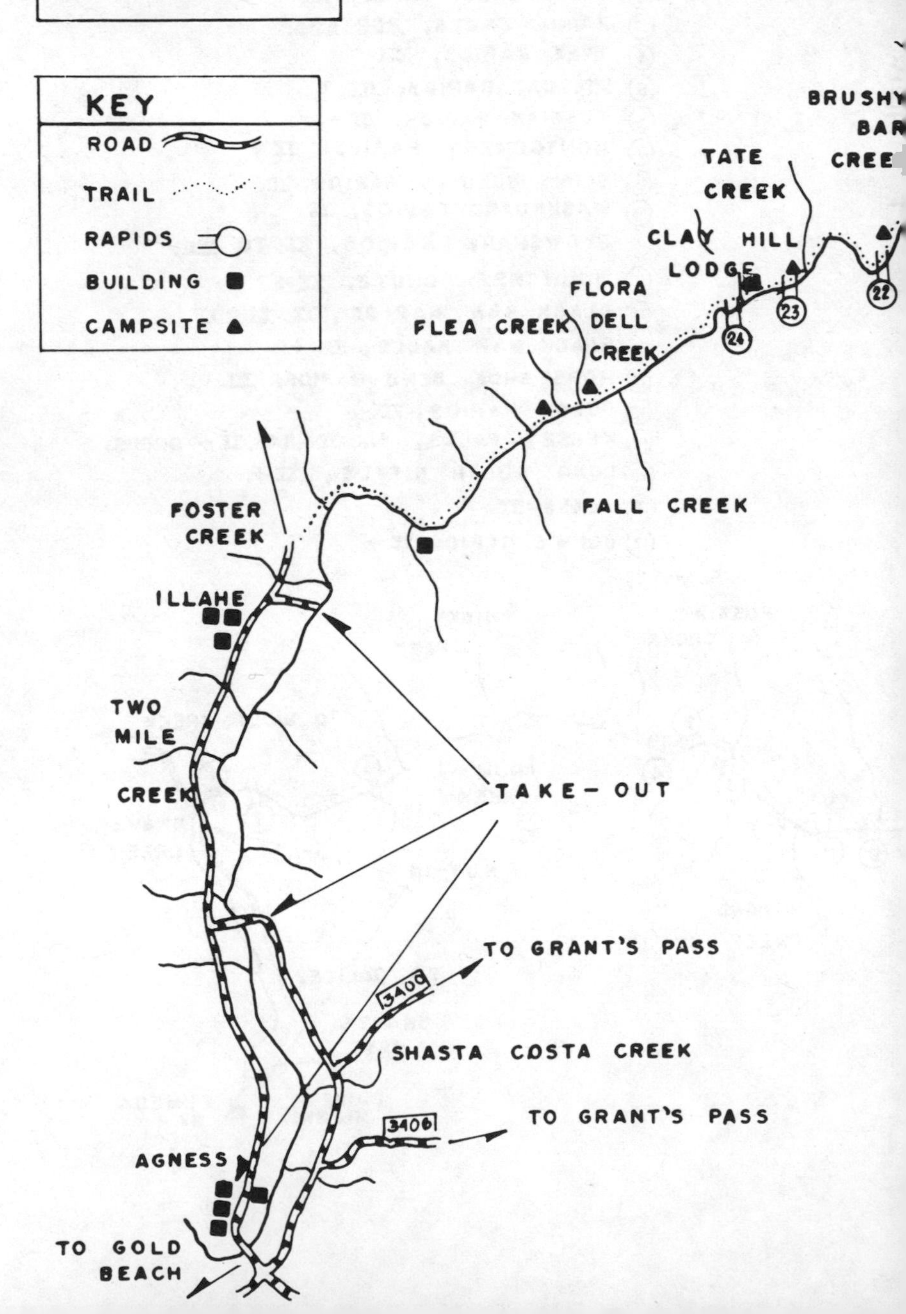
ROGUE RIVER
TOUR I
KEY
ROAD
TRAIL
RAPIDS
BUILDING
CAMPSITE
PARADISE
BRUSHY
BAR
CREE
TATE
CREEK
CLAY HILL
LODGE
FLORA
DELL
CREEK
FLEA CREEK
24
23
22
FALL CREEK
FOSTER
CREEK
ILLAHE
TWO
MILE
CREEK
TAKE-OUT
TO GRANT'S PASS
3400
SHASTA COSTA CREEK
TO GRANT'S PASS
3406
AGNESS
TO GOLD
BEACH

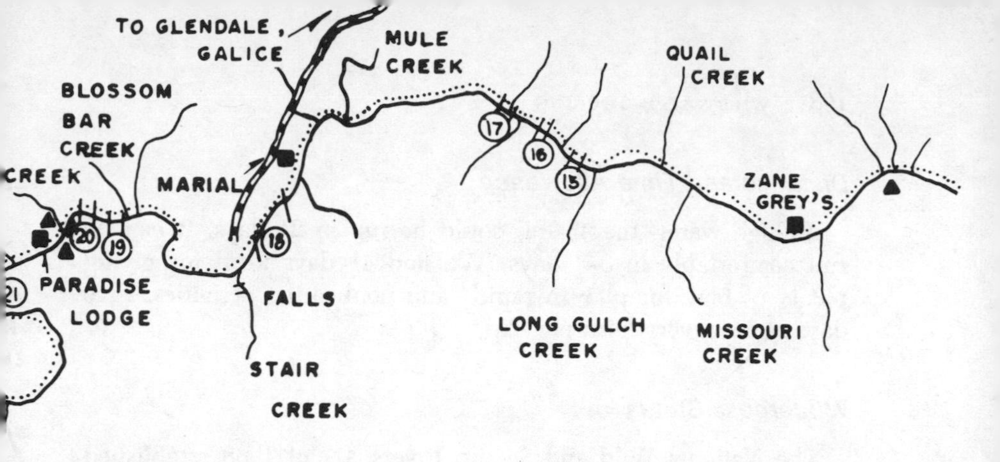

RAPIDS

15. LONG GULCH RIFFLE, II +.
16. CLASS II.
17. JOHN'S RAPIDS, II +.
18. MULE CREEK CANYON, III + TO IV -.
19. BLOSSOM BAR RAPIDS, IV - SCOUT.
20. DEVILS STAIRCASE, II +.
21. HUGGINS CANYON, II.
22. SOLITUDE RAPIDS, II.
23. CAMP TACOMA RAPIDS, II +
24. CLAY HILL RAPIDS, III -

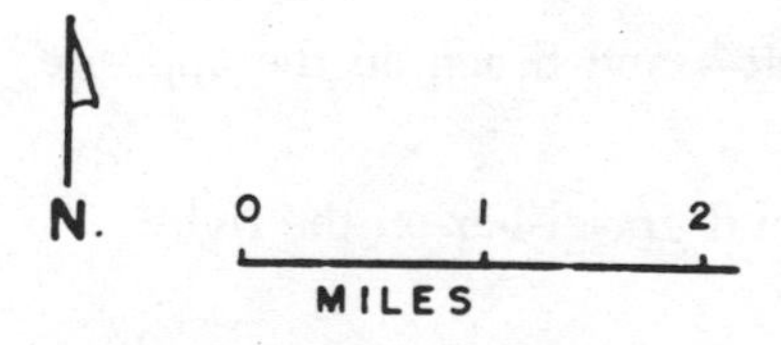

Distance and Time Allowance

At high water, the 45 mi. could be run in 2½ days. It can be run comfortably in 3–4 days. We find 4½ days ideal for giving plenty of time for play in rapids and nonboating activities. Five days allow a very leisurely trip.

Wilderness Status

The National Wild and Scenic Rivers Act of 1968 established the 33 mi. of the Rogue below Grave Creek as a Wild River. The Bureau of Land Management administers the section from Grave Creek to Marial, and the U.S. Forest Service administers the section downstream of Marial. This section of the Rogue is also classified as a wild river in the Oregon Scenic Waterways system. As a wild river, it will be preserved in a primitive condition, with no new building allowed except that needed for public outdoor recreation or for protection of the resources.

Guide

This applies only at recommended water levels. Rapids and campsites may change at any time due to flooding, landslides, and other phenomena.

MI. 0. Almeda Bar boat launching ramp and campground. From here to Grave Creek, Class II rapids alternate with some long pools. The road parallels the river in this stretch.

MI. 1. Bailey Creek on the left—sand beach on the opposite shore of the river.

MI. 2. Attractive little creek and gravel bar on the right.

MI. 4. Grave Creek on the right and a bridge across the river. Grave Creek is rather warm, and has a road along it. The road along the Rogue terminates here, and the hiking trail begins. Boats may be launched here.

MI. 4+. Grave Creek Riffle, a Class III– to III rock garden type of rapids around a gravel island. The main chute is on the left side of the island. The rapids can be fairly heavy, and some maneuvering is required. Less experienced boaters may wish to scout from the island. At high water, the right side of the island provides a good "chicken route."

MI. 4½. Grave Creek Falls, steep, short Class III– drop, about 200 yd. below Grave Creek Riffle.

MI. 5. Class II chute around a gravel island, which may be washed out eventually.

MI. 6. Rainie Falls. **CAUTION:** Class VI. The river drops vertically 10 ft. over boulders. A long quiet pool precedes the falls, so it is easy to hear it and land. Land on the left side to view the falls and fish trying to jump it. A spring about 75 yd. upstream of the falls provides drinking water. To line boats down the fishway, land on the right side.

MI. 7. Small creek and beach campsite on the left.

MI. 8. Whiskey Creek and campsite on the right. This is a large and popular campsite. It has a sand beach and a flat, shaded meadow area. There are several tables here. A herd of tame deer, some of which will eat out of your hand, make their home in the area.

MI. 8. Rum Creek and a small campsite on the left.

MI. 8+. Nice small camp with creek on left.

MI. 9. Tyee Rapids. Class III to III+. A rock garden with a huge boulder in the river towards the lower end of the rapid.

MI. 9+. Wildcat Rapids. Class III. About 200 yd. below Tyee. Very long rock garden. The first section consists of a rapid around a gravel island, take the right chute. The rapids continue after the island into the main drop, quite rocky.

MI. 10. Russian Creek on the right; nice beach campsite on the opposite side of the river.

MI. 10+. Russian Rapids. Class II+. Just after Russian Creek. Steep, quite heavy, but fairly clean drop.

MI. 10+. Montgomery Rapids, or Howard Creek Chute. Class II+. 200 yd. after Russian Rapids. Five steep but very short drops, separated by pools varying in length from about 50 to 150 yd.

MI. 11. Howard Creek on the left. Small, uninspiring camping spot.

MI. 11+. Slim Pickings Rapids. Class II.

MI. 12. Washboard Rapids. Class II. 100 yd. below Washboard: Plowshare Rapids. Class II at low water; Class III at moderate to high water, when it develops some tricky turbulence.

MI. 12+. Windy Creek Chute. Two drops; the first is Class II+, the second is Class II.

MI. 13. Bunker Creek on the right. No place to land.

MI. 13. Big Windy Creek on the left, small landing and possible camping spot.

MI. 13+. Black Bar Rapids. Class III. Those unfamiliar with

the rapids may wish to scout quickly. The route is on the extreme right. Very rocky.

MI. 13+. Black Bar Falls, 50 yd. below Black Bar Rapids. Class II+ to III−. Very steep but clean chute.

MI. 14. Black Bar Lodge on the left. This is not visible from the river, but usually one or more boats is moored there. Room and board available if you make reservations.

MI. 14+. Small beach campsite on the left. Little Windy Creek within walking distance downstream.

MI. 15. Jenny Creek and pleasant campsite on the left.

MI. 15+. Horseshoe Bend Rapids. Class III−. River curves to the right with some bad hydraulics on the left due to a canyon wall.

MI. 16. Francis Creek on the right. Possible campsite.

MI. 16+. Dulog Rapids. Two Class II drops separated by about 100 yd. Followed by Meadow Creek and a good campsite up a steep bank on the right.

MI. 17. Kelsey Falls. Six enjoyable drops of varying difficulty, but all in the Class II range, separated by about 100 yd. each. Some good play spots for kayaks.

MI. 18. Kelsey Creek on the right. Small campsite, but landing difficult except for kayaks.

MI. 19. Ditch Creek on the right by a large, steep meadow. Possible campsite here or on Battle Bar on the opposite side of the river where an abandoned cabin provides an emergency shelter.

MI. 20. Zane Grey's old cabin on the right. Airstrip and private hunting lodge.

MI. 20+. Spring on the right.

MI. 21. Missouri Creek and cabins on the left.

MI. 21+. Quail Creek on the right, sometimes dry, is rumored to have some arsenic content.

MI. 22+. Long Gulch Creek on the left. The creek is followed by two Class II drops and a Class II S turn separated by 100–200 yd. 100 yd. after the S turn is Long Gulch Riffle, Class II+, a steep drop through boulders.

MI. 23. Class II drop.

MI. 23+. John's Rapids. Steep Class II+ rapids.

MI. 24. Mule Creek on the right. Small campsite. This is the last camping possibility with water before Mule Creek Canyon.

MI. 24+. Marial on the right. This small colony of houses just around the corner from Mule Creek includes a lodge, make reservations. Although scouting is usually not helpful here, if a party wishes to scout Mule Creek Canyon this is the place to land. Climb up to the hiking trail, and follow it down the river. A rough road gives access here.

MI. 25. Mule Creek Canyon Rapids. Verges on Class IV−. A unique and challenging 1/4 mi. of rapids. The river drops into a narrow, rock-walled canyon, varying from about 15 ft. wide at the narrowest spot to about 35 ft. wide. The problem is not steep drops but the strange hydraulics that develop when the speeding narrow river makes a sharp turn and piles into the outside wall. Immediately after Marial are a few Class II rapids. About 1/4 mi. after Marial is the entrance to the canyon. The entrance is marked by a drop with large boulders on the right side and a wall just beyond them on the left. This drop is followed in a few yards by a sharp turn to the left with a wall on the right. The water shoots on, and in about 50 yd. hits a large, sharp, nasty rock about 6 ft. out from the left bank. At higher water this rock forms a hole, which it is wise to avoid. The rock is followed by about 200 yd. of small waves and turbulence. The canyon narrows toward the end of this 200 yd., "The Narrows," creating some interesting boils. After the Narrows, there is a long 200–300 yd. pause, with a good current but no rapids. The canyon walls remain steep, rising straight up from the water, so any swimmers at this point may have to continue swimming; the more athletic may be able to climb back into their boats. This quieter section ends in the Coffee Pot, a short rapids caused by the river passing through a narrow slot, about 15–20 ft. At very low water (1,000 c.f.s. or under) the Coffee Pot is reasonably straightforward, but at higher water, it can develop some very challenging eddies and boils. After this, the water is fairly quiet, and there are several landing spots. The canyon continues on another mile or two to Blossom Bar.

At the recommended water levels, we have seen a number of boaters swim most of Mule Canyon without problems *if* they were wearing lifejackets and hanging on to their overturned boats.

MI. 26. Staircase Creek and Falls on the left. Small, possible emergency camping spot on the right about 100 yd. below. There are several springs and two other small emergency camps in the canyon below this.

MI. 27. Blossom Bar Creek and possible campsite on the right at the head of the rapids.

MI. 27. Blossom Bar Rapids. **Scout** from the right bank. Class

IV–. A steep, very bouldery, very long, and relatively dangerous rapids. The normal route involves starting on the left, catching an eddy and crossing to the center to avoid a rock pile, and then running the center chute which is partially blocked by a boulder. This is followed by a long stretch of boulder-hopping. This is not a rapids for inexperienced boaters. Precise maneuvering is required, and mistakes are not easily forgiven. We usually run the weaker boaters' boats through the first, more difficult part of the rapids.

MI. 27+. Devils Staircase. 100 yd. below Blossom Bar. Two drops separated by 50 yd. The first is Class II+, the second is Class II. Avoid the wall. Immediately below Devils Staircase on the left is a small, pleasant beach campsite with a spring.

MI. 28. Paradise Creek on the right.

MI. 28+. Paradise Lodge on the right. Room and board if you have reservations.

MI. 29. Huggins Canyon. Class II S turn.

MI. 31. East Creek on the left.

MI. 31+. Brushy Bar Creek on the right. Possible campsite.

MI. 32. Solitude Bar and a good beach on the right. Solitude Rapids (Class II) at the end of Solitude Bar.

MI. 33. Tate Creek and a pleasant small campsite on the right.

MI. 33+. Camp Tacoma Rapids, or Tate Creek Rapids. Class II+ rock garden.

MI. 33+. Clay Hill Lodge on the right.

MI. 33½. Clay Hill Rapids. Class III–. About 100 yd. below the lodge, the river bends sharply to the left around an island. Run the main (right) chute, and then **cut sharply to the left** to avoid the bouldery ledge on the right and center.

MI. 34. Fall Creek on the left. Beautiful spot.

MI. 34+. Flora Dell Creek on the right. Lovely spot (if you walk up the creek a few yards) and a small campsite.

MI. 35. Flea Creek and a small campsite on the right. There are quite a few Class I to II rapids after Flea Creek, but most are too easy to record.

MI. 36+. Wild River Lodge on the left.

MI. 38. Road access and houses on the right.

MI. 39. Foster Creek and boat landing on the right. Possible take-out. A large Forest Service campground is located downstream.

MI. 40. Two Mile Creek on the right.

MI. 41. Two Mile Rapids. Class II+.

MI. 42. Bridge across the river. Possible take-out.

MI. 44. Shasta Costa Creek on the right.

MI. 44+. Agness jet boat landing on the right. Very steep. The beach just upstream on the left is a better take-out, but ask permission if it is posted.

TOUR TWO

Grande Ronde River

RECOMMENDED BOAT TYPE: *kayaks, rubber rafts, drift boats, inflatable kayaks. At low flows (under 2,000 c.f.s.) most of it is manageable by experienced whitewater boaters in open canoes.*

DIFFICULTY OF RAPIDS: *Class II−, II, with a little III−.*

AVERAGE GRADIENT: *21 ft./mi.*

WHEN TO RUN: *June, July, depending on water level.*

LENGTH IN MILES: *44.*

LENGTH IN DAYS: *2–4.*

Description

The Grande Ronde River in N.E. Oregon flows through a forested canyon, much of it national forest. Few rivers offer such

Figure T2-1 Typical Grande Ronde rapids

fine scenery combined with whitewater easy enough for the advanced novice. An occasional deserted cabin or logging road are the only reminders of civilization for most of the run. The dense forest at the put-in elevation of 2,500 ft. gradually thins out to grass-covered hills at the take-out, which is at elevation 1,580 ft. Somewhat discolored at high flows, the river clears as the water drops below about 3,000 c.f.s.

The put-in is actually on the Wallowa River, a tributary to the Grande Ronde, and from the put-in to Rondowa, where this tributary joins the main river, a railroad parallels the river. The railroad leaves the river at Rondowa, where the wild national forest section begins and continues for about 28 mi. to Wildcat Creek. Here a road enters the canyon and follows the river to the take-out at Troy.

Grassy meadows, open forest, and gravel beaches offer a variety of campsites. The river is relatively unknown, and few people run it as yet. We have not seen another party on it on any of our trips, the latest in 1973. In most areas campsites are numerous, but in a few they are quite scarce (see Guide). The river can be run at water levels higher than those recommended, but many of the campsites become unuseable.

The only problems associated with the camping are rattlesnakes and drinking water. The river water is probably unsafe to drink without some treatment, but we have had no trouble with the sidestreams. Unfortunatey there are very few good campsites located at the sidestreams. Almost invariably, however, there is a good campsite a short distance downstream of each sidestream. The technique we have adopted is to carry several one-gallon containers that we fill from a stream when we are ready to camp. We then drift down the river until we agree on a campsite.

The wildlife on the river is relatively undisturbed during the summer, and thus easy to spot. We have seen elk, deer, mink, bald eagles, and hawks. Although there are fish in the river, we have not had much success catching them. There is a good steelhead trout run in August, but usually the water is quite low by then. Other recreational activities include swimming and hiking which is difficult as there are no trails.

The weather in June is variable, mostly pleasant with occasional rainy periods. In July, it is usually hot and sunny. Nights can be cool; we had frost in July on one trip. The water temperature can be fairly cold, especially at high water, when the river is getting snow runoff, and lightweight wetsuit tops are recommended for kayakists. Other than a few flies insects are not usually a problem.

Nature of rapids

The Grande Ronde is a remarkable touring river in that it offers a large number of fairly easy, Class II rapids with only a few that are slightly more difficult, Class III−. Thus it is one of the few wilderness whitewater tours that is appropriate for the advanced novice.

The most difficult whitewater including two Class III− drops occurs in about the first 10 mi. of the trip before Rondowa. This section includes a large number of Class II rapids, mostly of the rock garden variety, and a number of good play spots for kayaks. After the confluence with the Grande Ronde at Rondowa the rapids become somewhat heavier due to the larger flow, although they are less frequent. No scouting or portaging has been necessary at the water levels that we have seen.

For flow readings we have used the reading at Troy (see Specific Information below), and have run the river at levels ranging from 1,000 to 4,000 c.f.s. At 4,000 c.f.s. the water is somewhat muddy and high, resulting in some holes, large waves, and powerful eddies. We find the river generally more enjoyable at lower water, especially with novices, as the rapids are less turbulent and easier to play in, not to mention the clearer water. Of course, rocks become more of a problem at lower water levels.

Although the Grande Ronde is well-suited to novice boaters (Class I+ and II), the party should include at least one experienced Class III boater for every three or four novices to aid with rescues, etc. It is an excellent and enjoyable training trip for the relatively inexperienced.

Road access at Rondowa after the most challenging section provides an escape opportunity if the river proves too difficult. For the next 28 mi. there is no road access, and hiking out would involve a very long bushwack through rugged country.

Specific information

Location: N.E. Oregon, northeast of La Grande

Put-in

Minam State Park on the Wallowa River 2 mi. north of the town of Minam (which in 1973 consisted of one motel). Follow the signs to the state park from Minam. The park is a pleasant camping spot.

Take-out

Troy bridge. There was no campground here in 1973, although there were several stores. It is possible to continue the trip for another 45 mi. to the confluence of the Grande Ronde with the Snake. We are not including that section in the guide because there is a dirt road along much of it, and camping is prohibited in some of it. It contains one difficult, Class III+ rapids which requires scouting, about 4½ miles above the confluence.

Shuttle

There are several routes from Minam to Troy. The shortest,

about 55 mi. one way, involves the road to Troy that leaves Highway 82 between the towns of Minam and Wallowa. The road is dirt and local inquiry should be made before attempting it. Bridges are occasionally washed out. The longer, but probably faster and more reliable route is to follow Highway 82 east of Minam 32 mi. to its junction with Highway 3 in the town of Enterprise. Drive north on Highway 3 about 35 mi. to the turn-off to Flora, and follow the turn-off west about 12 mi. to Troy. The last few miles are on a steep, winding dirt road, which is often impassable in passenger cars in bad weather. As an alternate route, continue beyond the Flora turn-off on Highway 3 for another 12 mi. to the bridge across the Grande Ronde and then follow the dirt road which goes along the river upstream to Troy. This route involves only about 13 mi. of fairly flat dirt road, passable for passenger cars in dry weather. The total distance one way for the longer routes is about 80–93 mi. and the round trip takes approximately 4 hr.

Maps

The National Forest maps including this section of river show sidestreams and approximate distances. The appropriate maps are:

1. Pomeroy Ranger District, Umatilla National Forest. Obtainable from:

   Forest Supervisor
   Umatilla National Forest
   P. O. Box 1208
   Pendleton, Ore. 97801

2. Bear Sleds District, Wallowa Whitman National Forest. Obtainable from:

Ranger Station
Wallowa Whitman National Forest
La Grande, Ore.

Unfortunately, as of 1973, very little of this section had detailed topographic mapping.

Water Level Information

Recommended water levels are 1,500–4,000 c.f.s. Ask for the flow in cubic feet per second at Troy from:

River Forecast Center
National Weather Service
320 Customhouse
Portland, Ore. 97209
(phone: 503-221-3811)

Distance and Time Allowance

The 44 river miles could be run in as little as 2 days at high water. 3 days gives an enjoyable trip with some leisure time. 4 days gives a very leisurely trip, even at low water.

Wilderness Status

At this time, the Grande Ronde is not included under either National or State Scenic River systems, so has no protection from these sources. Much of it flows through national forest, which does provide limited protection.

Figure T2-2 Lunch stop on the Grande Ronde

GRANDE RONDE RIVER
TOUR 2

RAPIDS

1. HOUSE ROCK DROP, III–
2. BLIND FALLS, III–
3. SHEEP CREEK RAPIDS, II+ TO III–
4. MARTIN'S MISERY, II+

Guide

This includes only major campsites and rapids and the descriptions apply only at recommended water levels. Rapids and campsites may change at any time due to flooding, landslides, and other phenomena.

MI. 0. Minam State Park. Pleasant camping area.

MI. 1. House Rock Drop. Short, heavy Class III– drop around a huge boulder. The chute is on the left side of the boulder. Good runout.

MI. 3. Blind Falls. Class III–. Class II– rock garden leads to an obscure ledge with a good chute in the center. The ledge is followed by a Class II+ to III– rock garden, then a long section of Class II rapids. Although scouting is not necessary, it is helpful to recognize this rapids in advance, as the ledge is very difficult to spot until you are almost on it, and you need to be near the center of the river to hit the center chute. Start watch-

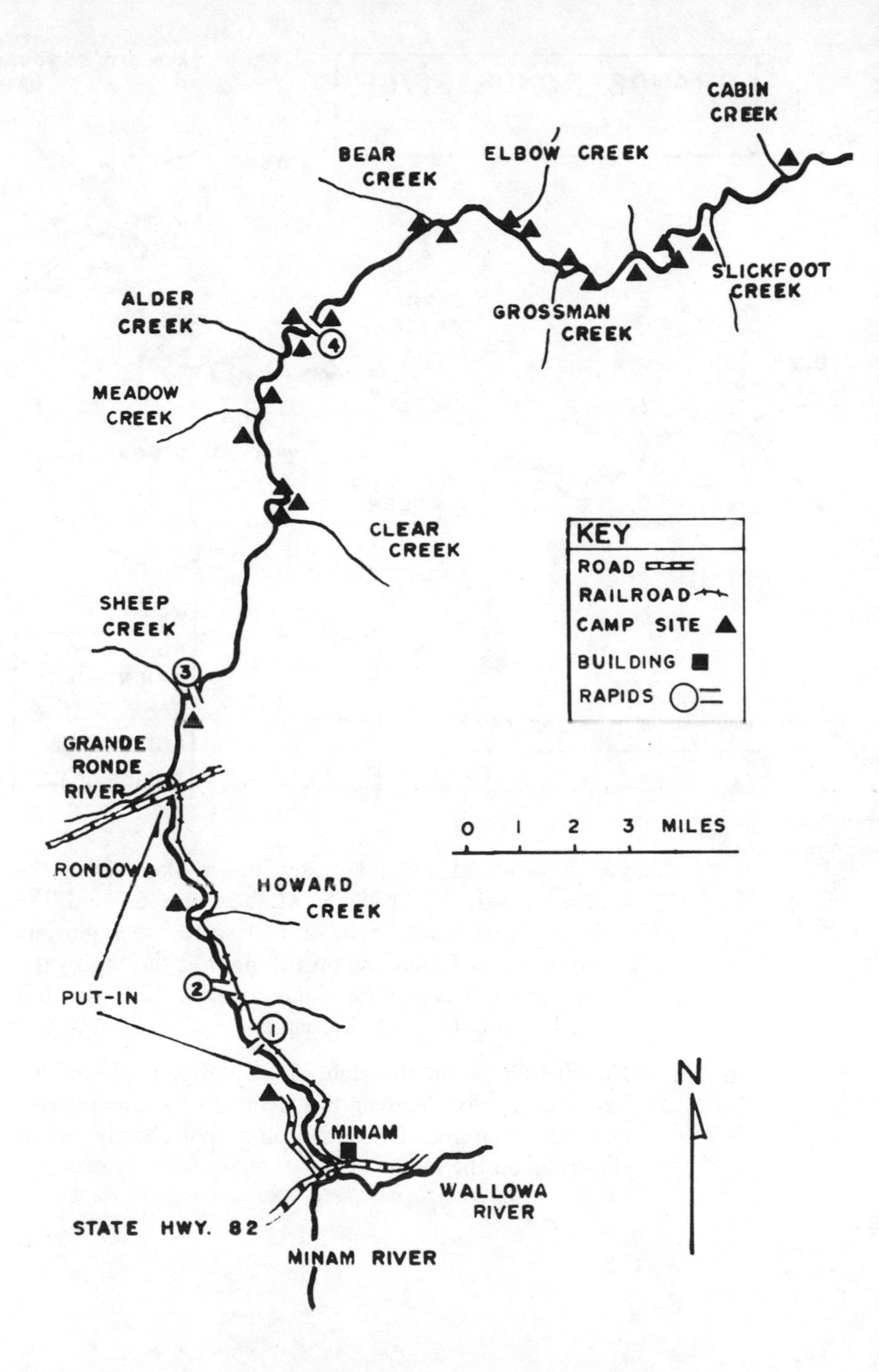

CABIN CREEK
BEAR CREEK
ELBOW CREEK
SLICKFOOT CREEK
GROSSMAN CREEK
ALDER CREEK
4
MEADOW CREEK
CLEAR CREEK
KEY
ROAD
RAILROAD
CAMP SITE
BUILDING
RAPIDS
SHEEP CREEK
3
GRANDE RONDE RIVER
0 1 2 3 MILES
RONDOWA
HOWARD CREEK
2
PUT-IN
1
N
MINAM
WALLOWA RIVER
STATE HWY. 82
MINAM RIVER

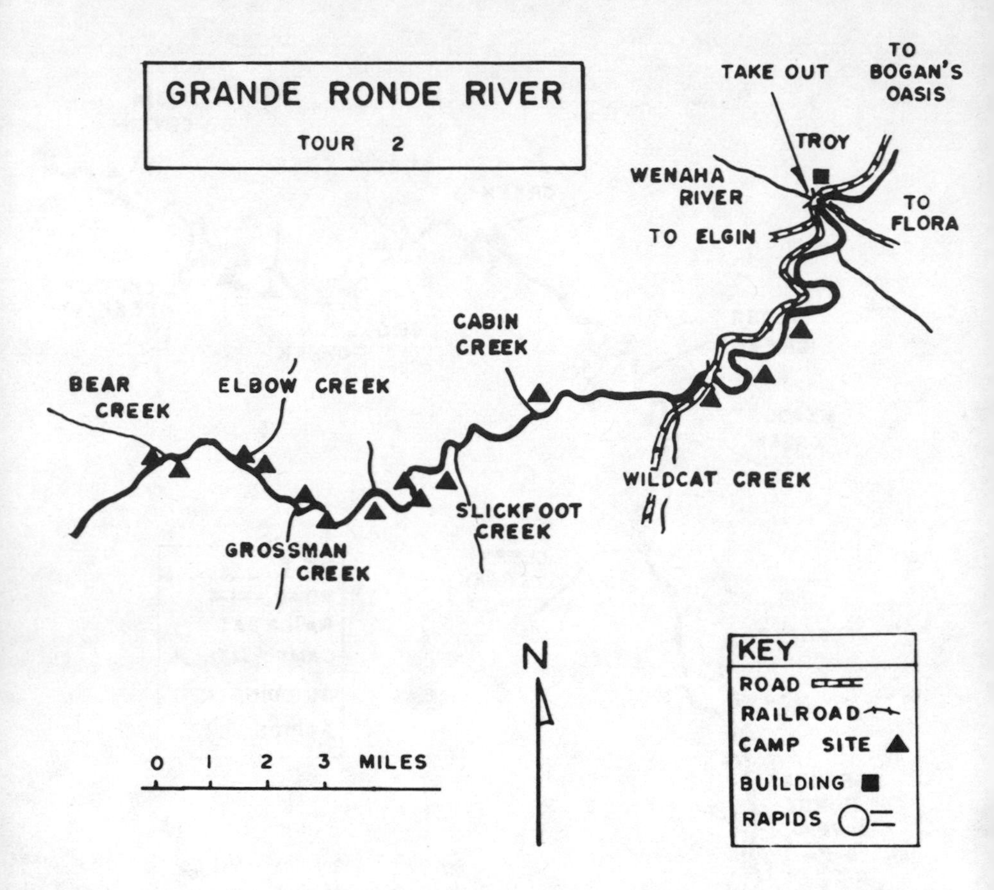

ing for it about 1/2 mi. below the marker 42 on the railroad on the right bank. At the entrance to Blind Falls the river bends right in a Class II− rock garden. There is a small meadow on the right at the top of the bend, and a steep rock slope is visible on the left towards the bottom of the bend.

MI. 5. Howard Creek on the right shortly after a power line has become visible over the river. Not recommended as a water source. Good camping spot shortly below the creek on the left.

MI. 8. Rondowa. Road and railroad bridges across the river. Grande Ronde River joins the Wallowa from the left. A gauging station for water level is shortly below the bridges on the right.

MI. 10. Sheep Creek on the left. There is a useable campsite opposite it on the right bank.

MI. 10. Sheep Creek Rapids. Class II+ to III−. Just after the creek. A long series of heavy rapids and chutes with some rock.

MI. 14. Clear Creek on the right. This is the first campsite after Sheep Creek. There is a small campsite on the creek, and a good, large campsite about a 5-min. paddle downstream on the right. This is followed by another good campsite on the left around the bend. Water must be transported from Clear Creek for these campsites.

MI. 15+. Marlene's Bar. Small sand bar and campsite on the left shortly before Meadow Creek.

MI. 16. Meadow Creek on the left. Good campsite on the right about a 10-min. paddle below the creek.

MI. 17. Alder Creek on the left. Good campsite about 5 to 10 min. below the creek following a short, heavy rapids.

MI. 18. Martin's Misery. Long, heavy Class II+ rapids with some rocks. This rapids is immediately after the Alder Creek camps, and has a good campsite on the right at the bottom. From here to Troy there are a number of Class II and easier rapids which should present no problems if you have gotten to here.

MI. 22. Bear Creek and campsite on the left. The campsite is a short distance downstream of an island, and a short distance upstream of the creek. It is sometimes rather littered. There is a good campsite just below Bear Creek on the right side of the river.

MI. 23+. Elbow Creek on the left. Small campsite on the creek, large campsite on the left a few minutes below the creek. This creek can dry up.

MI. 26. Grossman Creek on the right. At times the water is warm, milky, and unappetizing. The campsite opposite it on the left side of the river is followed by several more good campsites in the next half hour.

MI. 28. Small stream from the left about 20 to 30 min. below Grossman Creek, with an excellent campsite opposite it. Another good campsite lies around the bend just before an island. This is followed by still more campsites.

MI. 30. Slickfoot Creek on the right. There is a nice campsite just before the creek on the right within walking distance of the creek.

MI. 33. Cabin Creek on the left. Fair campsite on the left just below the creek.

MI. 36. Wildcat Creek on the right. A road enters and follows the river from here to Troy. There is a fair campsite (but on the road) at the bridge about 1/2 mi. below the creek.

MI. 38. Dam in the left channel: take the right!

MI. 39. Campsite on the right.

MI. 41. Campsite on the right.

MI. 44. Troy on the left where the Wenaha River joins the Grande Ronde. Troy is a *small* town with grocery stores, a bar, and cabins.

TOUR THREE

John Day River— Section I

RECOMMENDED BOAT TYPE: *rubber rafts, drift boats, kayaks; open canoes or inflatable kayaks (below 2,500 c.f.s.).*

DIFFICULTY OF RAPIDS: *Class I with a little Class II.*

AVERAGE GRADIENT: *8 ft./mi.*

WHEN TO RUN: *March through June depending on water level.*

LENGTH IN MILES: *44. Can be combined with the lower John Day for a total length of 114 mi.*

LENGTH IN DAYS: *2½–4.*

Description

The expert can choose from a variety of wilderness tours, but few river tours are as well suited to the novice as the upper John Day in north central Oregon. This desert canyon runs through a combination of de facto wilderness and cattle ranches. It makes a fascinating trip for the amateur geologist. Colorful strangely shaped rock formations are frequent, and several fossil beds lie near the river. There is even a good set of Indian paintings.

This is high desert country dotted with Ponderosa pine, juniper, and sage brush. The colorful rock formations and cliffs provide interesting vistas around every bend. Much of the trip is quite isolated with no road access, although there is a long section towards the middle in the Twickenham area, and another section

towards the take-out where there are ranches along the river. Also at Twickenham is road access to the river.

Campsites are plentiful except at ranches and are often quite beautiful—flat, open groves of trees with gravelly beaches. Wood is plentiful early in the season. Heavy use by cattle does detract

Figure T3-1 A John Day scene

somewhat from the attractiveness of these campsites but a paddle makes an excellent shovel. This is rattlesnake country. On this section either carry your own drinking water or be prepared to treat the river water by boiling for 20 min. At high water, the river is muddy; it clears up somewhat as the water drops. Early in the season, when few people are running the river, there is no trouble finding campsites.

Blue herons, eagles, chukar partridges, mule deer, mink, ducks, and Canada geese all are found along the river. In March, the steelhead fishing can be excellent if water conditions permit. As mentioned in Tour 1 steelhead are huge rainbow trout that return from the ocean to spawn in their native streams. Usually, however, the fishing is fairly poor. Because of the open, not too rugged terrain, hiking is a popular camp-time activity, and provides some magnificent panoramas of the canyon. Swimming, of course, is another popular activity when weather and water temperature permit. Fossil hunting is another of the extracurricular activities.

Weather on the river ranges from cool days in the 40's to 50's and cold nights below freezing in March to hot (100°) in June. This is generally a dry climate, but be prepared for a shower. Strong headwinds frequently occur during the day, usually in the slowest water sections, and can make paddling very difficult. Water temperatures range from very cold in March to comfortably warm in June. Insects are not usually a problem in this climate except for yellow jackets.

Nature of rapids

For most of its length, the upper John Day is simply moving water liberally endowed with Class I riffles and rapids. Even so at higher water, above 3,500 c.f.s., eddies can become quite turbulent, and at lower water, below 1,500 c.f.s., rocks can present problems. There are only three rapids on this section that are more difficult than Class I, and all three fall in the Class II category. Novices might wish to scout or carry these three rapids.

We have run this section at water levels at low as 900 c.f.s., which is very low, but still runnable, and as high as 6,000 c.f.s., very fast and quite turbulent. Most parties would probably prefer water levels of 1,500–4,000 c.f.s. At levels below 4,000 c.f.s., the John Day is ideally suited to the novice, but the party should include at least one person with considerable Class II experience. Ranches are frequent enough so that a 10-mi. hike in the proper direction would bring you to civilization any place along this section although it could be a very rugged 10 mi.

Specific information

Location: North central Oregon, northwest of the town of John Day.

Put-in

By the town of Service Creek, i.e., a gas station at the junction of Highways 19 and 207. There are no official campsites here, but there is a reasonably pleasant camping spot.

Take-out

Town, i.e. the ranches, of Clarno where Highway 218 crosses the river. There is no good place to camp here. The tiny state park nearby is closed to camping.

Shuttle

Highway 19 to the town of Fossil; then Highway 218 to Clarno. 40 mi. one way, all paved but fairly slow and winding. Allow 2½ hr. round trip. In the past, the Service Creek residents have been willing to shuttle the cars for a reasonable price.

Maps

The map of this tour contains the essentials, and most of the section is mapped by the U.S.G.S. (Clarno, Kinzua, and Mitchell quadrangles). The Bureau of Land Management also has a series of maps on the John Day River (P.O. Box 2965, Portland, Ore. 97208).

Water Level Information

Recommended level 1,500–4,000 c.f.s. Ask for the flow in c.f.s. on the John Day at Service Creek. Contact

River Forecast Center
National Weather Service
320 Customhouse
Portland, Oregon 97209
(phone: 503-221-3811 before 3:00 P.M.)

Distance and Time Allowance

44 mi. At high water, the section could be run in two days, but usually it will take 2½–3 days. A party running the river at low water, and wishing to allow ample time for exploring and fossil hunting, might want to allow 3½–4 days for the trip. The most scenic sections are the section between Service Creek and the Twickenham area, and the Big Bend area.

Wilderness Status

This section of the John Day is classified as a scenic river area

Figure T3-2 A John Day drift

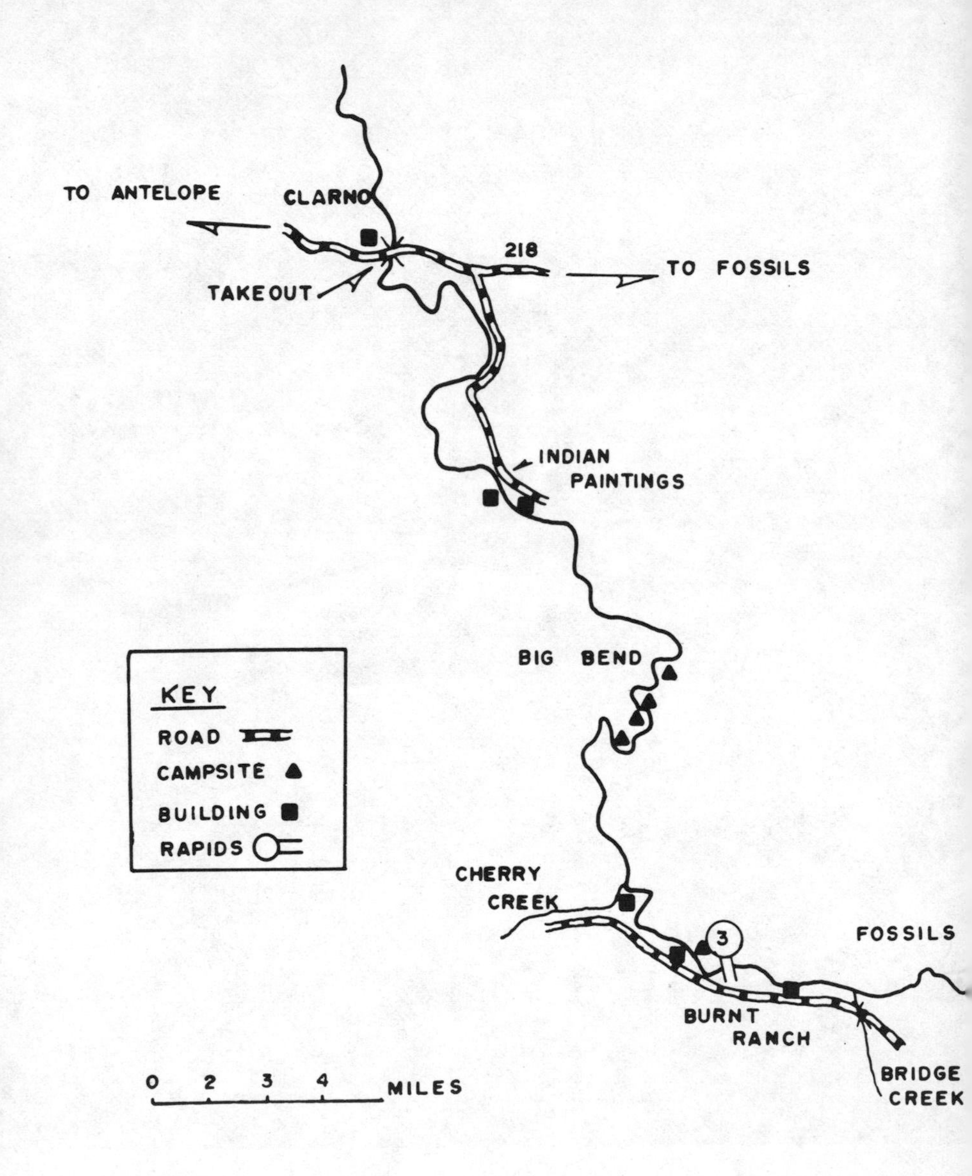
TO ANTELOPE
CLARNO
218
TO FOSSILS
TAKEOUT
INDIAN PAINTINGS
BIG BEND
KEY
ROAD
CAMPSITE
BUILDING
RAPIDS
CHERRY CREEK
3
FOSSILS
BURNT RANCH
BRIDGE CREEK
0 2 3 4 MILES

JOHN DAY RIVER – SECTION I
TOUR 3

RAPIDS

(1) RUSSO RAPIDS, II+.
(2) WRECK RAPIDS, II.
(3) SCHUSS RAPIDS, II.

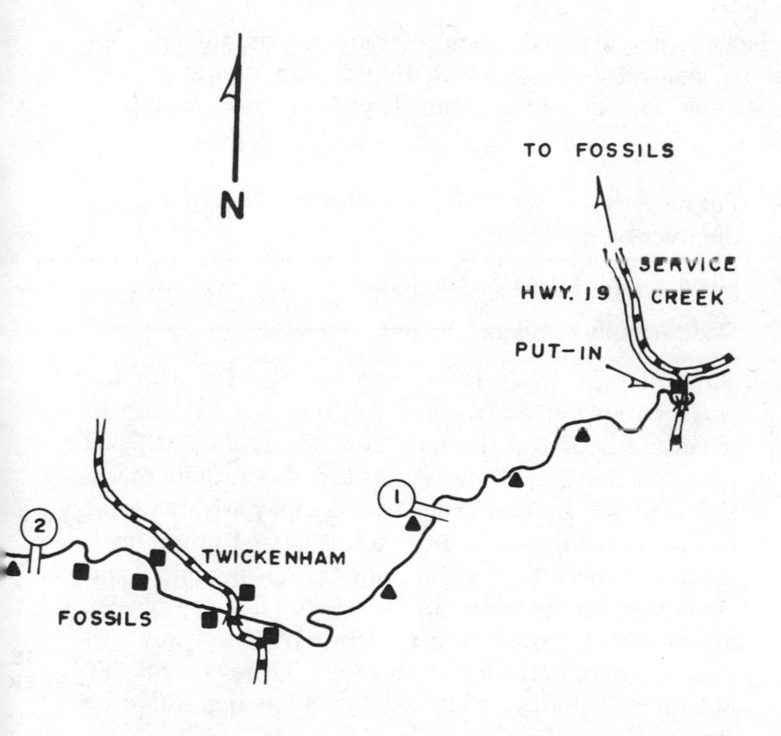

under the Oregon Scenic Waterways System. "Scenic river" sections are those that are largely primitive and undeveloped, except for grazing. Although they may be accessible in spots by road, they cannot be paralleled by long sections of well-traveled road. "Wild river" sections are less accessible, and do not have large grazing areas. As a scenic river, this section of the John Day can have no new buildings constructed along it, except those necessary for existing agricultural uses.

Guide

This includes only the major campsites and rapids, and only applies at recommended water levels. Rapids and campsites may change at any time due to flooding, landslides, and other phenomena.

MI. 0. Put-in. Service Creek. Reasonable camping spot along the river by the bridge.

MI. 2. Good camping area on the left.

MI. 4. Good camping area on the left.

MI. 6. Russo Rapids. Class II+. Steep rock garden with the current running into a rock wall that is fairly easy to avoid on the left at the bottom of the rapids. At 3,500 c.f.s. and above, quite heavy. At low water, quite rocky. Good runout. **Inexperienced boaters may wish to scout or line.** Landing is difficult as a fast Class I rapids leads around a curve to the left into the main rapids, and when you see the main rapids, it is too late to stop. So, if you wish to scout, stop well in advance of any suspicious curves to the left in this area. There is a possible but difficult portage route on the right; *impossible on the left.*

MI. 6. Good campsite at the foot of Russo Rapids on the right.

MI. 8. Campsite on the left.

MI. 12. Twickenham. Ranch community, bridge. There are no campsites in this area for about 2 mi. upstream and 2 mi. downstream.

MI. 14. Fossil beds on the left, quite a hike from the river. The clay in these fossil beds appears greenish from a distance.

MI. 15. Wreck Rapids. Class II. Fairly steep and short.

MI. 15. Good campsite on the left at the foot of the rapids.

MI. 17. Fossil beds on the right close to the river.

MI. 21. Burnt Ranch. Ranch on the left.

MI. 23. Schuss Rapids. Class II. Can be quite heavy.

MI. 24. Campsite on the right just after a rock pinnacle on the right. Ranch on the left.

MI. 27. Big Bend. The river makes a horseshoe-type bend to the right. For the next 2–3 mi., the river passes through a lovely, colorful wild canyon section. There are many excellent campsites and small rapids in this section.

MI. 34. Indian paintings on the right shore. You will pass a ranch on the right, and another will be visible on the left. Stop just after the ranch on the right ends, just across from the ranch on the left. Walk up to the dirt road a few feet above the river then downstream on the road for about 1/8 mi. Indian paintings are on the rock faces on the right side of the road. There are many ranches and few campsites from this point on.

MI. 44. Clarno bridge. Take-out.

TOUR FOUR

John Day River— Section II

RECOMMENDED BOAT TYPE: *rubber rafts, drift boats, kayaks; open canoes or inflatable kayaks (below 2,500 c.f.s.).*
DIFFICULTY OF RAPIDS: *Class I with a little Class III.*
AVERAGE GRADIENT: *11 ft./mi.*
WHEN TO RUN: *March through June depending on water level.*
LENGTH IN MILES: *70. Can be combined with the upper section for a total length of 114 mi.*
LENGTH IN DAYS: *3–5.*

Description

The lower John Day is very similar to the upper section, starting where the upper run ends, so in this discussion we will concentrate on the differences. The lower section is considerably longer and not suited to weekend trips. Like the upper section it runs through a combination of ranch lands and desert wilderness;

Figure T4-1 Typical John Day rapids

the wilderness portions on the lower section are considerably more extensive than those on the upper, giving a wilder feeling. Again, fossil beds are frequent and the geology is fascinating. In our opinion the Big Bend area on the upper section is the most scenic on the river, but the lower section has several areas (Red Wall, the Narrows, and Basalt Canyon) of great beauty.

Campsites are similar to those on the upper section, but trees become very sparse in the lower portion of the trip. Drinking water is again a problem, but a few inconspicuous springs help. If you must resort to the unappetizing river water, boil it for 20 min. The sidestreams are probably more dangerous than the river, due to the heavy grazing. The wildlife, extracurricular activities, and weather are similar to those on the upper section.

Nature of rapids

These are similar to those on the upper section except for one very long rapids about 1–mi. long with a moderately difficult drop of Class III in the middle. All boaters unfamiliar with this section should scout this rapids, and open canoeists or novices in kayaks will probably wish to portage. Basalt Rapids too is borderline Class III at high water, above 5,000 c.f.s., so this section on the whole is not as appropriate for novices as the upper section. However, with one carry, novices can run it below 3,000 c.f.s.

We have run this section as low as 1,200 c.f.s. and as high as 9,000 c.f.s., when it was very fast and rather turbulent. Occasional ranches provide possible escape routes at several points, and a rough road provides some access about midway in the section.

Specific information

Location: North central Oregon, northwest of the town of John Day.

Put-in

Clarno bridge where Highway 218 crosses the river. This is ranch land with no camping. Camping is not allowed in the state park a few miles away.

Take-out

Cottonwood bridge where Highway 206 crosses the river. A large parking spot with outhouses.

Shuttle

About 63 mi. 1½ hr., one way. Follow Highway 218 east from Clarno 18 mi. to Fossil. Then proceed north for 20 mi. on Highway 19 to Condon. Finally follow Highway 206 west from Condon for about 25 mi. until you reach the bridge across the John Day.

Maps

The attached map contains the essentials, or get the U.S. Geological Survey map for Clarno, which only covers the first part of the trip because the rest has not yet been mapped. The Bureau of Land Management sells a series of maps of the John Day (P.O. Box 2965, Portland, Ore. 97208).

Water Level Information See John Day River, Section I.

Distance and Time Allowance

70 mi. At higher water, it can be run in three full days. At lower water 4 or 5 days will be needed. The most scenic sections are the Red Wall-Narrows section, and the Basalt Canyon.

Wilderness Status

The first half of this section of the John Day is classified as a scenic river area, the second half as a wild river area under the Oregon Scenic Waterways system. The difference in classification is because of the heavy grazing on the upper section. Both sections are protected from new building unless it is needed for existing agriculture.

Guide

This includes only the major campsites and rapids, and only applies at recommended water levels. Rapids and campsites may change at any time due to flooding, landslides, and other phenomena.

MI. 0. Clarno bridge. Put-in. Clarno is not a town, just a few ranches. This all appears to be private property, so every courtesy should be exercised. The first few miles below Clarno pass through an agricultural valley with no good campsites.

MI. 3. Fossil beds on the left, recognizable by light green-gray clay. Fair camping spot on the right directly across from fossil beds. Good camping spot on the left immediately below the fossil beds, but a four-wheel drive road passes through it.

MI. 4. Clarno Rapids. Class III to III+. Groups including weak boaters or boaters unfamiliar with the rapids should scout. The safest place to land is a small sandy beach on the left 100–200 yd. above the first drop. The initial drop is easily recognizable, being an obvious rapids after several miles of flat water. The Class II drop is at the start of a curve to the left, and has a

Figure T4-2 John Day Canyon

JOHN DAY RIVER
SECTION II
TOUR 4

0 1 2 MILES

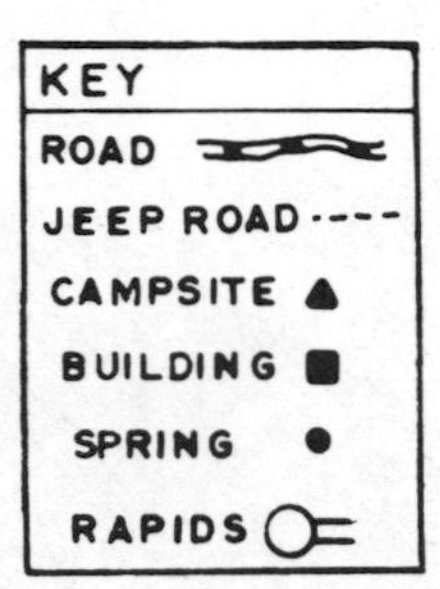

large but easily avoidable hole in the center at high water and many boulders at low water. The Class II rapids continue for about 1/3 mi. leading directly into the main drop. There are islands in the river directly above the main drop, and the preferred route is usually around their left side. The Class III–III+ main drop is very heavy but straightforward at high water; contains some large holes at low water. The runout is poor, being about 1/3 mi. of heavy Class II rapids. Part or all of the rapids can be carried on the left side, which also contains some pleasant camping spots.

MI. 5. Mulberry Spring campsite on the right at the foot of Clarno Rapids. Good camp (we found a small creek, but no sign of a spring). The camp is followed by about 1/2 mi. of Class I+ to II– rapids.

MI. 7. Fair campsite on the right.

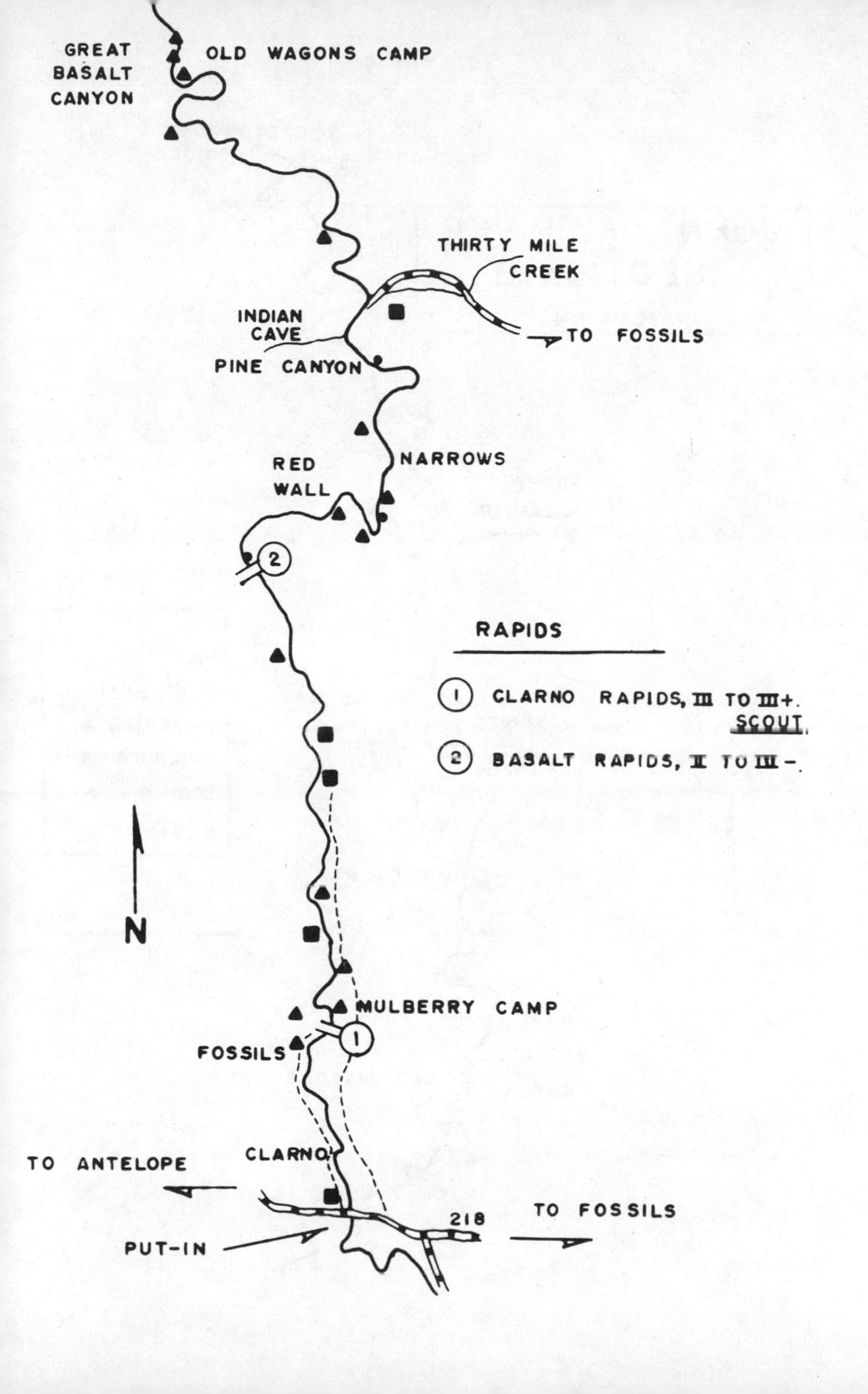
GREAT BASALT CANYON
OLD WAGONS CAMP
THIRTY MILE CREEK
INDIAN CAVE
TO FOSSILS
PINE CANYON
RED WALL
NARROWS
2
RAPIDS
1 CLARNO RAPIDS, III TO III+. SCOUT.
2 BASALT RAPIDS, II TO III -.
N
MULBERRY CAMP
1
FOSSILS
CLARNO
TO ANTELOPE
TO FOSSILS
218
PUT-IN

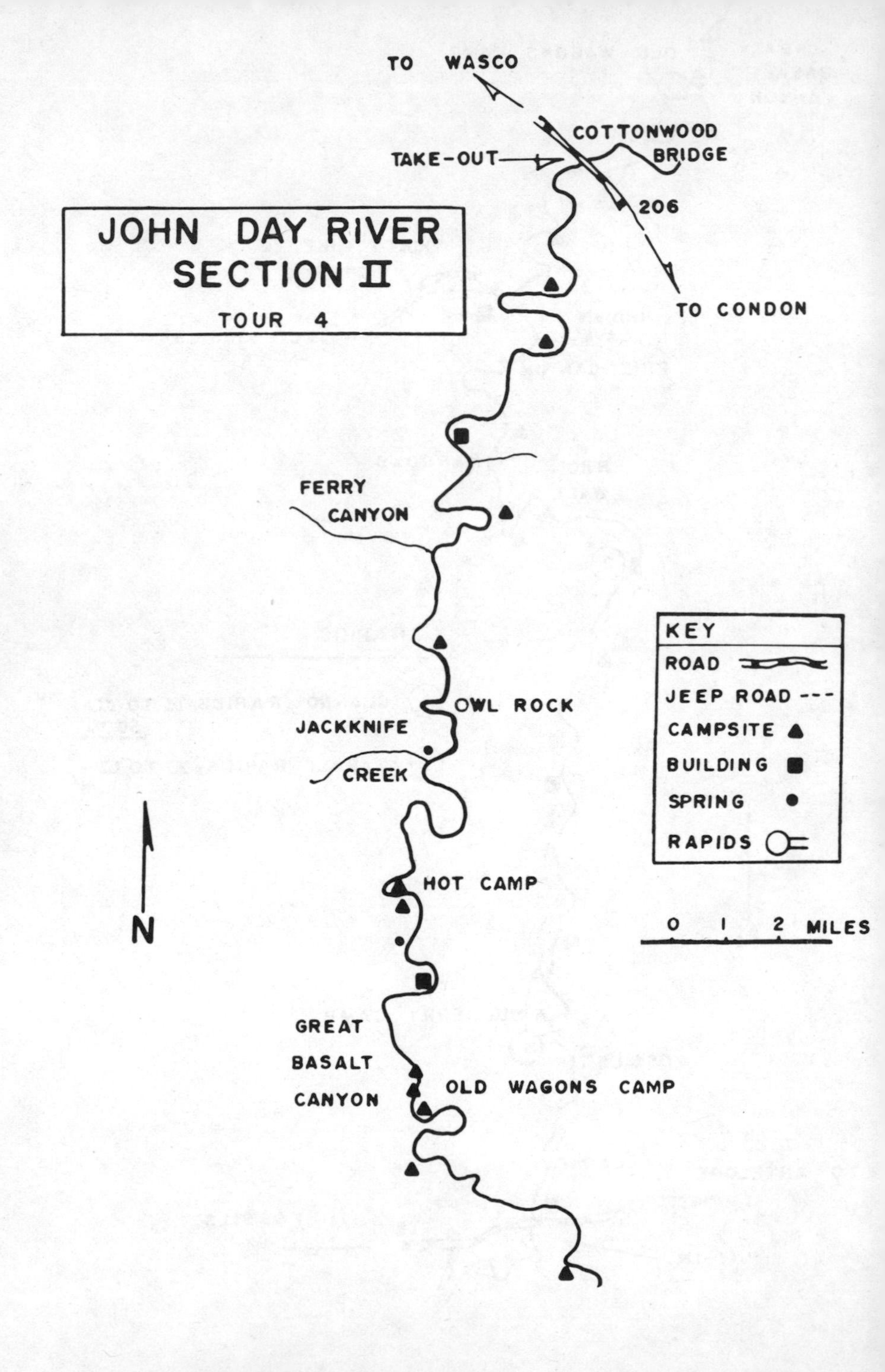
JOHN DAY RIVER
SECTION II
TOUR 4
TO WASCO
COTTONWOOD
BRIDGE
TAKE-OUT
206
TO CONDON
FERRY
CANYON
OWL ROCK
JACKKNIFE
CREEK
HOT CAMP
GREAT
BASALT
CANYON
OLD WAGONS CAMP
N
KEY
ROAD
JEEP ROAD
CAMPSITE
BUILDING
SPRING
RAPIDS
0 1 2 MILES

MI. 7+. Ranch buildings on the right.

MI. 8+. Ranch buildings on the left.

MI. 9+. Good campsite on the right point.

MI. 11. Ranch buildings on the right followed by 1/3 mi. of Class I+ to II− rapids.

MI. 12. Ranch on the right.

MI. 13. Campsite on the left.

MI. 15. Basalt Rapids. Class III− at high water, 9,000 c.f.s. At lower water it is considerably easier. Named for the large black basalt rocks that dot the rapids. The rapids start with a Class II+ heavy drop on a bend to the left followed by a 1/2 mi. series of rapids and drops, some quite heavy with tricky turbulence at high water. Routes are fairly obvious with a little maneuvering necessary because of the rocks.

MI. 15½. *Spring* at a small beach on the right just below the last big drop. Followed by two Class I+ to II− rapids.

MI. 17. Good campsite on the right, opposite the Red Wall. This section is quite scenic with good campsites for about 3 mi.

MI. 18. Good campsite on the right.

MI. 19. *Spring* on the right with a good campsite on the right about a 1/2 mi. below it.

MI. 20. Narrows. A scenic narrow section through basalt walls.

MI. 21. Good campsite on the left. Soon after this, you enter the agricultural land surrounding Thirty Mile Creek, and campsites are poor.

MI. 23. Spring on the right.

MI. 24. Pine Canyon on the left. There is supposed to be an Indian cave a mile or two up this canyon.

MI. 25. Thirty Mile Creek on the right. A rough road provides access to the ranches in this area.

MI. 27. Campsite on the left side. Poor camping for several miles.

MI. 31. Campsite on the left side.

MI. 33. Good campsite (Old Wagons) on the right near an old cabin. The canyon becomes scenic again with many good campsites in the next few miles through the Great Basalt Canyon.

MI. 39. Cabin on the left. Poor camping in this area.

MI. 41. Spring on the left.

MI. 42. Campsite on the left followed immediately by "Hot Camp" on the right. (The camp on the left has more trees.)

MI. 47. Jackknife Creek on the left. There is supposed to be a spring on the left just below the creek but we couldn't find it. The canyon becomes more scenic again, but good campsites are very scarce.

MI. 49. Owl Rock on the right. A striking rock formation looking exactly like an owl perched on top of a pillar.

MI. 51. Good campsite on the right. This is the last camp with a number of trees. All the campsites mentioned after this have only a few lone trees.

MI. 54. Ferry Canyon on the left side.

MI. 55. Fair campsite on the right side.

MI. 56. Creek on the right side.

MI. 61. Creek on the right; cabin on the left.

MI. 64. Fair campsite on the left. There are many camping spots between here and the take-out, but all are treeless and uninspiring. Power lines near Cottonwood Bridge become visible on horizon in distance.

MI. 70. Take-out. Cottonwood Bridge. There is a large parking area with outhouses here, but it is a dreary spot.

TOUR FIVE

Middle Fork of the Salmon River

RECOMMENDED BOAT TYPE: *fiberglass kayaks, six-man or larger rubber rafts equipped with frames and oars or sweeps.*
DIFFICULTY OF RAPIDS: *Classes III, III+ with some IV.*
AVERAGE GRADIENT: *35 ft./mi.*
WHEN TO RUN: *July through mid August depending on water level.*
LENGTH IN MILES: *96.*
LENGTH IN DAYS: *5–7.*

Description

A trip on the Middle Fork of the Salmon River in central Idaho offers inspiring and varied scenery as well as whitewater. The

Figure T5-1 Middle Fork campsite

96-mi. run is completely roadless, and passes through the Idaho Primitive Area.

At the put-in elevation of over 6,000 ft., the banks are heavily forested and the nights are crisp. The forest is broken by occasional meadows, and frequent hot springs provide luxurious baths or even a hot shower. As the elevation decreases, the forest changes to open Ponderosa pine. From MI. 23 to MI. 68 occasional widely separated ranches, many with airstrips, detract somewhat from the wilderness nature of the river.

The transition to a desert environment becomes evident in the region of MI. 60, as open sage brush-covered hills appear frequently. When you have passed the last ranch, at MI. 68, the scenery becomes increasingly wild and spectacular, as the river descends into a steep rock gorge which narrows as the mouth of the river is approached. Indian paintings occur on some of the cliff faces and in huge caves. The campsites include grassy meadows, pine flats, and sand beaches. A few come equipped with hot springs. There is a great variation in the size of campsites.

About 100 persons a day ran the river in July, 1971, and more in July, 1972, many traveling in large groups with commercial guides. Actually unless you stop for a day, you are not aware of the crowds. Because these large numbers approach the carrying capacity of the river, the Forest Service has taken steps to restrict the number of people on the river in the future. Trip permits must be obtained and campsites will be assigned (see Specific Information for this tour).

After about MI. 35, the elevation is low enough so that rattlesnakes should be watched for. (We almost stepped on one across from Marble Creek.) A few of the campsites in the last 20 mi. of the river support some lush growths of poison ivy.

The river itself is beautifully clear, and we have used it for drinking water with no ill effects. There are also an ample number of sidestreams which could be used for drinking water.

Although the Middle Fork passes through some very wild country, the crowds of people running it in July and August do not exactly encourage hordes of wildlife to remain in the area. We have, however, seen a few deer, mink, a bear, and several herds of mountain sheep. Trout fishing on the river can be excellent in spots; we caught a number of cutthroat trout weighing a pound or more. Current fishing regulations require releasing fish except those caught in sidestreams. Where to fish? Where no one else has!

A trail along much of the river, and trails up several of the sidestreams offer some hiking possibilities; but, after trying a few of these side trails, we concluded that the main river canyon was considerably more scenic and was cooler than most of the side canyons.

The weather is usually sunny and hot during the day, but evenings can be cool, especially at the higher elevations. The water temperature in mid-July on one trip varied from 58°F at Dagger Falls to 68°F at the confluence. Lightweight wetsuit tops are recommended for kayakists. We have found flies, yellow jackets, and a few No-see-ums in mid-July.

The history of the Middle Fork, like that of many other rivers, is connected with Indians and mining. The Sheepeater Indian war of 1879 was fought along the banks of the river and its tributaries, such as Big Creek. The gold miners also made their mark on the river, as shown by some placer mine diggings. But the Middle Fork has never been invaded by man as much as today, by people who wish to run a wild river.

Nature of rapids

The Middle Fork offers a real variety in types of whitewater. The first 6 mi. is virtually continuous Class III– to IV–, including some steep rock gardens and ending in a vertical drop at Velvet Falls (see Guide). This section gives a good test of a group's skill while it is still possible for them to turn back; a trail follows the west side of the river. At low water the rocks make this stretch particularly difficult for rafts, and many raft parties have their boats flown into Indian Creek, about 28 mi. downstream.

From MI. 6 to MI. 34, the rapids are easier, Class II–III, except for the drops listed in the guide. This section contains many rock gardens, although they are not as steep or continuous as those in the first 6 mi. The river increases markedly in size due to a large number of sidestreams.

From about MI. 34 to MI. 68, most rapids are still easier, Class I–II, except for those listed in the Guide. From MI. 68 to the mouth, however, the rapids become more challenging, Class III–IV, and the nature of the river changes. By MI. 68, its volume has increased considerably, and it begins dropping into a narrow rock gorge. The rapids are mostly the pool and drop type with some heavy turbulence and large holes. Kayak play spots abound.

Scouting is necessary at several rapids (see Guide), but most competent parties do not find portages necessary. The Middle Fork can be run over a wide range of water flows. Unfortunately, meaningful water flow data on the Middle Fork are difficult to get. The sole useable gauging station is at Middle Fork Lodge and this gauge was rebuilt and renumbered in 1973. Although the new gauge was installed in approximately the same place as the old one, the new numbers are between 1.0 and 1.5 feet larger than the old ones, and the gauge may change again. This problem illustrates the difficulty in using stage data, which we discuss more fully in Appendix C. To state a range of levels for which the Guide is valid, we think it is most conservative and appropriate to use the subjective "hazard" ratings formulated by the Forest Service from information furnished by the experienced outfitters who have used the river for years. For the gauge in use in 1973, a reading of 4.0 ft. to 5.5 ft. was considered "extremely hazardous," and above 5.5 ft. "impossible" or "suicidal." From our trips on the Middle Fork, we can phrase our flow-level range in which our Guide is valid in terms of these hazard levels as follows:

Water Level Range in Which Guide is Valid:
Maximum level: 2.3 ft. *below* the "suicide" level
Minimum level: 3.5–3.7 ft. *below* the "suicide" level

In 1973, *but perhaps never again,* the corresponding levels on the gauge were a maximum of 3.2 ft. and a minimum of 1.8–2.0 ft. We ran the Middle Fork most recently in 1973 at a level of 1.8 ft. on the new gauge and found it only marginally runnable, even for kayaks, for the first 30 miles. Rafters may find the trip more enjoyable if they fly into Indian Cr. to put in when the water level is more than 3.2 ft. below the "suicide" level. These recommended flows will give you a means of deciding whether the river is runnable and described by the Guides in spite of changes in the gauge (other than location) and resulting hazard levels listed by the Forest Service. A major change in location of the gauge would make this information useless, as we discuss in Appendix C. Flow data rather than stage data would eliminate the problem we have just discussed. By 1973, only a tentative rating of the Middle Fork Lodge gauge was available. **The rating is of questionable accuracy,** but is included to give you a rough idea of the flows that are run on the Middle Fork.

Middle Fork Lodge Gauge

Height, ft.	*Flow, c.f.s.*
2.0	480
3.0	1600
4.0	3000
5.0	4800
6.0	6900

The recommended range of flows occur from about July 10 or July 15 to about August 1 or August 15 in normal years. However, 1970, 1971, and 1973 were all abnormal years; the first two abnormally high and the latter abnormally low. Always check the water level before you leave for the river. Parties should be careful to run *after* the peak of runoff, as the river can rise amazingly fast in one day.

The Middle Fork is a difficult river, and is for experienced boaters only. Novices can expect to lose or damage their equipment, and perhaps endanger themselves. Boaters should have considerable experience on rapids of Class III difficulty and some experience on Class IV. Although there is no road within reason-

able hiking distance of the Middle Fork, rescue possibilities in case of disaster are better than on most wilderness rivers because of a number of ranches with airstrips, trails, and the large number of boaters.

Specific information

Location: Central Idaho, north of Stanley.

Figure T5-2 Kayak in Rubber Rapids

Put-in

Dagger Falls campground, about 50 mi. northwest of Stanley.

Take-out

Confluence of the Middle Fork with the main Salmon about 40 mi. west of the town of North Fork, Idaho. The take-out here is very hot, dusty, and unpleasant.

Shuttle

About 220 mi. one way, including about 30 mi. of dirt road into Dagger Falls and 40 mi. of dirt road into the confluence. Both dirt roads are slow but passable in passenger cars.

Follow Highway 21 west from Stanley for 15–20 mi., and take the road turning off to the right marked Dagger Falls. To get to the take-out, drive northeast of Stanley on Highway 93 to North Fork; drive west on the road following the Salmon from North Fork to the confluence.

Maps

The Forest Service distributes an excellent free map of the river, including location of campsites and major rapids. Write:

Wild River Manager
Challis National Forest
Forest Service Building
Challis, Idaho 83226

Water Level Information

Recommended flows are between 2.3 ft. *below* "suicide" level to 3.5–3.7 ft. *below* "suicide" level. Current and projected readings from the gauge at Middle Fork Lodge may be obtained from the manager whose address is listed above.

Distance and Time Allowance

Time for running the 96 mi. varies from as little as 3 days at high water, to 5 days for a normal trip at moderate water, to 7 days for a leisurely trip at low water. We found the most scenic and enjoyable areas to be MI. 1–MI. 38 and MI. 68–MI. 96.

Wilderness Status

The 1968 National Wild and Scenic Rivers Act established the Middle Fork of the Salmon as a Wild River, and it is therefore protected from further development. It also enjoys a rather unique protection among the Wild Rivers in that it flows through the Idaho Primitive Area. This means that all forms of motorized vehicles including jet boats are prohibited.

Special Restrictions

Because the mushrooming popularity of the Middle Fork is threatening to destroy its wilderness character, the Forest Service has placed a number of much-needed restrictions on its use. The most important restrictions* for the 1973 season are summarized as follows:

1. You may run the Middle Fork only if you have made a reservation in advance with the Forest Service.
2. Maximum party size will be 15.
3. A maximum of seven parties will be allowed to put in each day.

*These may be changed in future years, so check before you plan your trip.

4. Approximately 36 percent of the reservations will be assigned to private parties, based on past usage by private parties (about 30 percent) and anticipated increased usage by private groups. Use it or lose it.
5. Parties will be assigned campsites according to their preferences.
6. There will be restrictions on type and condition of equipment for private parties. In our opinion, the specifications for equipment, which will not be given here, are very reasonable for this river. Chapters 4 and 5 discuss equipment, nearly all of which meets the specifications. Inflatable kayaks do not meet them. For detailed information, get an up-to-date information sheet from the address given below.
7. Important: "A competent, experienced boatman must be present in each boat. Competent is defined to mean 'having run a boat equal in size, make and handling characteristics as the one taken on this trip.' Experienced is defined to mean 'having run 50 miles of a classified river of similar character and hazardous conditions as is found on the river to be run.' "

To obtain a detailed information sheet with all the regulations write:

Wild River Manager
Salmon National Forest
Salmon, Idaho 83467

Guide

This includes only the major campsites and rapids, and only applies at recommended water levels. Rapids and campsites may change at any time due to flooding, landslides, and other phenomena.

MI. 0. Dagger Falls campground and boat launching ramp. The campground is crowded on summer weekends.

The next 6 miles contain almost continuous steep, rocky Class III and Class IV rapids, some of which should be scouted at low water.

MI. 3. Long, steep drop which usually requires scouting. You will recognize this drop by the difficulty that you have in seeing the whole drop from the top.

MI. 4. Gardell's Hole. Steep drop into a pool. The pool is a popular salmon fishing hole. The steep drop is particularly difficult at low water.

MI. 6. Velvet Falls. **Scout.** Class III+ to IV− if run in the proper spot. Vertical drop of about 4 ft.; dangerous holes at some water levels. Must be approached with great caution as it is very difficult to see in time to stop. Even experienced boaters may not realize the Falls is present until they are within 20 yds. of it. To aid recognition, look for a truck-sized boulder on the far left side of the river. The Falls is about *20 ft.* below this boulder. You will be in Class II water at this point, and the river will be bending gently left. Stop to scout *above* the boulder. It is possible to stop below the boulder at very low flows, but not at higher flows. The usual route for small boats at our recommended flows is toward the far left side of the Falls. At flows higher than our recommended range, you may not be able to stop at all.

MI. 6. Campsite at the foot of Velvet Falls on the right. This is a pleasant camp for kayaks, or a good emergency camp for other boats at low water. Landing is difficult.

MI. 7. Big Bend Campsite on the right. Good camp.

MI. 7+. Trail Flat Campsite on the left. Good camp with excellent hot springs.

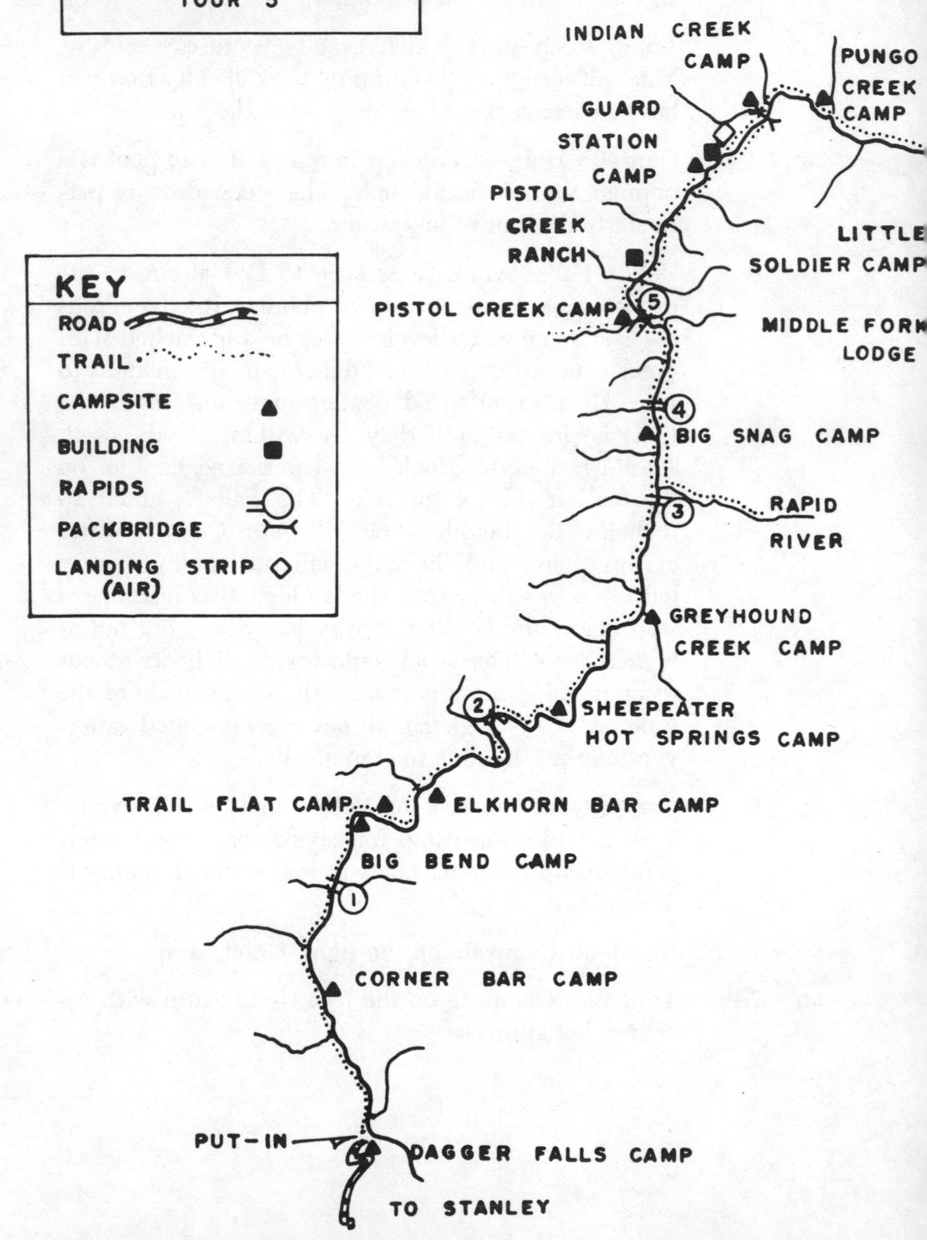
MIDDLE FORK
SALMON RIVER
TOUR 5
KEY
ROAD
TRAIL
CAMPSITE
BUILDING
RAPIDS
PACKBRIDGE
LANDING STRIP (AIR)
INDIAN CREEK CAMP
PUNGO CREEK CAMP
GUARD STATION CAMP
PISTOL CREEK RANCH
LITTLE SOLDIER CAMP
PISTOL CREEK CAMP
5
MIDDLE FORK LODGE
4
BIG SNAG CAMP
3
RAPID RIVER
GREYHOUND CREEK CAMP
2
SHEEPEATER HOT SPRINGS CAMP
TRAIL FLAT CAMP
ELKHORN BAR CAMP
BIG BEND CAMP
1
CORNER BAR CAMP
PUT-IN
DAGGER FALLS CAMP
TO STANLEY

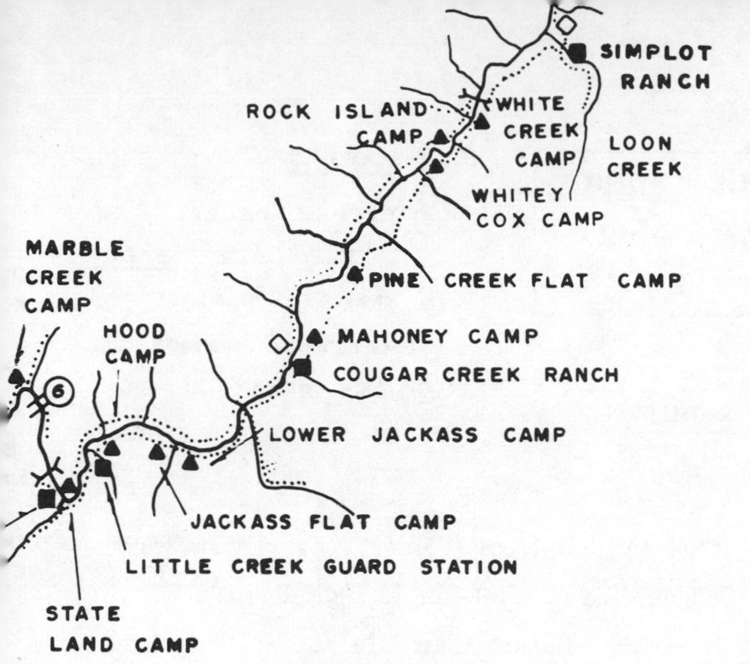

RAPIDS

1. VELVET FALLS. III+ TO IV−, SCOUT.
2. POWERHOUSE RAPIDS. III+ TO IV−.
3. ARTILLERY RAPIDS. II+ TO III−.
4. CANNON CREEK RAPIDS. III.
5. PISTOL CREEK RAPIDS. III+ TO IV−. SCOUT.
6. MARBLE CREEK RAPIDS. III−.

0 1 2 MILES

N.

MIDDLE FORK
SALMON RIVER
TOUR 5

RAPIDS

⑦ TAPPEN FALLS.
III− TO IV−. SCOUT.

⑧ APAREJO RAPIDS. III−.

⑨ HAYSTACK RAPIDS. III.

⑩ JACK CREEK RAPIDS.
III−.

0 1 2 MILES

MI. 8+. Chutes Rapids. Nasty (Class IV−) at very low water.

MI. 9. Elkhorn Bar Campsite on the right. Fair camp.

MI. 11. Powerhouse Rapids. Class III+ to IV−. Very long, heavy, rocky rapids with a poor runout. Scouting unnecessary. A conspicuous rockslide forms the left bank as the river bends to the right, and drops down a heavy Class III rapids past an old paddle wheel on the right bank. It is followed immediately by a longer, more difficult rapids of Class IV− with a very long Class II+ runout.

MI. 14. Sheepeater Hot Springs Campsite on the left. Excellent camp and hot springs. This is a large and very popular camp; the hot springs are located on the shelf behind the meadow. At low water, it is difficult to land here unless you watch carefully for a big meadow on the left, as the water is very shallow and fast by the camp.

MI. 15+ Greyhound Creek Campsite on the right. Good camp.

MI. 17. Artillery Rapids. Very long, about 1-mi., continuous enjoyable Class II+ to III−.

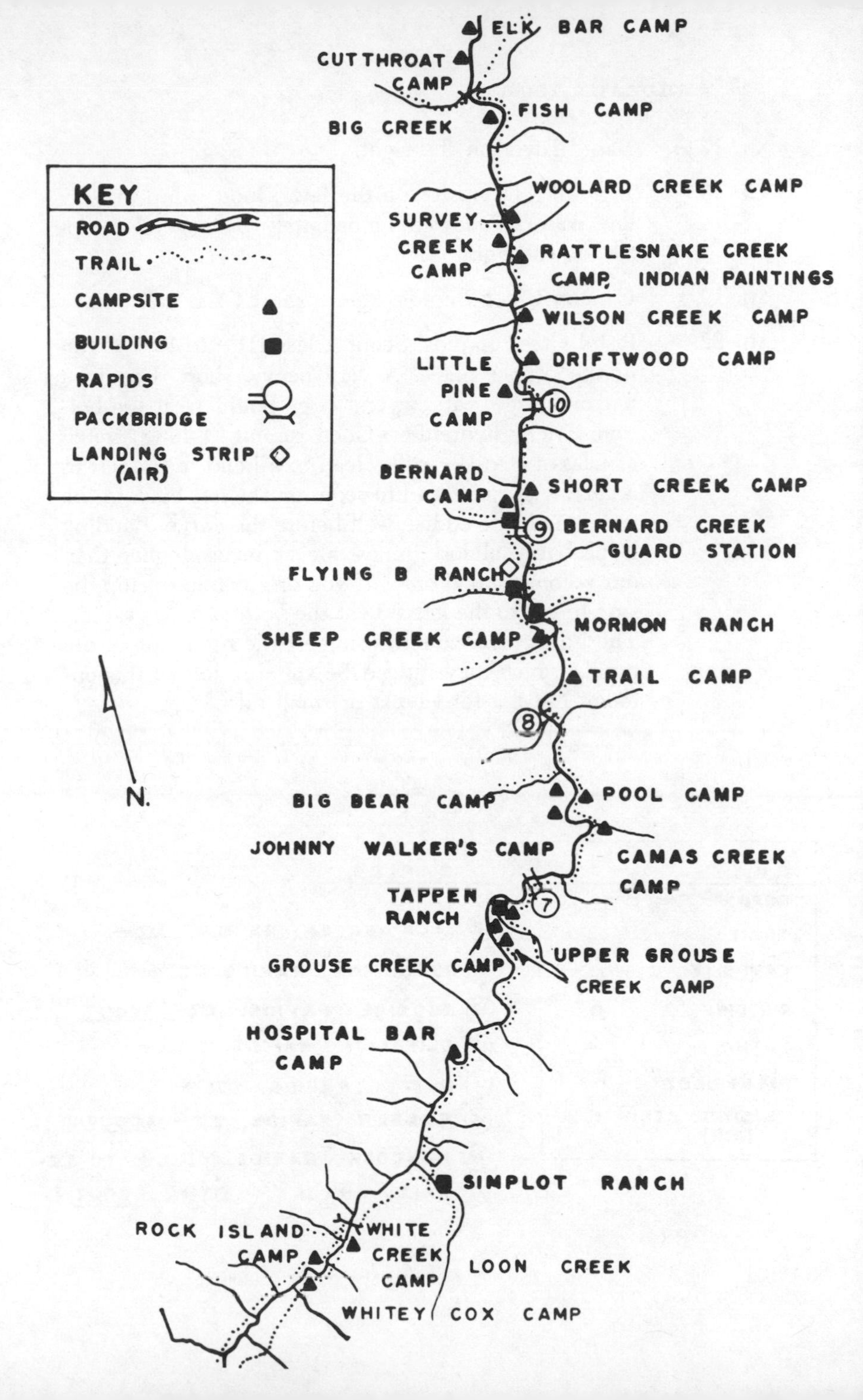
ELK BAR CAMP
CUTTHROAT CAMP
FISH CAMP
BIG CREEK
KEY
ROAD
TRAIL
CAMPSITE
BUILDING
RAPIDS
PACKBRIDGE
LANDING STRIP (AIR)
WOOLARD CREEK CAMP
SURVEY CREEK CAMP
RATTLESNAKE CREEK CAMP, INDIAN PAINTINGS
WILSON CREEK CAMP
DRIFTWOOD CAMP
LITTLE PINE CAMP
10
BERNARD CAMP
SHORT CREEK CAMP
9
BERNARD CREEK GUARD STATION
FLYING B RANCH
MORMON RANCH
SHEEP CREEK CAMP
TRAIL CAMP
N.
8
BIG BEAR CAMP
POOL CAMP
JOHNNY WALKER'S CAMP
CAMAS CREEK CAMP
TAPPEN RANCH
7
GROUSE CREEK CAMP
UPPER GROUSE CREEK CAMP
HOSPITAL BAR CAMP
SIMPLOT RANCH
ROCK ISLAND CAMP
WHITE CREEK CAMP
LOON CREEK
WHITEY COX CAMP

MI. 17+. Rapid River on the right.

MI. 18+. Big Snag Campsite on the left. Good camp at very low water. Followed immediately by a good campsite on the right.

MI. 19. Cannon Creek Rapids. Sharp, short Class III drop.

MI. 22. Pistol Creek Rapids. **Scout.** Class III+ to IV− if run in the proper place. A very heavy, short drop in a narrow gorge, with several large boulders at the bottom. Tricky hydraulics. Good runout. A long stretch of Class I+ to II− riffles lead to a bend to the left in a narrow gorge. Land to scout on the left bank in the very small side eddies well before the curve. Landing is probably almost impossible at levels higher than our recommended ones. If you are unable to stop, be sure to get to the left side at the *bottom* of the rapids. The Forest Service notes suggest the right side of the rapids which may indeed be suitable for 22 ft. pontoons, but not for kayaks or small rafts.

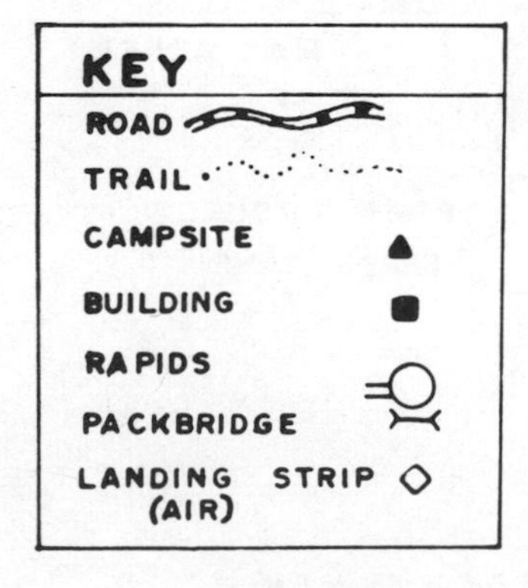

RAPIDS

(10) JACK CREEK RAPIDS. III−.

(11) PORCUPINE RAPIDS. III−.

(12) REDSIDE RAPIDS. III. SCOUT.

(13) CLIFFSIDE RAPIDS. III−.

(14) OUZEL RAPIDS. III−.

(15) RUBBER RAPIDS. IV− SCOUT.

(16) HANCOCK RAPIDS. III+ TO IV−.

(17) EXIT CRACKS. III+ SCOUT. ?

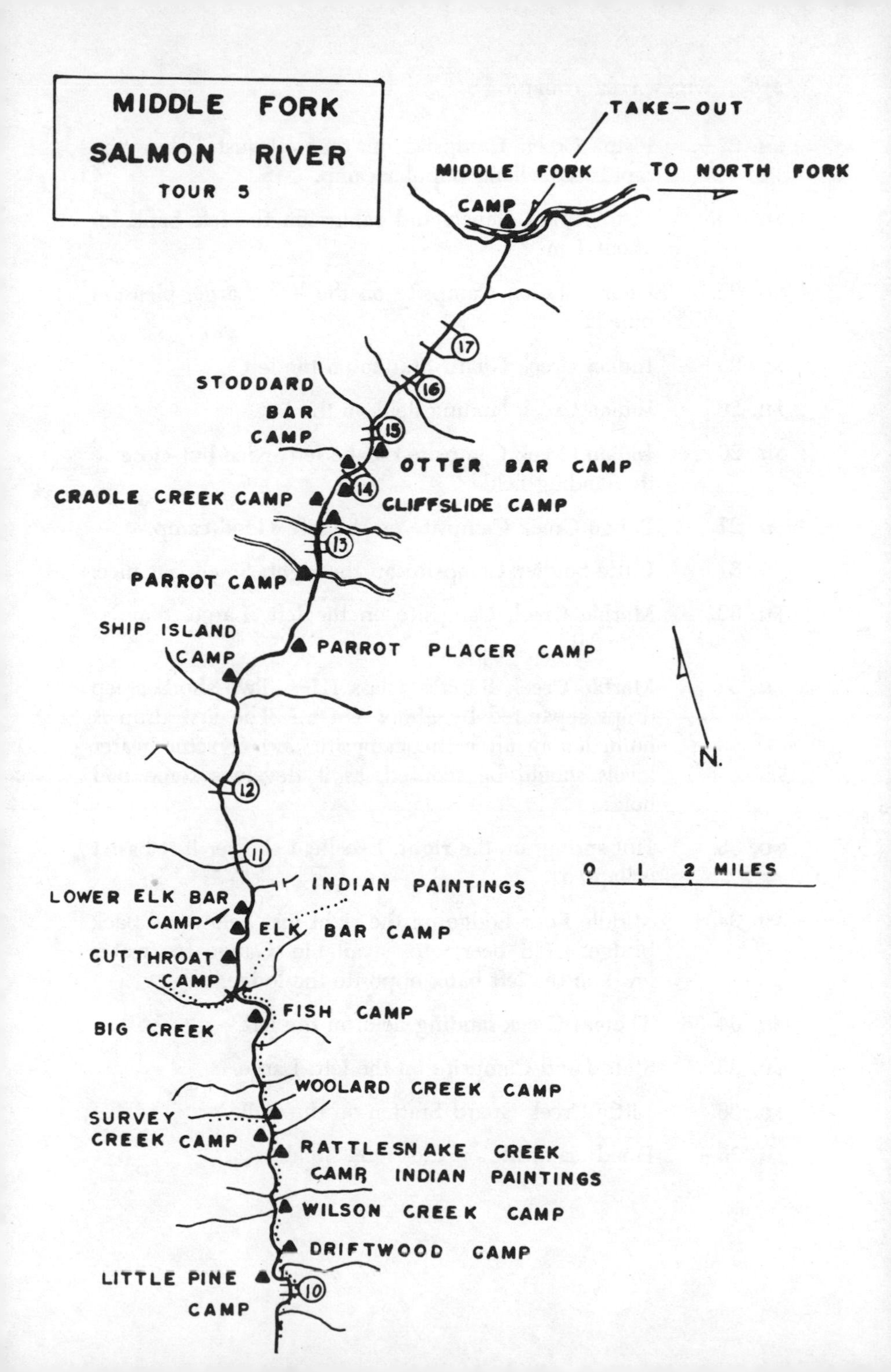
MIDDLE FORK
SALMON RIVER
TOUR 5
TAKE-OUT
MIDDLE FORK
CAMP
TO NORTH FORK
17
16
STODDARD
BAR
CAMP
15
OTTER BAR CAMP
14
CRADLE CREEK CAMP
CLIFFSLIDE CAMP
13
PARROT CAMP
SHIP ISLAND
CAMP
PARROT PLACER CAMP
N.
12
11
0 1 2 MILES
INDIAN PAINTINGS
LOWER ELK BAR
CAMP
ELK BAR CAMP
CUTTHROAT
CAMP
FISH CAMP
BIG CREEK
WOOLARD CREEK CAMP
SURVEY
CREEK CAMP
RATTLESNAKE CREEK
CAMP, INDIAN PAINTINGS
WILSON CREEK CAMP
DRIFTWOOD CAMP
LITTLE PINE
CAMP
10

MI. 22+. Pistol Creek Campsite on the left just below the rapids. Excellent, popular camp.

MI. 23. Pistol Creek Ranch and cabins on the left bank for about 1 mi.

MI. 25. Guard Station Campsite on the left. Large, pleasant pine flat.

MI. 25+. Indian Creek Guard Station on the left.

MI. 26. Indian Creek landing field on the left.

MI. 26+. Indian Creek Campsite on the left. Nice but close to the landing field.

MI. 27+. Pungo Creek Campsite on the left. Good camp.

MI. 31. Little Soldier Campsite on the right. Small but nice.

MI. 32. Marble Creek Campsite on the left. Large, popular pine flat.

MI. 32. Marble Creek Rapids. Class III−. Two short, steep drops separated by about 1/4 mi. The first drop is immediately after the campsite and at some water levels should be scouted, as it develops some bad holes.

MI. 33. Hot springs on the right. Excellent shower if it hasn't collapsed.

MI. 34. Middle Fork Lodge on the right just below the pack bridge. Cold beer, etc., available. Gauge for water level on the left bank opposite the lodge.

MI. 34–36. Thomas Creek landing field on the left.

MI. 35. State Land Campsite on the left. Large.

MI. 36. Little Creek Guard Station on the right.

MI. 36+. Hood Campsite on the right. Small.

MI. 37+. Jackass Flat Campsite on the right.

MI. 38+. Lower Jackass Campsite on the right. Large and popular.

MI. 41. Cougar Creek Ranch on the right. Mahoney landing field on the left. Neither obvious from river.

MI. 41+. Mahoney Campsite on the right. Small and nice.

MI. 43. Pine Creek Flat Campsite on the right. Large.

MI. 44+. Whitey Cox Campsite, grave, and hot springs on the right. Small camp.

MI. 45. Rock Island Campsite on the left. Small and pleasant.

MI. 47+. White Creek Camp on the right. Small and nice.

MI. 48. White Creek Pack Bridge.

MI. 50. Simplot Ranch, landing strip, and Loon Creek on the right.

MI. 53. Hospital Bar Campsite and hot springs on the left. Large and deservedly popular camp. Watch for mountain sheep in this area.

MI. 56+. Upper Grouse Creek Campsite on the right.

MI. 57. Tappen Ranch on the right. Not visible from the river.

MI. 57+. Grouse Creek camp on the right. Has a good beach at low water in the middle of a stretch of rapids. Followed by a good island camp.

MI. 58. First of the Tappen rapids. Class III−.

MI. 58+. Tappen Falls. **Scout.** Class III− to IV− if run in proper chutes. 5 ft. vertical drop over boulders, some dangerous holes. Several interesting runnable chutes. Good runout. The short pool following the first Tappen rapids leads to the falls. The falls is followed by several tricky Class III drops in the next mile.

MI. 60. Camas Creek Campsite on the right. Small.

MI. 61. Johnny Walkers Campsite on the left. Large and pleasant.

MI. 61+. Pool Campsite on the right.

MI. 62. Big Bear Campsite on the left.

MI. 62+. Funston Campsite on the left. Fair.

MI. 64. Aparejo Rapids. Straightforward Class III−.

MI. 65. Trail Campsite on the right. Small and nice.

MI. 66. Sheep Creek Campsite on the left. Fairly large, pleasant.

MI. 66+. Mormon Ranch on the right.

MI. 67+. Flying B Ranch on the left and Bernard Bridge.

MI. 68+. Flying B landing strip on the left.

MI. 69. Haystack Rapids. Class III rock garden.

MI. 69. Bernard Creek Guard Station on the left just after the rapids.

MI. 69+. Bernard Campsite on the left.

MI. 70. Short Creek Campsite on the right.

MI. 72. Jack Creek Rapids. Heavy Class III−.

MI. 72+. Little Pine Campsite on the left. Fair.

MI. 73. Driftwood Campsite on the right. Good. Watch for mountain sheep in this area.

MI. 74. Wilson Creek Campsite on the right. Small and nice.

MI. 75. Rattlesnake Creek and cave on the right. Huge cave with Indian paintings. Landing is difficult at low water as it is very rocky.

MI. 75+. Survey Creek Campsite on the left. Large and fairly nice.

MI. 76. Woolard Creek Campsite on the right. Small and pleasant.

MI. 77+. Fish Campsite on the left. Very small.

MI. 79. Big Creek Bridge and Big Creek.

MI. 80. Cutthroat Campsite on the left. Good.

MI. 80+. Elk Bar Campsite on the left. Beautiful, very popular camp.

MI. 81. Lower Elk Bar Campsite on the left.

MI. 81+. Veil Falls on the right cliff. Indian paintings in cave behind falls about 150 ft. above river.

MI. 82. Porcupine Rapids. Class III−.

MI. 83. Redside Rapids. **Scout** to determine route if unfamiliar with river. Class III. Steep, short drop among huge boulders. Followed shortly by a heavy Class III to IV drop which may require scouting.

MI. 85. Ship Island Campsite on the left. Good.

MI. 86. Parrot Placer Campsite and Historical Site on the right.

MI. 87. Parrot Campsite and cabin on the left.

MI. 88. Cliffside Rapids. Class III−. The river runs into a cliff on the left and has some bad holes, but they are fairly easy to avoid.

MI. 88. Campsite on the right just below Cliffside Rapids. Small.

MI. 89. Cradle Creek campsite on the left. Small, with poison ivy.

MI. 89+. Cliffside Campsite on the right. Nice, small. People tend to pile up in the next few campsites as they are the last ones available above the mouth.

MI. 90. Ouzel Rapids. Class III−.

MI. 90. Stoddard Bar Campsite on the left. Large flat several feet above the river towards the lower part of Ouzel Rapids. Excellent Indian paintings—walk a few hundred yards up the trail on Stoddard Creek to the cliffs. Stoddard Creek is at the upper end of the campsite.

MI. 90+. Otter Bar Campsite on the right. Small sand bar.

MI. 91. Rubber Rapids. **Scout.** Class IV−. Heavy waves and a fast pool lead to the main drop. Steep, short, very heavy drop over boulders, heavy runout. This is the first major rapids after Otter Bar. Much easier at very low water.

MI. 92.+. Hancock Rapids. Class III+ to IV−. Long rock garden, quite heavy at the bottom.

MI. 93. Exit Cracks Rapids. Class III+. Steep drop through huge boulders. *Quick scout is helpful.* Followed by several more heavy Class III to IV drops in the next 1½ mi. Some may require scouting.

MI. 96. Confluence with the main Salmon River. Middle Fork boat launching ramp on the right side of the main Salmon. Ugly, dusty, and very hot.

TOUR SIX

River of No Return— The Main Salmon River

RECOMMENDED BOAT TYPE: *rubber rafts equipped with frame and oars, kayaks, wooden drift boats*
DIFFICULTY OF RAPIDS: *Class III with a little IV–.*
AVERAGE GRADIENT: *12 ft./mi.*
WHEN TO RUN: *late July through September.*
LENGTH IN MILES: *79–153 mi. depending on put-ins and take-outs.*
LENGTH IN DAYS: *4–8.*

Description

The section of the Salmon River known as the "River of No Return" cuts its path from east to west across central Idaho through the second deepest canyon in the United States, 1/5 mi. deeper than the Grand Canyon. A dirt road follows it for the first 8 mi. from the confluence with the Middle Fork, and another dirt road

comes in at the end for the last 28 mi. before Riggins. But between these roads are 79 mi. of nearly roadless wilderness. (Rough roads do come into the river at two points.) The scenery is a compromise between the more heavily forested Middle Fork and the desert-like Lower Canyon. The No-Return canyon has a semi-forested environment; large grassy areas alternate with sparse to heavy forest. Occasionally the canyon narrows down between dark rock walls, but usually it is fairly open, with steeply sloping hills forming its sides. It has one good hot spring.

Campsites vary from gravel beaches and grassy flats to some lovely sand beaches. We have found the wood supply adequate. Sidestreams provide an ample supply of good water. The main river probably should be treated before drinking, especially toward the beginning of the section. Although this is a fairly popular river run, it is not nearly as crowded as the Middle Fork, and in August we have seen only a few other parties on the river.

Wildlife includes mule deer, mountain sheep, and a few rattlesnakes. Although this section is famous for salmon and steelhead fishing, in late summer fishing is fairly poor except in the sidestreams. Trails descend to the river at points and offer good opportunities for hiking. And in August the water temperature is usually comfortable for swimming.

The weather is normally hot and sunny during the summer, but nights can be cool since the elevation at the confluence is 3,000 ft. Rain is possible, however. We ran this section one August when we had rain every day. Insects are usually not bothersome at this time of year.

The first inhabitants of the canyon lived 8,000 years ago. More recently, the Salmon was a favorite of several Indian tribes. With the arrival of the white man, there were several Indian wars in the period 1877–79. *If* you're lucky you'll find some Indian paintings. We once stumbled across some in a cave by accident, but don't remember where.

Figure T6-1 "River of No Return" scene

Clark (of Lewis and Clark) scouted the first part of the "River of No Return" as a possible route to the west. But he retreated after 14 mi. convinced that the river was impassable on foot or by boat. In 1832 the first known attempt to boat the river was made by four Hudson Bay Company trappers in small boats constructed from hides. Two of the men drowned, and the other two arrived at their destination "quite naked." The first successful boating trip down the Salmon was thought to be in 1862, but it was not until this century that the river was commonly run. The Salmon took heavy pressure from miners, starting with the 1866 gold rush, and there are still some relics from mining days along the river.

Nature of rapids

The rapids are of the pool and drop type, and are frequent enough to make this an interesting whitewater trip. There are a few relatively long "quiet" sections, but they have a reasonable current except at very low water. Most of the drops contain a few huge though easily avoidable boulders and some heavy water, waves up to 7–8 ft. A few are quite rocky and require scouting, and a few contain some dangerous holes. Most rapids have good runouts.

We have run this section as low as 3,500 c.f.s. and as high as 10,000 c.f.s. on the Whitebird gauge (see Specific Information). On the whole, the run was much more exciting at 10,000 c.f.s. Highly experienced boaters would probably prefer water levels of 7,000 c.f.s. and above. Less experienced groups would probably prefer much lower water (below 4,500 c.f.s.).

This section requires boaters of very strong Class III ability and the party should include some Class IV boaters. Several rather inconspicuous ranches along the roadless section might provide help in case of an accident. Otherwise it would be a very long hike out. The two access roads at MacKay Bar and at Whitewater Ranch are very rough and not heavily used, but might provide a ride out.

Specific information

Location: Central Idaho. northwest of the town of Salmon.

Put-in

The many possibilities give a great variety of trip lengths. It is possible to put in at the town of North Fork on Highway 93. This adds 38 mi. to the trip, down to the mouth of the Middle Fork, the normal put-in. We have run this section and consider it rather unattractive; a fairly heavily used dirt road follows the river, and although there are a few good rapids, e.g., Long Tom, Pine Creek, for the most part the rapids are uninspiring. The river is, of course, much smaller in this section than below the confluence with the Middle Fork. It is possible to put in at a number of points along this stretch.

The confluence with the Middle Fork is a very popular put-in, complete with tables and a boat ramp. This put-in contains all the essentials, but is very dusty, very hot, and very unappealing. The road continues for 8 mi. beyond the confluence, but is much less heavily used. There are boat launching ramps and more pleasant campgrounds at Cache Bar (4 mi. downstream of the confluence) and Corn Creek (8 mi. downstream of the confluence).

The first few miles of the road from North Fork to the Middle Fork are paved and another section was being paved during our last visit in the summer of 1973. The road was slow and bumpy in the past, although quite passable in passenger vehicles. Its being paved should make the drive considerably more pleasant, but unfortunately may increase litter and vandalism.

Take-out

A variety of spots are again possible. A dirt road runs upriver for 28 mi. from Riggins to just upstream of Vinegar Creek. It is all passable by passenger vehicle, but the last section is rather rough. If you take out at Vinegar Creek you will miss several interesting rapids that follow it in quick succession. There are several possible take-out spots as you proceed downstream. We like to run about 7 mi. downstream from Vinegar Creek to the vicinity of the Manning Bridge. Downstream from the bridge, the rapids are less frequent although there is a very nasty Class IV rapids at Lake Creek bridge several miles downstream from Manning Bridge. Some parties prefer to run all the way down to the Riggins boat launching ramp to take out; the last 6 mi. is slow and boring.

Shuttle

This section has a very time-consuming shuttle, 7–10 hr. one way. There are several ways to shorten your driving time:

1. Local residents are often willing to shuttle cars for you at a reasonable price.
2. If you combine this trip with one down the Middle Fork, the shuttle is much more reasonable, especially considering the added length of the river trip.
3. Starting at North Fork and taking out at Riggins cuts off a little of the shuttle, the slowest part, but adds several days of rather uninspiring boating to the trip.

For the trip on the main Salmon alone, drive north on Highway 93 for about 110 mi. from North Fork to the town of Lolo. Follow Highway 12 west for about 130 mi. to the town of Kooskia. Follow Highway 13 south for 26 mi. to Grangeville, and then proceed south on Highway 95 for 53 mi. to Riggins. This gives a total of about 320 mi. over paved highway, which would take

6–7 hr. one way. To this must be added whatever mileage you wish on the dirt access roads at 10–25 mi./hr.

If you combine this section with the Middle Fork, the shuttle involves following Highway 21 from the Dagger Falls area to the town of Lowman, and then taking the good dirt road from Lowman to Banks. From Banks, Highway 55 leads north to Highway 95 which continues to Riggins. Total distance one way is about 185 mi. for which you should allow 5–6 hr.

Maps

The Forest Service distributes free an excellent river map, showing location of major rapids, campsites, and trails. Request the river map of the Salmon, the River of No Return, from:

Forest Supervisor
Salmon National Forest
Salmon, Idaho 83467

Water Level Information

Recommended flows 10,000 c.f.s. and below. You can probably obtain general information on the water level from the Forest Supervisor at the address given above under "Maps." The exact current flow in c.f.s. and a rough projected flow can be obtained for the Salmon at Whitebird from:

River Forecast Center
National Weather Service
320 Customhouse
Portland, Ore. 97209
(phone: 503-221-3811 before 3:00 P.M.)

Distance and Time Allowance

Shortest trip: Corn Creek Campground to Vinegar Creek, 79 mi.

Longest trip: North Fork to Riggins, 153 mi.

Allow 12–15 mi. a day for a fairly leisurely trip; 15–20 for a faster but still unhurried trip. If time allows, plan to look at, then run, the 5-mi. section below Riggins. It is along the highway, but contains some of the biggest water on the Salmon.

Wilderness Status

This section of the Salmon was designated for study in the National Wild and Scenic Rivers Act of 1968. Classification under this Act will probably take place in 1974. The Salmon is bor-

dered on the north by the Salmon River Breaks Primitive area, and on the south by the Idaho Primitive area.

Special Restrictions

The pressure on the River of No Return section was great enough by 1973 to make it a reservation-only river like the Middle Fork, effective in 1974. Its popularity is increasing, so if you plan to run it, check well in advance. Contact:

Figure T6-2 "River of No Return" rapids

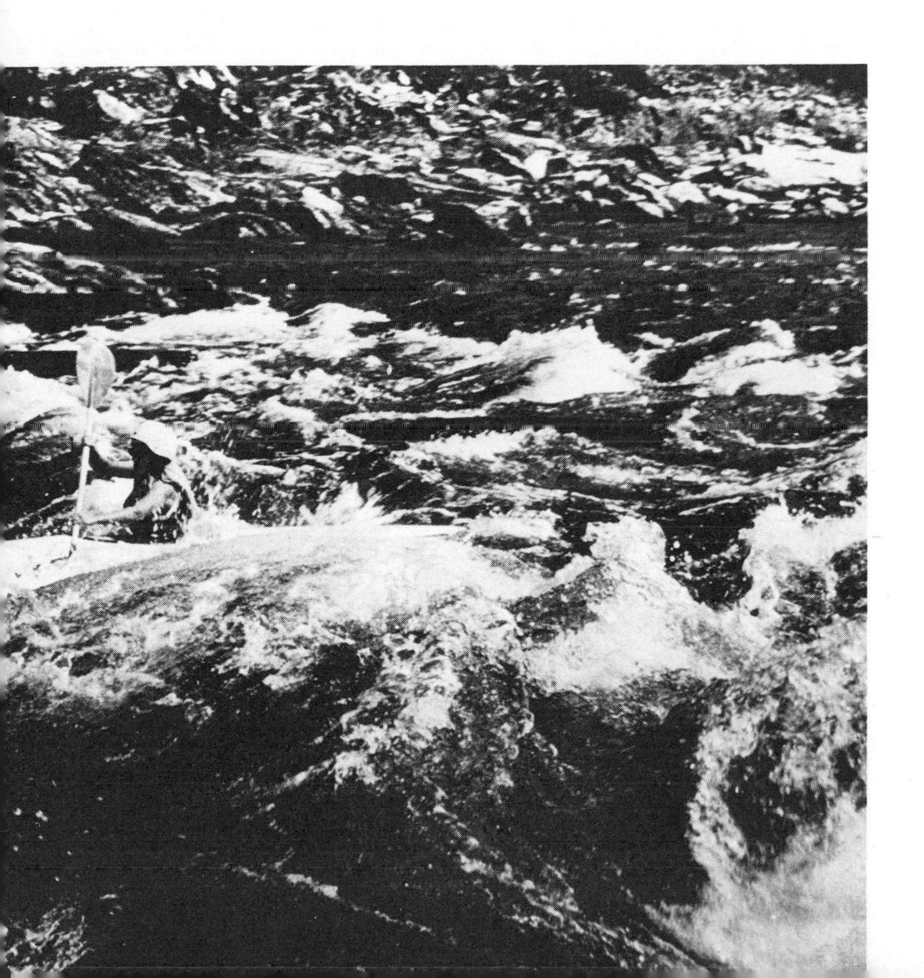

SALMON RIVER

RIVER OF NO RETURN

TOUR 6

RAPIDS

(1) GUNBARREL RAPIDS. II.

(2) RANIER RAPIDS, III TO III +.

(3) DEVILS TEETH RAPIDS. II +.

Wild River Manager
Salmon National Forest
Salmon, Idaho 83467

Trip permits are required, and will be issued only to parties with suitable equipment and experience. See items 5, 6, 7 under the "Special Restrictions" section for Middle Fork (Tour 5). For further information concerning these restrictions, as well as information about how, where and when to obtain trip permits, contact the Wild River Manager at the address given above.

Guide

This includes only major campsites and rapids, and the descriptions apply only at recommended water levels. Rapids and campsites may change at any time due to flooding, landslides, and other phenomena. Only the larger creeks and creeks with campsites are listed.

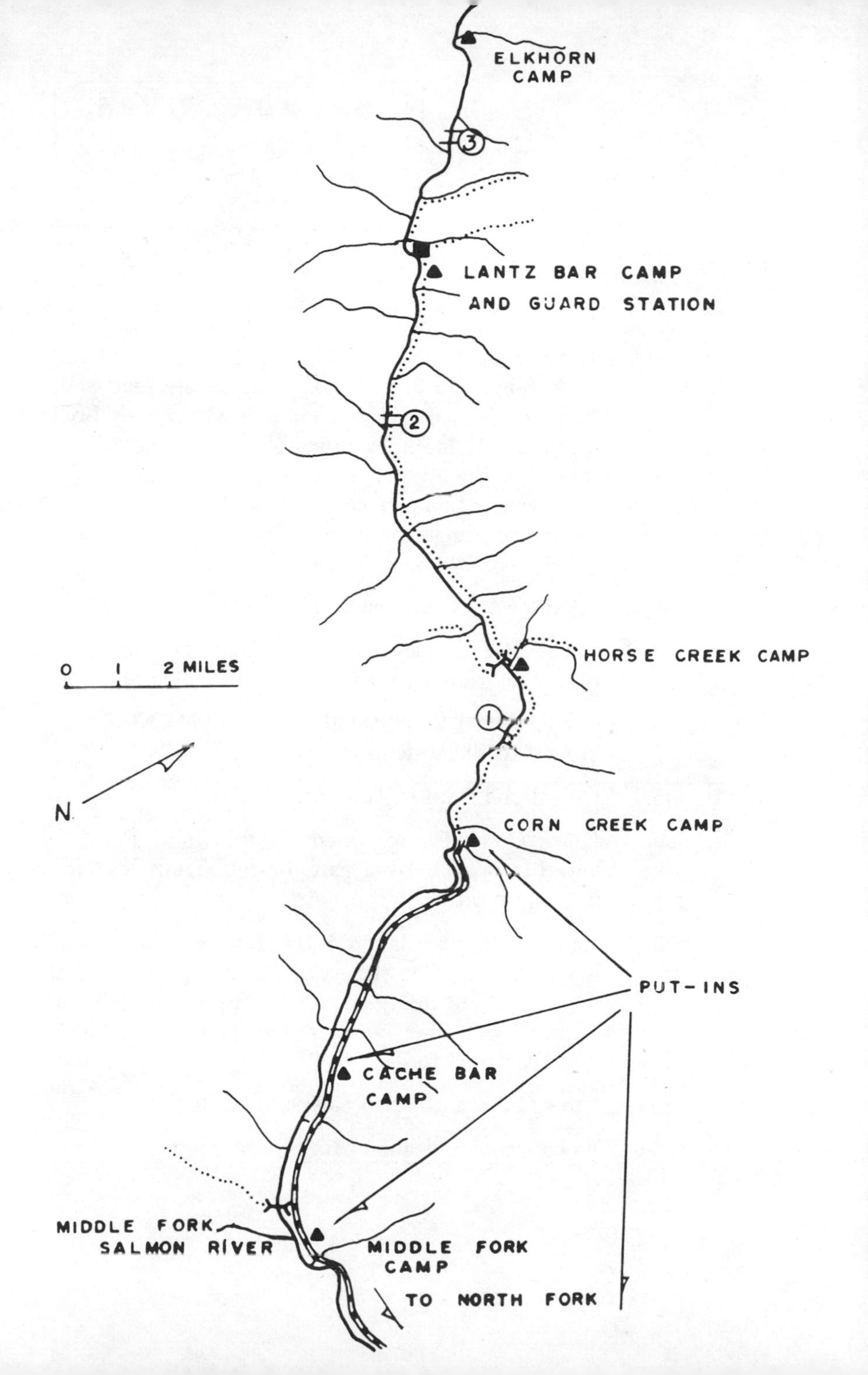
ELKHORN
CAMP
3
LANTZ BAR CAMP
AND GUARD STATION
2
0 1 2 MILES
HORSE CREEK CAMP
1
N
CORN CREEK CAMP
PUT-INS
CACHE BAR
CAMP
MIDDLE FORK
SALMON RIVER
MIDDLE FORK
CAMP
TO NORTH FORK

SALMON RIVER

RIVER OF NO RETURN

TOUR 6

MI. 0–38. Town of North Fork to confluence with the Middle Fork. Since the first 38 mi. parallels the road and is in no sense a wilderness section, it will be only briefly described. It includes Indianola Ranger Station, the "town" of Shoup, three Forest Service campgrounds (Ebenezer, Long Tom, and Middle Fork), some Indian paintings, and one challenging rapids, Pine Creek, a rocky Class III–IV.

MI. 38. Middle Fork Confluence. Boat launching ramp.

MI. 42. Cache Bar Campground and boat landing on the right. The campground is reasonably pleasant.

MI. 46. Corn Creek Campground on the right. Nice campground. Boat launching.

MI. 48. Gun Barrel Rapids. Class II to III−.

MI. 50. Horse Creek Campground on the right. Fair. Followed in 0.2 mi. by a pack bridge. Trails lead from here up into the high country.

MI. 55. Ranier Rapids. Class III–III+. Very heavy with a few holes. The Forest Service actually provides warning signs on many rapids: "Approaching Ranier Rapids." But the signs are usually much harder to spot than the rapids.

MI. 55+. Otter Creek and small campsite on the left.

MI. 56+ Fawn Creek and good campsite on the right.

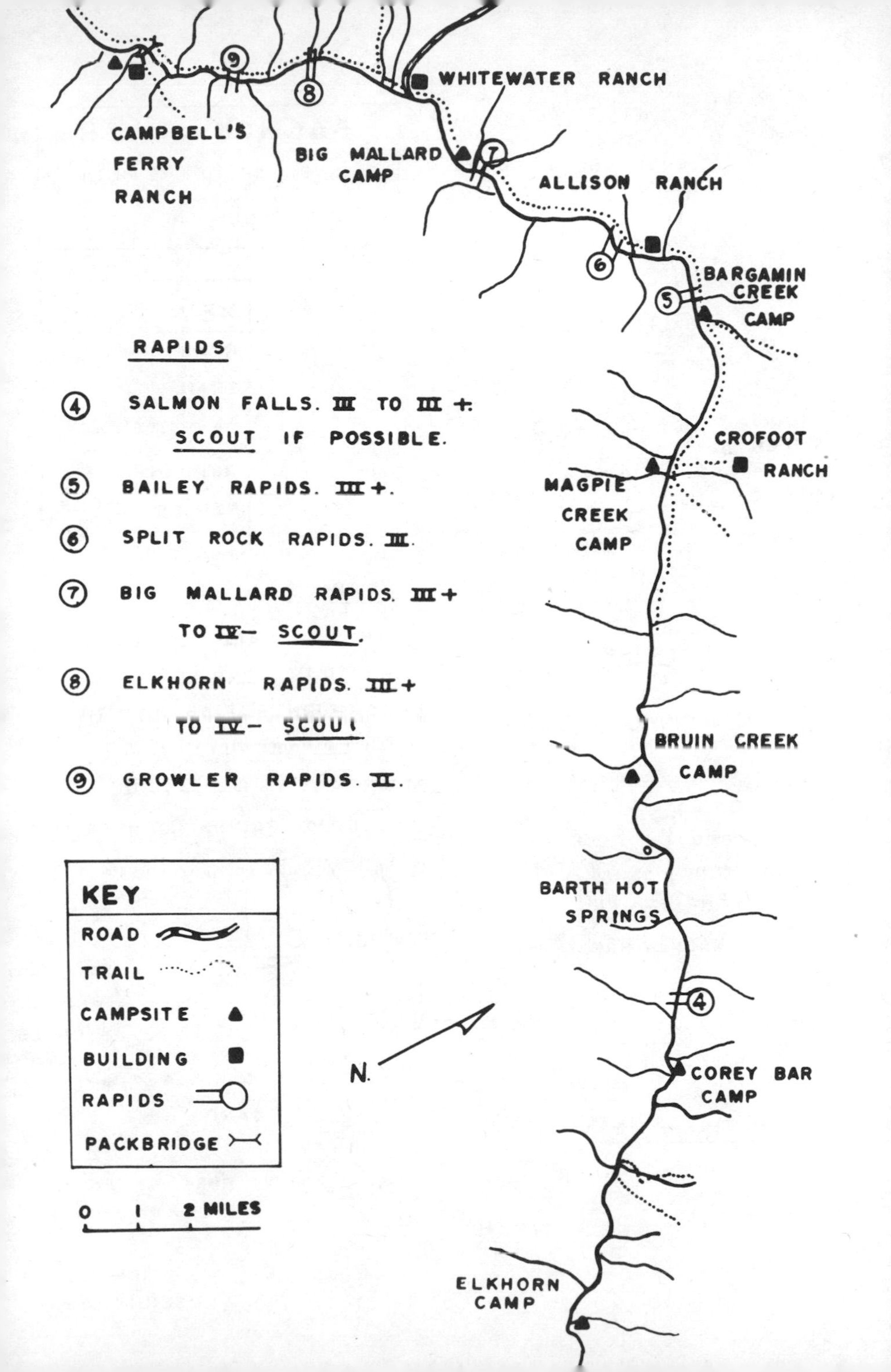

WHITEWATER RANCH
CAMPBELL'S FERRY RANCH
BIG MALLARD CAMP
ALLISON RANCH
BARGAMIN CREEK CAMP
CROFOOT RANCH
MAGPIE CREEK CAMP
BRUIN CREEK CAMP
BARTH HOT SPRINGS
COREY BAR CAMP
ELKHORN CAMP
N.
RAPIDS
4 SALMON FALLS. III TO III +. SCOUT IF POSSIBLE.
5 BAILEY RAPIDS. III +.
6 SPLIT ROCK RAPIDS. III.
7 BIG MALLARD RAPIDS. III + TO IV – SCOUT.
8 ELKHORN RAPIDS. III + TO IV – SCOUT
9 GROWLER RAPIDS. II.
KEY
ROAD
TRAIL
CAMPSITE
BUILDING
RAPIDS
PACKBRIDGE
0 1 2 MILES

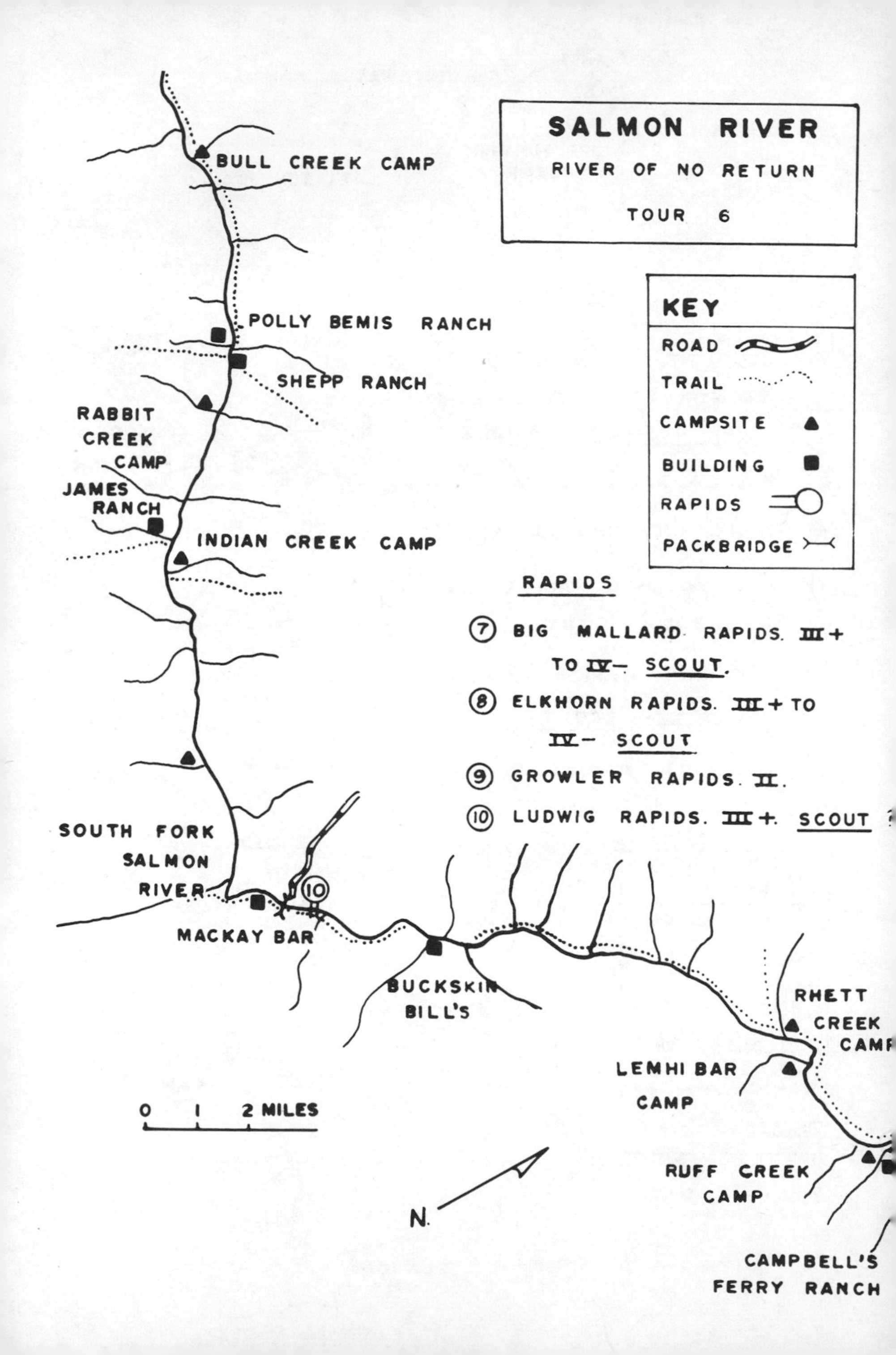
SALMON RIVER
RIVER OF NO RETURN
TOUR 6
KEY
ROAD
TRAIL
CAMPSITE
BUILDING
RAPIDS
PACKBRIDGE
RAPIDS
7 BIG MALLARD RAPIDS. III+ TO IV- SCOUT.
8 ELKHORN RAPIDS. III+ TO IV- SCOUT
9 GROWLER RAPIDS. II.
10 LUDWIG RAPIDS. III+. SCOUT
BULL CREEK CAMP
POLLY BEMIS RANCH
SHEPP RANCH
RABBIT CREEK CAMP
JAMES RANCH
INDIAN CREEK CAMP
SOUTH FORK SALMON RIVER
10
MACKAY BAR
BUCKSKIN BILL'S
RHETT CREEK CAMP
LEMHI BAR CAMP
RUFF CREEK CAMP
CAMPBELL'S FERRY RANCH
0 1 2 MILES
N.

MI. 57. Lantz Bar Campground and Guard Station on the right. Fair. Another trail comes down from the mountains here. A beach below this on a creek entering from the left is a good campsite.

MI. 57+. Lantz Rapids. Class III.

MI. 58. Disappointment Creek on left.

MI. 60. Devil's Teeth Rapids. Class II+ with rocks.

MI. 61. Elkhorn Campground and Creek on the right. Fair.

MI. 62. Chamberlain Creek on left.

MI. 66. Corey Bar Campground on the right. Looks inviting.

MI. 68. Salmon Falls. Class III to III+. A sharp drop over a ledge with several chutes. *Scouting is difficult but possible and recommended on the right.* It involves some rock scrambling, as the river is in a rock gorge at this point. The most commonly run chute is just to the right of center on the left side of the exposed rock. At many water levels there is a good chicken route on the far right. Avoid the far left. It's unfriendly.

MI. 69. Sabe Creek on right.

MI. 70+. Hot Springs Creek on the left. Excellent bath temperature.

MI. 71. Barth Hot Springs on the left. Watch for mountain sheep. Very hot for bathing.

MI. 72. Bruin Creek Campsite on the left. Nice camp.

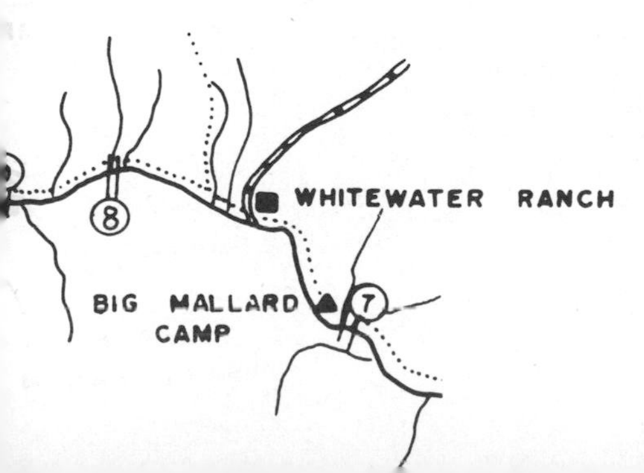

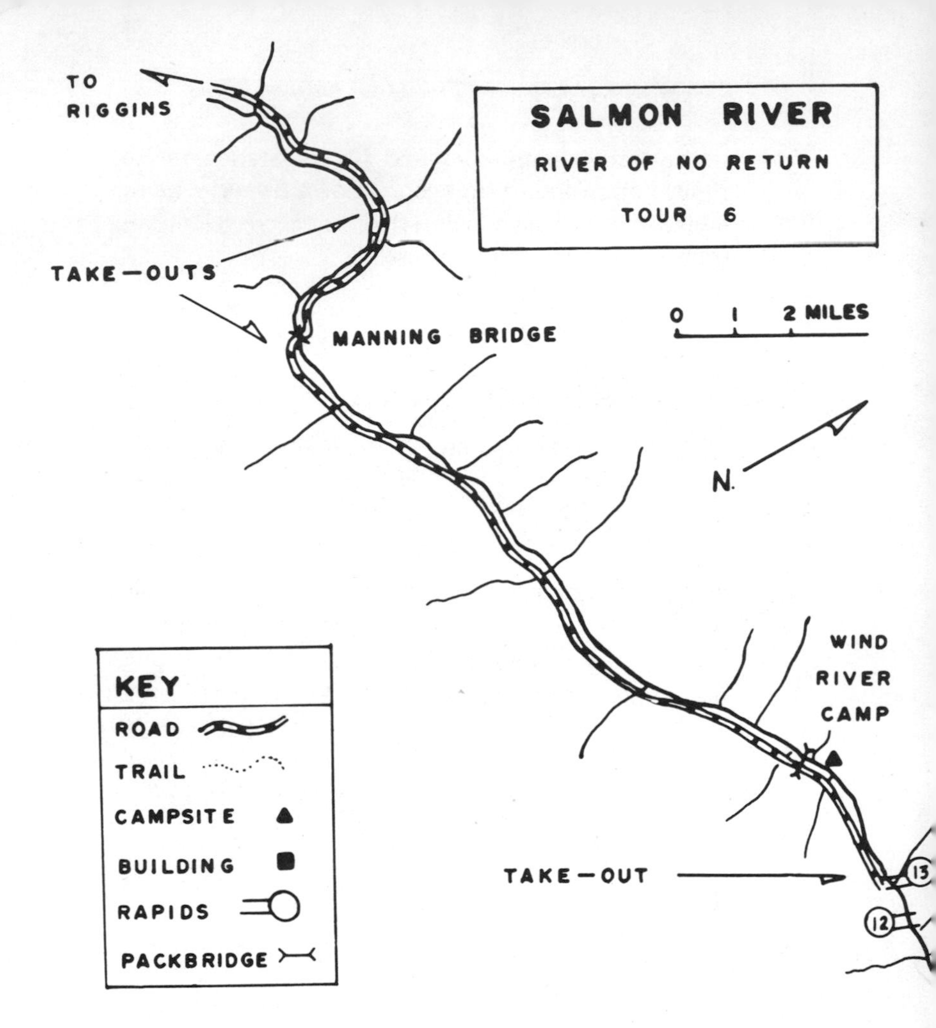

JOHNSO
CREEK CAM

RAPIDS

(11) DRIED MEAT RAPIDS. III TO III +.

(12) CHITTAM RAPIDS. III.

(13) VINEGAR CREEK RAPIDS. III +. SCOUT

MI. 76. Magpie Creek and Bar on the left. Good camp. Rattlesnake Creek and trail to Crofoot Ranch on the right.

MI. 78. Bargamin Creek Campsite and trail on the right. Good camp.

MI. 79. Bailey Rapids. Class III+. Big rock on the left. Big waves.

MI. 80. Myers Creek and Allison Ranch on the right.

MI. 80+. Split Rock Rapids. Class III. Two drops with some enjoyable waves.

MI. 83. Big Mallard Rapids. Class III+ to IV. **Scout.** Big rock and hole at the bottom left. Many smaller rocks and holes on the right. Can be tricky.

MI. 83+. Big Mallard Campsite on the right. Nice.

MI. 85. Whitewater Campground, ranch, and road access on the right.

MI. 87. Elkhorn Rapids. Class III+ to IV. **Scout** from the left side. Quite heavy and rocky.

MI. 88. Growler Rapids. Class II chute on the right side. Very rocky elsewhere.

MI. 89. Campbell's Ferry bridge and ranch on the left.

MI. 90. Ruff Creek and small but nice campsite on the left.

MI. 91+. Small creek and good campsite on the right.

11

CALIFORNIA CREEK CAMP

BULL CREEK CAMP

MI. 92. Lemhi Creek and Bar on the left.

MI. 93. Rhett Creek Campground on the right. Good. Trail junction.

MI. 95. Blowout Creek, Bar, and Indian paintings on the right.

MI. 99. Jersey Creek and Painter Mine on the right.

MI. 99+. Buckskin Bill's Cabin on the left. Fascinating "hermit" makes his own guns, beautiful teapots, etc., a real craftsman. He lives there by choice, and may not always appreciate visitors, so use discretion. Followed by Five Mile Creek on left.

MI. 101. Ludwig Rapids. Class III+. *Scouting may be useful.* Huge waves and holes. Followed by many miles of scenic but relatively calm canyon.

MI. 102. MacKay Bar pack bridge, ranch, and road access.

MI. 102+. South Fork of Salmon River on the left.

MI. 105. Unnamed creek on the left. Good campsite.

MI. 107. Warren Creek on left.

MI. 108. Indian Creek and Campground on the right. Fair.

MI. 109. James Creek and ranch on the left.

MI. 111. Rabbit Creek on the left. Good campsite.

MI. 112. Shepp Ranch on the right. Polly Bemis Ranch on the left.

MI. 116. Bull Creek Campsite on the right. Nice.

MI. 118. California Creek Campsite on the left. Nice.

MI. 121. Dried Meat Rapids. Class III–III+. A lovely, very

heavy chute with man-eating holes on either side. Easier at lower flows (Class II+).

MI. 121+. Johnson Creek on the right. Good campsite.

MI. 122+. Bear Creek on left with a nice camp below.

MI. 124. Chittam Rapids. Class III. This one sneaks up on you on a blind curve to the right. To avoid some very nasty holes, sneak up on it on the far right, next to the gravel bar.

MI. 125. End of the road from Riggins on the left.

MI. 125+. Vinegar Creek Rapids. Class III+ to IV. **Scout** from the right side. Run tongue on the right. Very rocky and nasty on the left. Interesting turbulence.

MI. 126. Huntz Gulch boat landing on the left.

MI. 126+. Wind River pack bridge. Good campsite on the right.

MI. 127–134. A number of pleasant rapids. None require scouting.

MI. 134–153. (To Riggins.) Some nice beaches get considerable use by the townspeople and tourists; a campground; a few easy rapids and one nasty one which you should **Scout** at MI. 147, under Lake Creek Bridge.

TOUR SEVEN

Salmon River— Lower Gorge

RECOMMENDED BOAT TYPE: *kayaks, rubber rafts equipped with frame and oars, rigid drift boats.*
DIFFICULTY OF RAPIDS: *Class II and III, with a little IV.*
AVERAGE GRADIENT: *10 ft./mi.*
WHEN TO RUN: *August-September depending on water level.*
LENGTH IN MILES: *71–75 depending on put-in.*
LENGTH IN DAYS: *3½–5.*

Description

The lower Salmon River carves its way through a unique desert canyon as it approaches the Snake in western Idaho. This is not a Grand Canyon type river with colorful rocks and tourists everywhere. The rare somber beauty of the lower Salmon stems mostly

Figure T7-1 Kayak in Devil's Slide Rapids

from the impression it gives of a vast, lonely wilderness. Although an occasional jeep track or cabin dots the river, they are rare, and the lack of fellow travelers adds to the sense of isolation in this seldom run section. The scarcity of sidestreams and other landmarks adds to this feeling of isolation; it is difficult to tell where you are in this huge canyon. The last 20 mi. of the trip are on the Snake River, including the last few miles of Hells Canyon. The isolation ends when you join the Snake, as it is heavily traveled by power boats.

For days you follow a narrow cleft, your vision limited to a narrow strip of sky, the steeply sloping grass-covered canyon, and the river. Lovely huge white sand beaches are frequent, making perfect campsites. Beware of rattlesnakes there. These beaches usually have a few trees that provide welcome shade. In several sections, the canyon passes through somber narrow basalt gorges. Sidestreams are scarce, and are probably more polluted than the main river. We have always used the main river for drinking water without treatment with no ill effects, but, of course, it is safer to boil it or use Halazone first. The Snake is not safe to drink; treat it, or carry water from the Salmon.

The wildlife along the river includes eagles, deer, mink, and even a few mountain lions. Fishing is poor in summer except for warm water fish. Lack of trails and an abundance of heat discourage hiking, but the combination of sand beaches, hot weather, and warm water makes swimming popular.

Daytime temperatures often soar over 100°, but the combination of dry air and river breeze makes the heat bearable, even delightful, especially while on the water. However, this river is not a good choice for someone who is very sensitive to the sun or heat, and all members of the party should be adequately protected against it. The night temperatures are a comfortable 60–75°F. This is desert country, and rain is very rare in the summer, but. . . .

Nature of rapids

Although the small gradient of 10 ft./mi. might indicate that this section of the Salmon is flat, it has some magnificent rapids. It is a pool and drop section with some very long pools that have good current. And the rapids are well worth the wait. At moderate flows of 7,000–10,000 c.f.s., most rapids develop huge well-spaced waves that are a boater's dream. This stretch makes an excellent introduction to heavy water boating as most of the rapids are Class II–III, not particularly difficult, requiring a good brace, a powerful stroke, and very little maneuvering. There is one nasty boulder-strewn rapid (Class IV−) that can be portaged only with difficulty, but it does have a fairly straightforward chute. Only a few rapids require scouting. One word of caution: as always these ratings refer to the easiest route through the rapids. On big rivers like this, the more sporting routes can be very dangerous due to house-sized holes, so stick to the friendly obvious green tongues.

The 20 mi. on the Snake have many small rapids. They are usually more interesting than they look because of the strange boils and turbulence that develop with large flows of water.

We have run the river from 5,000 to 9,500 c.f.s. In general, of course, the rocks are more of a problem at lower water, and turbulence is worse at higher water. We found the trip most enjoyable above 7,000 c.f.s. (see Specific Information).

The lower Salmon is an outstanding trip for an experienced intermediate boater who wants a "big water" wilderness trip. The average skill of the boaters should be a strong Class III or medium Class III with a reliable roll, and the party should include several Class IV boaters. The minimum boater skill should be a Class III−.

A rough ranch road parallels the river for 15 mi. below Whitebird. After this, a few jeep roads provide limited access to the Salmon, and jet boats could provide necessary aid on the Snake.

To accustom the party to big water before the trip starts, run the 5-mi. section of the Salmon immediately below the town of Riggins. It contains some huge water as big as or bigger than any on the lower canyon and slightly more difficult.

Specific information

Location: Western Idaho, South of Lewiston.

Put-in

Skookumchuk campground on Highway 95 about 4 mi. upstream of the bridge across the river at Whitebird. This is a popular swimming spot with the local people and is often rather noisy. But it does have a beautiful beach for boat-launching. Starting at the Whitebird bridge instead of the campground eliminates 4 mi. of rather dull paddling.

Take-out

Confluence of the Grande Ronde from the west with the Snake. There are several boat launching areas near here, one right at the confluence. They are not pleasant spots to camp. The trip may be extended by paddling part or all of the remaining 25 mi. or so into Lewiston, but this stretch is heavily traveled by jet boats, is along the road, and although it has one good rapids is not particularly interesting.

Shuttle

The lower Salmon shuttle is only moderately long; allow $8\frac{1}{2}$ hr. round trip. A direct bus connection from Lewiston to Whitebird simplifies the shuttle immensely. We unload all gear at the put-in early in the morning, and leave by 6:00 A.M. to drive all the cars to Lewiston. We leave one at the junction of the Grande Ronde, and the rest in Lewiston, catching the bus at 11:00 A.M. and arriving back at the put-in about 2:00 P.M. to begin the trip, with no shuttle to do at the end. (Check the bus timetable.) Highway 95 is an excellent road from Whitebird to Lewiston, but it includes one very long, steep, slow grade climbing out of the Salmon Canyon, and takes about 3¼ hr. one way. To get to the mouth of the Grande Ronde from Lewiston, cross the Snake River on Highway 12 to Clarkston, and turn south on Highway 129 to Asotin. At Asotin, leave Highway 129 and follow the unmarked road along the river to the mouth of the Grande Ronde River. Allow 2 hr. for the Lewiston-Grande Ronde round trip. The last 10 mi. of this is on good gravel road.

Maps

U.S. Geological Survey Idaho quadrangles: Whitebird, Fenn, Moughmer Point, Boles, Westlake, Hoover Point.

Water Level Information

Recommended flows 10,000 c.f.s. and below. Ask for the flow in c.f.s. on the Salmon at Whitebird. Contact

River Forecast Center
National Weather Service
320 Customhouse
Portland, Ore. 97209
(phone: 503-221-3811 before 3:00 P.M.)

Distance and Time Allowance

71 mi. from Whitebird to the Grande Ronde. This can be run

hurriedly in $3\frac{1}{2}$ days, very comfortably in 4 to $4\frac{1}{2}$ days, and at a leisurely pace in 5 days. Most parties will not want to spend much more time than this, as the hot weather makes the river the most pleasant place to spend the time.

Wilderness Status

The lower Salmon is not protected at present, but it is included in the Salmon River study under the Wild River Act of 1968, and will probably be classified under this Act in 1974.

Guide

This includes only major campsites and rapids, and applies only at recommended water levels. Rapids and campsites may change at any time due to floods, landslides, and other phenomena.

MI. 0. Whitebird Bridge. This is a useable put-in for small boats, but is not a pleasant spot to spend much time. Parties with larger boats or parties planning to spend some time at the put-in should start about 4 mi. upstream at the campground at Skookumchuk Creek. Just below the Whitebird bridge is a rapids with holes on the far right.

MI. $\frac{1}{4}$. Whitebird Creek on the right followed by campsites on both the right and the left for the next mile or so.

MI. 2. Rollercoaster Rapids. A string of huge, enjoyable waves. Followed by several fair campsites.

MI. 3. Good campsite on the left following some large black

Figure T7-2 Typical Lower Salmon scene

rocks on the left shore. This campsite is followed immediately by a large and pleasant one on the left.

MI. 4½. Good campsite with a possible spring.

MI. 5. Class III− rapids with a good play spot at the bottom.

MI. 6½. Campsites on the left and right.

MI. 8. Short's Bar and cabin on the right. This is the last good spot to camp until the end of the Green Canyon.

MI. 8¼. The Green Canyon starts immediately after Short's Bar. It is a scenic narrow canyon with fairly steep rock walls, lasting 2–3 mi., and containing four Class III rapids.

MI. 8½. Class III− rapids.

MI. 9. Wright-Way Drop. Class III. Sharp drop with big waves. Avoid the wall on the left at the bottom. *You may wish to scout quickly.* This is followed in about 100 yd. by a long Class III− rapids.

MI. 9½. Demon's Drop. Class III. Big rock in the left center at the top.

MI. 10. Small stream on the left followed in 1/4 mi. by a spring on the right.

MI. 11. Pine Bar Rapids. Class III. **Scout on the right.** Steep rock garden littered with boulders and holes. Recognize by a large sand bar on the right with a house on it. This is the end of the Green Canyon. The rapids is followed by a small camping beach on the left. Road from Rice Creek ends here.

MI. 12. Good campsite on the left with pine trees. No more good camps for a few miles.

MI. 12½. Shack on the right.

MI. 14. Spring on the left.

MI. 15½. Cabins and John's Creek on the right. These are followed by a ranch on the left and a Class II+ rapids with sporty swirlies.

MI. 16. Rice Creek Bridge and Creek.

MI. 17. Class III− rapids followed by a cabin on the right. The dirt road that has been paralleling the river ends in this vicinity. Watch for twisted and upended basalt columns in this area.

MI. 19. Campsite on the right.

MI. 20. Campsite on the right. The last campsite before Cougar Canyon.

MI. 20½. Cougar Canyon starts with a Class III rapids followed closely by a Class III− rapids. The narrow canyon lasts for several miles and contains a few campsites.

MI. 22. Stream on the right.

MI. 23. Class II+ rapids with a wall followed by a Class III rapids.

MI. 24. Lorna's Lulu. Class III rapids with good waves. Campsite on the left at the bottom.

MI. 25. Heavy Class III− rapids followed by two small campsites on the right.

MI. 26. Whitehouse Bar on the right. Large beach. The last campsite before Snohole Canyon. The best landing spot is at the lower end of the beach.

MI. 26½. Snohole Canyon. Narrow canyon with challenging rapids and no good campsites for several miles.

MI. 27. Class III− rapids with a huge hole on the far right.

RAPIDS

1. ROLLERCOASTER RAPIDS, III.
2. III –.
3. III –.
4. WRIGHT WAY DROP, III, III –. SCOUT.
5. DEMON'S DROP III.
6. PINE BAR RAPIDS. III. SCOUT.
7. III –.
8. III, III –.
9. III –.
10. LORNA'S LULU, III.
11. III –.
12. III –.
13. BODACIOUS BOUNCE, III.
14. HALF AND HALF, III +.
15. GOBBLER III –.
16. SNOHOLE, IV – SCOUT.
17. CHINA RAPIDS, III – TO IV SCOUT.
18. III –.
19. III.
20. III.
21. DEVIL'S SLIDE, III.
22. III –.
23. III.
24. BJERKE'S BOULDER, III +. SCOUT ?

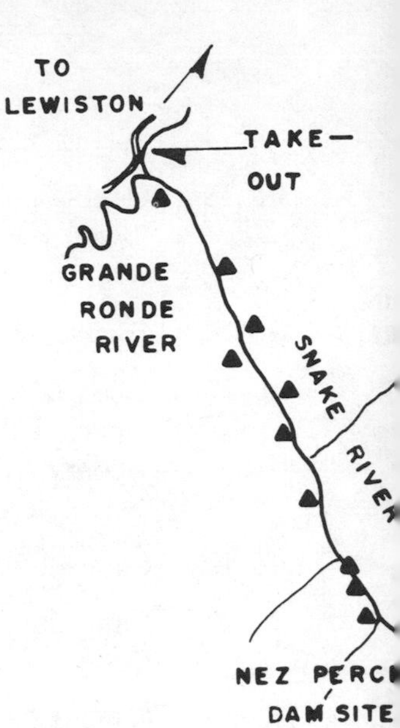

N

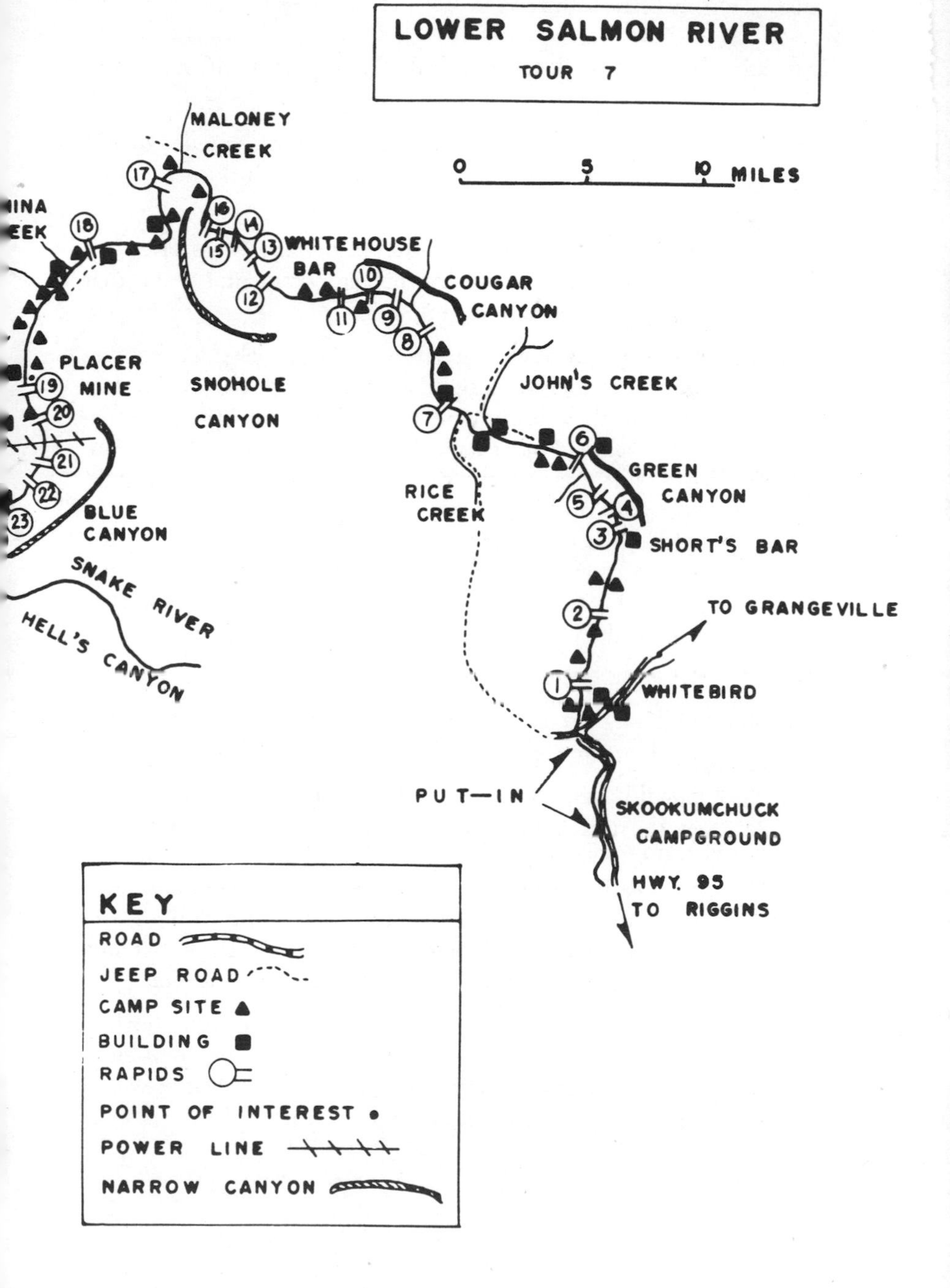
LOWER SALMON RIVER
TOUR 7
0 5 10 MILES
MALONEY CREEK
WHITE HOUSE BAR
COUGAR CANYON
SNOHOLE CANYON
PLACER MINE
JOHN'S CREEK
GREEN CANYON
RICE CREEK
SHORT'S BAR
BLUE CANYON
SNAKE RIVER
HELL'S CANYON
TO GRANGEVILLE
WHITEBIRD
PUT-IN
SKOOKUMCHUCK CAMPGROUND
HWY. 95 TO RIGGINS
KEY
ROAD
JEEP ROAD
CAMP SITE
BUILDING
RAPIDS
POINT OF INTEREST
POWER LINE
NARROW CANYON

MI. 28. Bodacious Bounce. Class III rapids with huge fun waves.

MI. 29½. Half and Half Rapids. (Half the time you make it!) Class III+. Some big holes, requires a little maneuvering in heavy water.

MI. 30. The Gobbler. This is a straightforward Class III– unless you get gobbled by the temperamental wave that appears at certain water levels.

MI. 30½. Class II drop with a large vertical rock face coming into view below it on the right bank. 100 yd. of fast current then bring you to **Snohole. Scouting mandatory.** *Scout from the left side.* Class IV–. Very dangerous if run in the wrong spot. If you are in the right spot, the run is reasonably straightforward. Steep drop with huge boulders and holes. The chute is just to the right of center. *This drop cannot be portaged or lined without great difficulty at flows over 6,000 c.f.s.* It is followed by several small beaches in the next mile.

MI. 32. Nice campsite on the left.

MI. 33. Maloney Creek and a nice campsite on the right. Rough road on the right. Good marker for China Rapids.

MI. 33½. Small beach on the left followed by China Rapids. Stop at the beach to **scout** if you are unfamiliar with the rapids. The river curves to the left so that **the rapids is not really visible until you are in it.** It contains some dangerous holes in the center and on the right. There is a good Class III– chicken route on the far left. There are springs on the right 100 yd. below the rapids.

MI. 34½. Cabins on the right just after a campsite on the left. They are followed by several campsites on both sides and then a good campsite on the left. There are several more good campsites in the next 2 mi.

MI. 37½. House high on the left side with a rough road paralleling the river.

MI. 38½. Class III− rapids followed by several campsites on the right.

MI. 39. Creek and a nice small campsite on the right followed by a house on the right. Several good campsites in the next 1/2 mi.

MI. 39½. A Bureau of Land Management jeep road and sign become visible on the right. The road follows the river for several miles. They are followed by a nice campsite on the left.

MI. 41. Creek and Bureau of Land Management campsite with outhouses on the right.

MI. 41½. Bureau of Land Management campsite on the right opposite a Class II+ rock garden. The main chute is on on the right. This is followed by another B.L.M. campsite on the right, a Class II+ rapids, and a nice campsite on the left.

MI. 43. Good campsite on the left. Just downstream of it are some placer mining ruins within walking distance. A cabin is visible on the right side downstream. The placer mine is followed by a Class III chute.

MI. 44½. House high on the right side, and camping beaches on both sides at a long Class III rapids. The Blue Canyon starts here, and there are no more good campsites for several miles.

MI. 45. Start of the Blue Canyon.

MI. 45½. Power lines cross the river.

MI. 46. Devil's Slide. Class III, heavy drop. Recognize by the rock slide on the left. This is supposed to become quite difficult at very high water. It is followed by a Class II+ rapids and two small campsites on the left.

MI. 47. Long 1/2 mi. heavy Class III− rapids.

MI. 48½. Small beach on the left and a cabin on the right mark the entrance to a heavy Class III rapids.

MI. 49. Beach on the left and a cabin on the right signal the approach to Bjerke's Boulder. Class III+. *A quick scouting might be useful.* This is quite turbulent, and harder than it looks!

MI. 50½. Snake River junction. Pick up drinking water from the Salmon. The junction is followed by a long Class II rapids and several beaches.

MI. 51½. Start of a gorge with no campsites for about 2 mi. The Nez Perce Damsite is located about 1/2 mi. down this gorge. Look for writing on the rocks.

MI. 53. Stream on the left.

MI. 53½. Geneva Bar (good campsite) on the left. Geneva Bar is followed by about 5 mi. of flat water and several other campsites.

MI. 58. Leaving national forest sign on the left. Shortly after this Class II rapids begin again (some of these are quite heavy at high water). Good campsites are spaced at reasonable intervals until the junction with the Grande Ronde at MI. 71.

TOUR EIGHT

Owyhee River—Section I

RECOMMENDED BOAT TYPE: *slalom kayaks, 8–12 ft. rafts equipped with frame and oars.*

DIFFICULTY OF RAPIDS: *Class III and IV, with some Class V and VI.*

AVERAGE GRADIENT: *22 ft./mi.*

WHEN TO RUN: *early May to early June (depending on water level).*

LENGTH IN MILES: *35.*

LENGTH IN DAYS: *2–4.*

A NOTE OF CAUTION: *Even an experienced whitewater boater could be killed on this section if he became careless. If the Middle Fork of the Salmon is a pleasant play river for you, you may be ready for this tour.*

The Owyhee River between Three Forks and Rome in southeast Oregon combines a deep, magnificent steep-walled canyon with

35 mi. of difficult whitewater. The narrow river snakes its way between vertical basalt walls that rise as much as 1,000 ft. from the water's edge in some areas. Desert wildflowers, hot springs, and Indian petroglyphs add to the fascination of this gorge.

The difficulty of the rapids, the short boating season, and the steepness of the canyon make this river the wildest of those described in this guide. In our four trips on this section we have seen no one, not fishermen, nor boaters, nor ranchers.

In some areas, campsites are limited; but in others, there are a number of pleasant sand beaches, some with trees. Drinking water is obtained from springs, which are numerous except in the last few miles. Water containers should be carried and filled at each opportunity. The river itself is quite muddy and unappetizing, some tributaries coming from grazing country.

Wildlife includes deer, coyotes, mink, otter, eagles, chukar partridge, Canada geese, and occasional antelope, bobcats, and wild horses. Rattlesnakes are common. The river has been planted with trout in the vicinity of Rome, and trout fishing in that area is reputed to be good. The canyon also contains black bass. After mid May, the water is usually warm enough for swimming, and several abandoned homesteads and apparent Indian caves make interesting side trips.

The weather in May and June is variable, ranging from rainy to very hot and sunny. Nights can be frosty. In May, the water temperature is cold enough that lightweight wetsuit tops are recommended for kayakists. Insects are usually not a problem in May and June.

Nature of rapids

This section of the Owyhee has the most difficult whitewater of any river described in this guide, in spite of its relatively mild

Figure T8-1 Owyhee Canyon

gradient. It is a pool and drop river, with some long sections of flat water, and some drops that make up for the pools with a vengeance. The rapids include long, heavy boulder gardens, and some sharp drops. The boulder-strewn rapids and one very nasty portage preclude large rafts and McKenzie boats, and the hydraulics preclude small rafts. So this river is strictly for medium-sized, 8–12 ft., rafts, and for kayaks.

The one Class VI rapids apparently cannot be lined, so must be portaged, and most parties will probably wish to line or portage a few other rapids as well. Most of the rapids are Class III and IV, but there is a long Class V rapid as well as the Class VI.

We have run the river in the range from 1,200 to 2,500 c.f.s. (see Specific Information). It is somewhat easier at the lower end of this range, as the hydraulics become less powerful as the water drops. The river becomes quite dangerous at levels above 3,500 c.f.s.

This section of the Owyhee is obviously for experts only. The weakest member of the party should be capable of handling Class III+ to IV− water reliably. Although very few people run this section, several boats have been lost. It will not tolerate incompetence. And if a boat is lost, it's a long, tough hike out, through roadless, rattlesnake-infested desert.

Specific information

Location: S.E. Oregon, south of Ontario, Ore.

Put-in

Three Forks, Ore. (pop. 26 packrats, 2 deer), at the confluence of the North, Middle, and Main Owyhee Rivers. This is a perfectly reasonable spot to camp.

Take-out

Rome, Ore. (pop. about 50 human beings). Rome has a cafe and a gas station, but no good place to camp.

Shuttle

In the past it has been possible to hire local drivers to drive your car to the take-out or to pick you up in their trucks. The price was $30–$40 in 1973. Contact:

Mrs. Norman Easterday
Jordan Valley, Oregon 97910
(phone: 586-2352)

Follow Highway 95 east of Rome for about 17 mi., where a dirt road marked Three Forks heads south. Follow this dirt road using any available signs, common sense, and your map for about 30 mi. until you reach the rim of the canyon overlooking the three forks. This section of road, from Rome to the rim, was manageable when dry for passenger cars in 1973. But we had considerable difficulty with even a four-wheel-drive truck that had chains on all four wheels when the road was wet. Usually roads are passable again 8–12 hrs. after the rain stops. The one mile from the canyon rim to the river requires a truck or jeep, preferably four-wheel drive, in dry weather. In wet weather, wait! If necessary, boats and gear can be portaged down the road to the river.

Maps

U.S. Geological Survey: Jordan Valley, 1:250,000. And Bureau of Land Management Quads. S.E. 19, S.E. 20 of Oregon (B.L.M., P.O. 2965, Portland, Ore.)

Water Level Information

Recommended water level: 1,000-3,000 c.f.s. Ask for the net inflow to Owyhee Reservoir in c.f.s. from:

River Forecast Center
National Weather Service
320 Customhouse
Portland, Ore. 97209
(phone: 503-221-3811)

Distance and Time Allowance

The 35 mi. can be run in 2–4 days, depending on the strength and ambition of the party.

Wilderness Status

Unfortunately this section was not included in the Oregon Scenic Waterways system, although it is a magnificently wild river. So at this time, it has only its isolated and rugged setting to protect it.

Guide

This includes only the more obvious rapids and campsites, and applies only at recommended water levels. Rapids and campsites may change at any time due to flooding, landslides, and other phenomena.

MI. 0. Three Forks confluence. Reasonable campsite.

Figure T8-2 Kayak in Halfmile Rapids

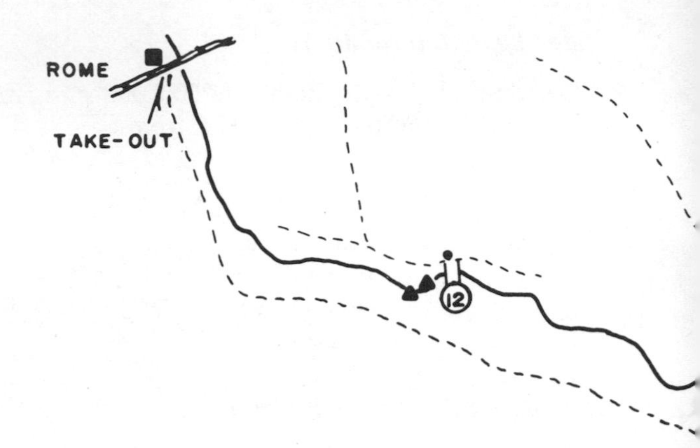

RAPIDS

1. LEDGE RAPIDS, IV+ TO V–. SCOUT.
2. HALFMILE RAPIDS, V. SCOUT.
3. RAFTFLIP DROP, IV. SCOUT.
4. SEVERAL III –.
5. SUBTLE HOLE, III TO IV –. SCOUT.
   BOMBSHELTER DROP. IV—. SCOUT.
6. III +.
7. FINGER ROCK RAPIDS. III–. SCOUT ?
8. BOULDER. II ON LEFT.
9. III+, III, III –.
10. WIDOW MAKER RAPIDS, VI. PORTAGE.
11. III+ TO IV–.
12. III –.

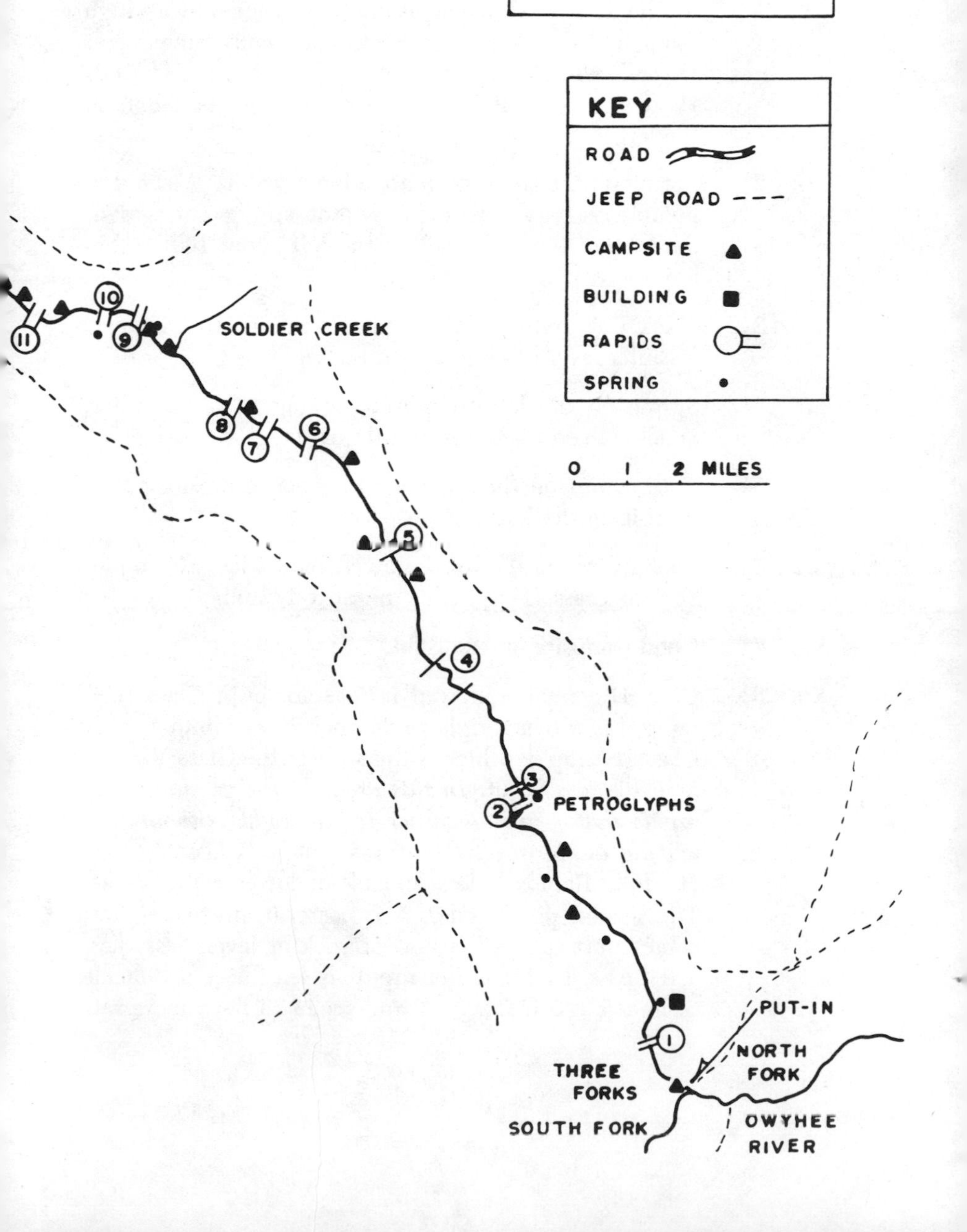
OWYHEE RIVER
SECTION I
TOUR 8
KEY
ROAD
JEEP ROAD
CAMPSITE
BUILDING
RAPIDS
SPRING
0 1 2 MILES
SOLDIER CREEK
PETROGLYPHS
PUT-IN
NORTH FORK
THREE FORKS
SOUTH FORK
OWYHEE RIVER
1
2
3
4
5
6
7
8
9
10
11

MI. 1½. Ledge Rapids. Class IV+ to V−. **Scout.** Recognize by the large rock slide on the right. A Class II rapids leads to the ledge. The center chute is runnable at high flows, and the right chute looks marginally runnable at lower flows. The ledge is followed by 1/4 mi. of Class IV rock garden. It is possible to portage the ledge on the left.

MI. 2½. Spring on the right at an abandoned cabin. Warm, but potable water. A moderately hot spring emerges at the base of the rock wall on the left about 100 yd. below the cabin.

MI. 3½. Door in its frame on the right. Formation that appears fossiliferous up the gulley on the right.

MI. 4½. Spring on the left. Requires digging to reach water. Small canyon for the next mile or so.

MI. 5½. Cabin ruins on the right, and a good campsite across from it on the left.

MI. 6½. Poor spring on the left followed by a Class II− rapid. Several Class II rapids in the next 1/2 mi.

MI. 7. Good campsite on the right.

MI. 8½. Class II+ rapid followed in 200 yd. by a Class III− rapid. River bends right in another 200 yd. into a small Class II+ rapids which is the start of the Class V Halfmile Rapids. **Scout.** *In this area do not go down any rapids that round a corner to the right without first looking at the rapids.* The first pitch (Class V−) of Halfmile Rapids is less difficult at lower water levels. The second pitch (Class V), nasty at any water, becomes unrunnable because of rock at levels less than 1,400 c.f.s. Right side of rapids is feasible but difficult to line. The left is worse, and seems to have more rattlesnakes. Muddy spring on the right at the second pitch, and petroglyphs on the rocks near the bottom of the second pitch on the right side. Campsites are very poor for the next few miles.

MI. 9. Raftflip Drop. Class IV. About 100 yd. below the second pitch of Halfmile Rapids. **Scout.** Steep, nasty, but short drop, with good runout.

MI. 11½. Steep walls on the left. Several Class III− rapids in the next 1½ mi.

MI. 13½. Campsite on the right.

MI. 14. Subtle Hole (Class III at low water to Class IV− at high water). Followed in 100 yd. by Class IV− Bombshelter Drop. Bombshelter Drop is harder than it looks. Scouting recommended for both rapids if the party is unfamiliar with the river. About 100 yd. below Bombshelter is a large cave on the left in which you could camp in bad weather.

MI. 15½. Several fair to poor campsites on the right

MI. 16. Steep Class III+ rapid.

MI. 17. Finger Rock Rapids. Class III−. Fairly easy rapids, but difficult to see. You may scout easily from the left side.

MI. 17½. Good campsite on the right. A Class II rapids above it and a Class II− rapids below it.

MI. 17¾. Large boulder blocks most of the river. Easy chute on left. Class II.

MI. 19. Large gravel and rock bar on right where Soldier Creek enters river. Good campsite on the right just below the creek.

MI. 19¾. Springs on the right which dry up early. Several nice campsites in this area.

MI. 20. Class III+ rapids followed in 100 yds. by a Class III rapids, and in about 1/4 mi., a heavy Class III− rapids. Spectacular steep canyon continues for about 1/4 mi., leading to the Widowmaker.

MI. 20½. Widowmaker Rapids. Class VI. *Portage.* The rapids begins with a Class III+ to IV− drop followed by 30 yd. of Class III and 30 yd. more of Class II which lead directly into the Class VI, 8-ft. vertical drop over boulders. **Scout.** Unless you have an extremely strong party, *don't even attempt to enter the first drop without scouting the entire rapids.* Most of the section leading up to the Class VI drop can be lined, but the Widowmaker itself must be carried and is a miserable carry. The right side is the best of the poor choices. There are warm springs on the left side immediately above the Class VI drop (the last springs for many miles). It is possible (although of course somewhat dangerous) to ferry across to these springs at lower flow levels. The Widowmaker is followed immediately by a Class III rapids.

MI. 21. Small beach on the right. Emergency campsite.

MI. 22. Class III+ to IV− rapid.

MI. 22½. Several good campsites on the right. Campsites become scarcer, and then nonexistent in the next 6 mi. Several rapids from here to Rome, none more difficult than Class III.

MI. 29. Class III− rapid on a right bend with grassy springs on both sides. Several campsites in this area.

MI. 35. Rome bridge.

TOUR NINE

Owyhee River— Section II

RECOMMENDED BOAT TYPE: *kayaks, rubber rafts equipped with frame and oars, wooden drift boats at medium-high water only. Open keel-less canoes have run this successfully with numerous portages, but it is only recommended for open canoeists who are highly experienced on whitewater.*

DIFFICULTY OF RAPIDS: *Class II+ with a little Class III and one class IV−.*

AVERAGE GRADIENT: *15 ft./mi.*

WHEN TO RUN: *April to early June depending on water level.*

LENGTH IN MILES: *38–63 depending on put-in and take-out.*

LENGTH IN DAYS: *3–6.*

This section of the Owyhee River in S.E. Oregon combines moderate whitewater with fantastic canyon scenery. It offers a greater variety of desert scenery than any other river described in this guide. Sagebrush hills and sand beaches alternate with intricately carved clay badlands, and spectacular colorful rock gorges. The trip can even include a huge lake rimmed by massive rock formations and distant mountains. The remote location of the Owyhee and its early boating season make it less heavily run than many rivers although its use increases each year. Except in the lower part of the section, where a few buildings and jeep roads can be seen, the canyon is wild and isolated.

Campsites are frequent except on the lake and are usually sand beaches. The better ones are shaded by trees, refreshing after the heat of the canyon. Of course this is excellent rattlesnake habitat, so step carefully. Springs are frequent on the first half of the trip; the group should carry sufficient water containers to supply dinner and breakfast, and fill them from springs before making camp. The river itself is muddy, and somewhat polluted from heavy agricultural use. It should be treated by boiling or using Halazone before use.

The canyon wildlife includes eagles, deer, buzzards, coyotes, hawks, ducks, geese, mink, and occasional bobcats, antelope, desert sheep, and herds of wild horses. The river is full of fish, trout in the vicinity of Rome, and bass and catfish further downstream. The lake has large numbers of carp and crappie. Muddy water makes spinning gear the best choice in fishing equipment.

The canyon is a rock-hound's paradise. In spots the beaches are strewn with agates and other colorful rocks. Fossil hunting in the clay areas, and hikes up the fascinating side canyons provide other diversions. And the warm water temperatures in late May and June make swimming enjoyable.

By June, daytime temperatures can reach the 100's, but in April, it can be quite cool. Night temperatures can vary from the 30's to the 60's. Kayakists in April or early May will probably want wet suits. Rain is a distinct possibility in the early part of the season, so parties should be prepared.

Figure T9-1 Riffle on the Owyhee

Nature of rapids

This section of the Owyhee makes an excellent tour for a boater who is just reaching the intermediate stage. The rapids are of the pool and drop type. Usually quiet water extends to the lip of the rapids, which drop sharply over Class II to III rock gardens into a pool. Most rapids are reasonably short. At just the right water level it might be possible to run everything on this stretch, but usually at least one portage is necessary.

The river is enjoyable to run at flows from 900 to 3,000 c.f.s. Below about 1,500 c.f.s., rocks are numerous, and wooden drift boats may have problems. The optimum water level is probably about 1,500–2,500 c.f.s.

The average skill of boaters on this trip should be at least a strong Class II, but because the pool and drop rapids make scouting and portaging easy, a few weaker boaters can accompany the group. The party should include several Class III boaters as there are several Class III rapids. There is no access to the river between MI. 5–MI. 40, so parties should be prepared for a long hike if they have serious problems.

Specific information

Location: S.E. Oregon, south of Ontario.

Figure T9-2 Owyhee scene

Put-in

Bridge at Rome, Ore., or bridge 2 mi. downstream from Rome. The latter put-in is private property—ask permission to use it. Neither spot is good for camping.

Take-out

1) Hole-in-the-Ground Ranch. Private property—obtain permission to use it. This take-out has the advantage of shortening the trip by 23 mi., 10 of them with very flat water, but it also has the disadvantage of a very steep clay road, barely passable for passenger cars when the road is dry and not passable in anything when it is wet. Inquire locally at Rome or Jordan Valley for the condition of the road, and instructions for finding it. The road to Hole-in-the-Ground Ranch is shown on the Boise, 1:250,000 quadrangle. The road leaves the main highway near Sheaville and later parallels Mahogany Creek for a short distance.

2) Leslie Gulch. A gravel road passable in passenger cars leads to this spot about 9 mi. down Lake Owyhee. This is a popular spot with fishermen and power boaters, and camping is shadeless, waterless, and generally unpleasant. There are some attractive potential camping spots and a spring in the scenic gorge area a mile or two up the road from Leslie Gulch.

Shuttle

The shuttle to Leslie Gulch is about 75 mi., $2\frac{1}{2}$ hr. one way from Rome. You may be able to hire a local driver in Rome or Jordan Valley to drive your car for you or to pick you up in a truck. Prices as of 1972 were $30–$40. Contact:

Mrs. Norman Easterday
Jordan Valley, Ore. 97910
(phone: 586-2352)

Drive northeast from Rome on Highway 95 through Jordan Valley. Turn left on the road to Succor Creek State Park, 6 mi. north of Sheaville. Follow signs to Leslie Gulch (bear left at most major junctions).

Maps

U.S. Geological Survey topographic maps: Jordan Valley, Boise, 1:250,000. The sketch map included in the guide has the essentials. The Bureau of Land Management also publishes a map of this area: Central Vale District (B.L.M., P.O. 2965, Portland, Ore.).

Water Level Information

Recommended flows: 900–3,000 c.f.s. Ask for the net inflow to Owyhee Reservoir (which is almost the same flow that is registered at Rome during the recommended running period). Contact:

River Forecast Center
National Weather Service
320 Customhouse
Portland, Ore. 97209
(phone: 503-221-3811 before 3.00 P.M.)

Distance and Time Allowance

About 40 mi. from Rome to Hole-in-the-Ground. This can be done comfortably in 3 days, and at quite a leisurely pace in 4 days. From Rome to Leslie Gulch is about 63 mi. It can be run comfortably in 4 days, and at a leisurely pace in 5–6 days.

Wilderness Status

The Lower Owyhee from Crooked Creek to Birch Creek is classified as a Wild River under the Oregon Scenic Rivers system. This prohibits new building or development other than those needed for existing agricultural uses, for public outdoor recreation, or for resource protection.

Guide

This includes only the more obvious rapids and campsites, and applies only at recommended water levels. Rapids and campsites may change at any time (due to flooding, landslides, and other phenomena).

MI. 0. Rome bridge put-in. Flat water paddle through agricultural land.

MI. 2. Bridge, with a water gauge on the right just below it. This is an alternate put-in, but permission should be obtained from the property owner. Agricultural land continues for about two more miles.

MI. 4+. Spring on the left where a steep-walled canyon becomes visible ahead. Camping beach on the right.

MI. 5. Crooked Creek enters from the left at the start of the canyon. The canyon is narrow and scenic with vertical rock walls, and continues for about a mile. Springs enter from the right about 1/4 mi. below the creek, and continue for the next 1/2 mi.

MI. 5½. Campsite on the right. Usable at low water only.

MI. 6. Class I rapid.

MI. 6½. Canyon opens. Campsite on the left and spring on the right.

MI. 7. Class I rapid.

MI. 8. Two Class I rapids. Just below the lower rapid is a

good spring on the right with campsites on the right and the left below the spring.

MI. 8½. Class II− rapid, followed by two Class 1+ rapids.

MI. 9. Class II rapid followed by a Class 1+ rapid. Spring on the right about 50 yd. below the Class I+ rapids.

MI. 9½. Campsite on the right.

MI. 10. Class II rapid with a good spring on the left at the bottom. Class III− rapid below the spring. Route on the left. Followed by 1/4 mi. of Class I+ rapids.

MI. 10½. Class III rapids just after a right bend in the river. Quite rocky at low water. *Inexperienced paddlers might wish to scout.*

MI. 11. Class II rapid.

MI. 11½. Class II+ rapid with a campsite on the left at the bottom. Good spring on the left about 100 yd. below the campsite just above a Class I+ rapid.

MI. 12. Campsite on the left followed by a Class II and a Class II rapids.

MI. 12½. Good small campsite with trees on the right.

MI. 13. Class II rapids and a good campsite with trees on the left below it.

MI. 13½. Class II− rapid.

MI. 14. Good campsite on the right, followed by a Class II+ rapid with a spring on the right at the bottom. Followed shortly by another Class II rapid.

MI. 14½. Vertical rock wall rising from the river on the left, with many springs and a good, scenic campsite opposite it on the right.

OWYHEE RIVER
SECTION II
TOUR 9

0 1 2 MILES

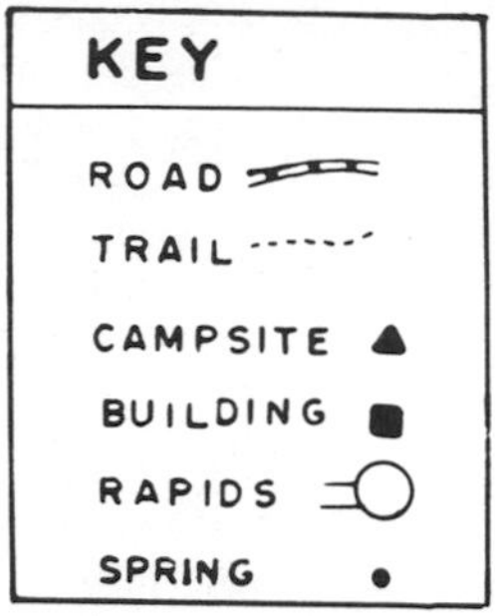

KEY

ROAD
TRAIL
CAMPSITE
BUILDING
RAPIDS
SPRING

MI. 15. Class II+ rapid.

MI. 15½–17. Three Class II rapids, and a few treeless campsites.

MI. 17. Small clay badlands on the right, and treeless campsites on both the right and the left.

MI. 17½. Long Class III− rapid, with a spring on the right at the foot. Class III+ rapid shortly below the Class III− rapid. Very steep and heavy. **Scouting recommended.**

MI. 18½. Class II− rapid with spring on the right at the foot.

MI. 20. Abandoned rustler's cabin high on the right side, with several springs in the area.

MI. 20½. Several hot springs on the left recognizable by orange algae-covered rocks. Big enough for sponge baths.

MI. 21. Cold spring from a pipe and a treeless campsite on the right.

MI. 21½. Spectacular clay badlands area on the left, lasting for about 1/2 mi.

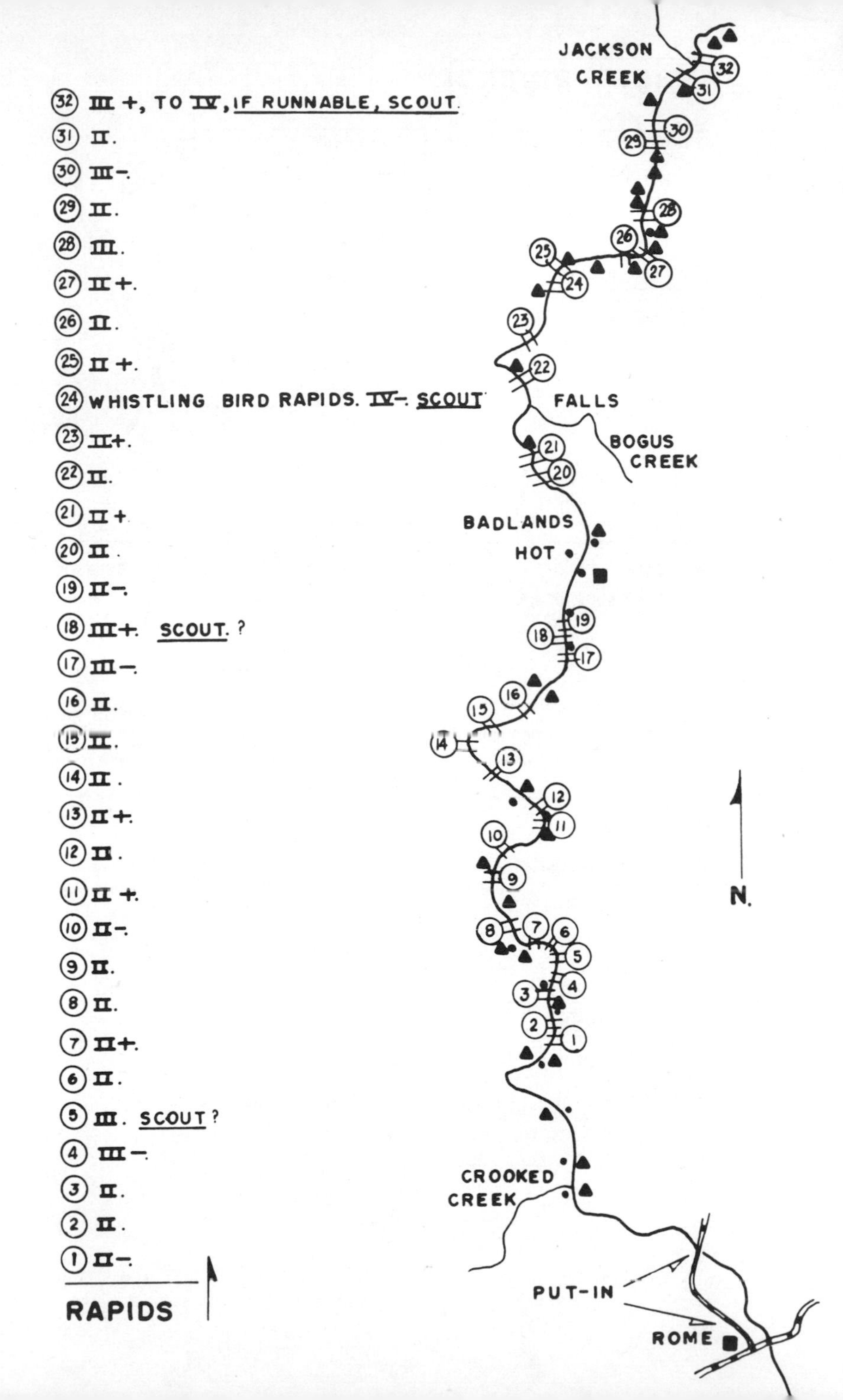

JACKSON CREEK
(32) III +, TO IV, IF RUNNABLE, SCOUT.
(31) II.
(30) III–.
(29) II.
(28) III.
(27) II +.
(26) II.
(25) II +.
(24) WHISTLING BIRD RAPIDS. IV–. SCOUT
(23) II+.
(22) II.
(21) II +
(20) II .
(19) II–.
(18) III+. SCOUT. ?
(17) III –.
(16) II.
(15) II.
(14) II .
(13) II +.
(12) II .
(11) II +.
(10) II–.
(9) II.
(8) II.
(7) II+.
(6) II.
(5) III. SCOUT ?
(4) III –.
(3) II.
(2) II.
(1) II–.
RAPIDS
FALLS
BOGUS CREEK
BADLANDS
HOT
N.
CROOKED CREEK
PUT-IN
ROME

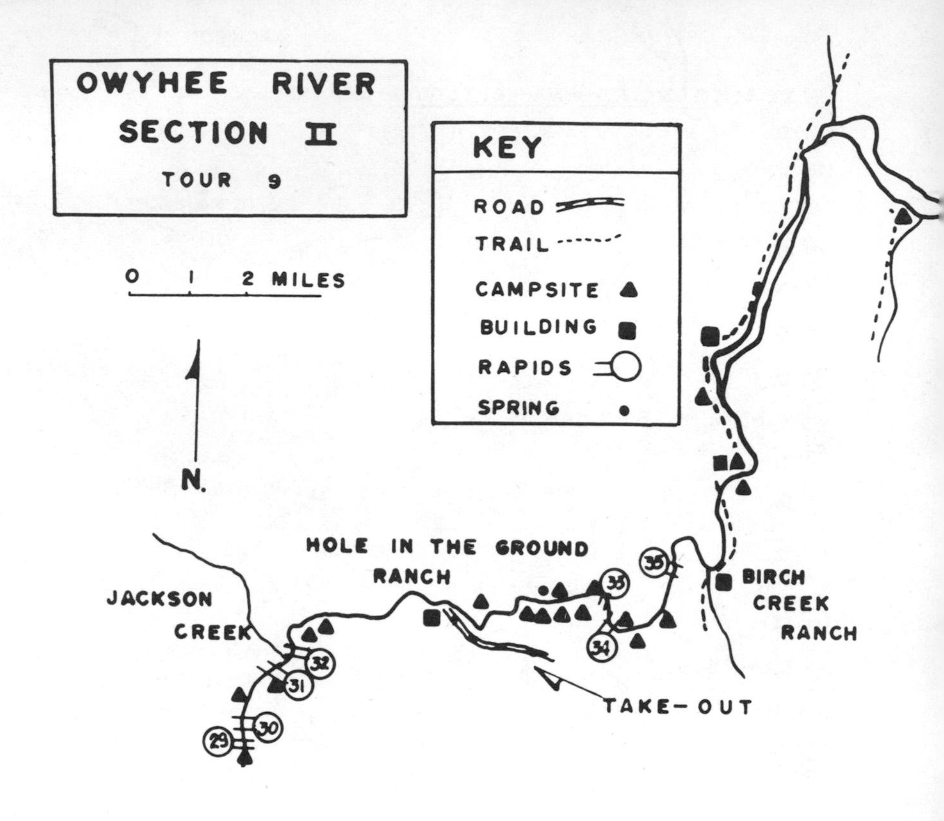

MI. 23–24.	Class II and a Class II+ rapids, followed by a good campsite on the right.
MI. 24–26.	Bogus Creek Falls on the right. Several Class II– rapids.
MI. 27.	Class II rapids followed by a good campsite on the right.
MI. 28.	Long Class II+ rapids.
MI. 29.	Small campsite on the left. Gorge begins and continues for about 1/4 mi. Lovely vertical red rock wall on the left.

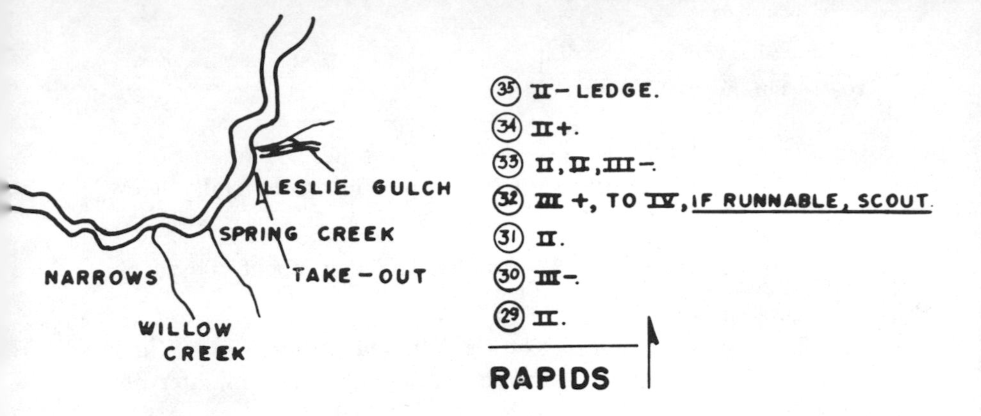

MI. 29½. Whistling Bird Rapids. Class IV–. **Caution: this must be scouted, and many parties may prefer to line or portage.** Recognize it by 1) the red rock wall on the left 1/2 mi. above it and 2) the obvious drop by a rock wall on the right. A huge rock slab has fallen into the river, and the current flows directly into the slab; at high water it may be possible to run down the left side of the river, avoiding the slab area. Good campsite on the left at the foot of the rapids, with small Indian caves behind, and an interesting 1/4-mi. hike up a narrow gully just above the campsite.

MI. 30. Class II+ rapid with a good campsite on the left at the foot.

MI. 30½. Class II– rapid with a campsite on the right at the foot. Spectacular steep walled canyon (most scenic of trip) begins and continues for about 3 mi. Just after the entrance to the canyon is a low-water campsite on the left in a cave.

MI. 31. Class II rapid with a good campsite on the right at the foot. The campsite is followed by a Class II+ rapids.

MI. 31½. Good campsite on the right followed in about 200 yd. by a Class II– rapids.

MI. 32. Warm springs on the right (these seem to be the last reliable springs). Campsite on the right below the springs.

MI. 32½. Long Class II– rapid followed in about 200 yd. by a Class III rapid.

MI. 33. Good campsite on the left. This is followed by three more good campsites on the left at 1/4 mi. intervals.

MI. 34½. Canyon opens. Numerous campsites in the next 2–3 mi.

MI. 36. Two Class II rapids.

MI. 36½. Class III– rapid.

MI. 38. Large beautiful campsite on the left.

MI. 39. Class II rapid with a campsite on the right just above it. Followed in 100 yd. by a Class II– rapid.

MI. 39½. Creek cascading down a gully on the left. **DANGER:** immediately below this is a broken dam obvious from the roar. **Scout; and carry on the right, if you are so inclined.** A Class IV center chute is runnable at high water.

MI. 40. Class II– rapids followed in the next 1/4–1/2 mi. by several campsites on the right.

MI. 40½. Hole-in-the-Ground Ranch on the right. Possible take-out is private property; *obtain permission.*

MI. 41. Campsite on the left. Dubious springs on the right just below this campsite.

MI. 41½. Class II– rapids with several campsites on the right and several more Class II– rapids in the next 1/4 mi.

MI. 42. Cold but feeble spring on the left below a Class II–

rapid. Campsites on both the right and the left below the spring.

MI. 42½. Class II− rapid with a good campsite on the right below it, followed by another Class II− rapid.

MI. 43. Class I+ rapid with a good campsite about 200 yd. below it on the left. The campsite is followed by two Class II rapids and a Class II− rapids at 100-yd. intervals.

MI. 44. Class II− rapid with a poor warm spring on the right about 200 yd. below it.

MI. 44½. Class II+ rapids if you run the right side; steep ledge on the left. Beautiful campsite on the left at the bottom in a scenic canyon area.

MI. 45. Beautiful campsite on the right.

MI. 45½. Good campsite on the right—the last good one.

MI. 46. Road becomes visible on the right, and a poor spring comes down a gully from the right.

MI. 47½. Class II− ledge.

MI. 49. Hayfield on the right.

MI. 50. Birch Creek, ranch, and road on the right. This is a fly-in dude ranch; please respect their privacy. Large waterwheel on the right.

MI. 53. Deserted ranch on the left with campsites on the right and the left. These campsites are uninspiring, but are the only ones for the next 2 mi.

MI. 54½. Waterwheel on the right. Jeep road becomes visible on the left in this area.

MI. 55. Campsite on the left at an interesting gully with a prominent rock pillar and many large boulders.

MI. 55–56. Current ceases; river gradually widens; the lake begins. The lake includes back-breaking paddling, power boats, and poor campsites (although it does have some excellent scenery, and a good gravel road into Leslie Gulch). Plan to paddle the lake in the early morning or late evening to avoid headwinds. Lake paddle took us four hours without a headwind.

MI. 55½. Cabin on the left.

MI. 58. Root cellar and campsite on the right.

MI. 60. Narrows. Narrow slot towards the left side of the lake with a red rock wall rising vertically on the left.

MI. 63. Leslie Gulch on right inlet. Outhouse visible from the lake. Camping possible but unpleasant and crowded. No water available.

APPENDIX A

Equipment and Food Sources

1. *General backpack, climbing, and lightweight equipment, as well as boats*—mail-order

   a. L.L. Bean, Inc.
   Freeport, Me. 04032

   b. Recreational Equipment
   1525–11th Ave.
   Seattle, Wash. 98122

   c. Eastern Mountain
   Sports, Inc.
   1041 Commonwealth Ave.
   Boston, Mass. 02215

   d. Moor and Mountain
   Main St.
   Concord, Mass. 01742

   e. Sierra Designs
   4th and Addison
   Berkeley, Calif. 94710

   f. Cloud Cap Chalet
   625 S.W. 12th Ave.
   Portland, Ore. 97205

2. *Boats and Boating Equipment*

   a. Amerimex
   124 West 30th St.
   New York, N.Y.
   (rubber kayaks)

   b. BlueWater Marine Supply
   1000 Broadway
   Houston, Texas 77012
   (rubber rafts)

c. Custom Boats
5115–55th Ave. NE
Salem, Ore. 97303
(McKenzie River boats)

d. Eastside Boats
Third and Kennedy
Duvall, Wash. 98019
(McKenzie River boats)

e. Easy Rider Fiberglass Boat Co.
4802 B East Mercer Way
Mercer Island, Wash. 98040
(kayaks and canoes)

f. Hauthaway Kayaks
640 Boston Post Road
Weston, Mass. 02193

g. High Performance Plastics, Inc.
Hingham Industrial Center, Bldg. 56
Hingham, Mass. 02043
(kayaks and canoes)

h. Imtra Corporation
151 Mystic Ave.
Medford, Mass. 02155
(rubber rafts)

i. Inflatable Boats Unlimited
Box 21021
Salt Lake City, Utah 84121
(rubber rafts)

j. Inland Marine
79 E. Jackson St.
Wilkes-Barre, Pa. 18701
(rubber rafts)

k. Leisure Imports, Inc.
104 Arlington Ave.
St. James, N.Y. 11780
(rubber kayaks)

l. Hans Klepper Corporation
35 Union Square, West
New York, N.Y. 10003
(kayaks and foldboats)

m. Old Town Canoe Company
6083 Mill St.
Old Town, Me. 04468
(kayaks and canoes)

n. Plasticrafts, Inc.
2800 N. Speer Blvd.
Denver, Colo. 80211
(kayak and canoe kits)

o. Seagull Marine Sales
3107 Washington Blvd.
Venice, Calif. 90291
(rubber rafts)

p. Vega Integral Plastics Co.
P.O. Box 55342
Indianapolis, Ind. 46205
(kayaks and canoes)

q. American Water Works, Inc.
P.O. Box 5084
Terminal Annex
Denver, Colo. 80217
(kayaks, canoes, rafts)

r. Alumaweld Boats, Inc.
1158 Court St.
Medford, Ore. 97501
(aluminum drift boats)

s. Smokecraft, Inc.
New Paris, Ind.
(aluminum drift boats)

3. *Miscellaneous boating equipment* (see previous suppliers, as well)

a. *Flotation bags*
(kayak and canoe)

Harvest Enterprises
3976 East Ave.
Hayward, Calif.

Sims Flotation Bags
P.O. Box 8979
Vancouver, B.C.
Canada

b. *Waterproof Equipment Bags*

Voyageur Enterprises
P.O. Box 512-A1
Shawnee Mission, Kan. 66201

c. *Paddles*

Illiad, Inc.
168 Circuit St.
Norwell, Mass. 02061

Sportglass
6709 11th Ave.
Los Angeles, Calif. 90043

Sawyer Custom Paddles
Sawyer Woodworking
101 Mill St.
Oscoda, Mich. 48750

Timberline Sports Inc.
P.O. Box 426
West Hartford, Conn. 06107

Seda Products
P.O. Box 369
La Mirada, Calif.

Voyageur Enterprises
P.O. Box 512-A1
Shawnee Mission, Kan. 66201

4. *Dehydrated Foods* (suppliers in Appendix A.1. carry extensive lines, as well)

   a. Chuck Wagon Foods
   Micro Drive
   Woburn, Mass. 01801

   b. Dri Lite Foods
   11333 Atlantic
   Lynwood, Calif. 90262

   c. Stow-a-way Products Co.
   103 Ripley Road
   Cohasset, Mass. 02025

We have found that Chinese and Japanese food stores, located in some of the larger cities, often have very useful dehydrated foods, some at very low prices. Try your local outlet if one is available.

APPENDIX B

Selected Recipes*

LOGAN BREAD

This bread is high in energy content, filling, lightweight, and good. Fills two normal bread pans.

4 cups whole wheat flour	½ cup dark molasses
1 cup instant Ralston, uncooked	1½ cups honey
1 tsp. baking powder	2 cups water
½ tsp. salt	¾ cup melted lard
½ cup powdered milk, dry	nuts, raisins to taste
2 cups dark brown sugar	

Mix in any order, place in greased pans, and bake at 325°F for 1¾ hr. or until done. Cool, remove from pan, and slice. Dry on oven racks for 2–3 hr. with the oven on its lowest setting (150°F) and the oven door open a few inches. The bread should be fairly brittle, but not so rock-like that it can't be chewed at all! Cool, store in plastic bags. Keeps for months. Eat plain or with jelly.

*Tbs. = tablespoon; tsp. = teaspoon.

FODDER

Another high energy, filling food. For 9 cups (most people aren't interested in more than 2/3 cup for lunch).

5 cups *uncooked* oatmeal (instant)
1 cup white sugar
1 cup brown sugar
1 tsp. salt
1 cup nuts
1 cup chopped dates or other dried fruit

Mix, package in plastic bags. Ready to eat (most people find it too dry straight, and prefer to lubricate it with jelly, milk, or just plain water.

JERKY

Very popular eaten straight at lunch, or in the dinner "glop." Lean meat only should be used for jerky, for any meat marbled with fat will go rancid fairly quickly. Venison and horse meat make excellent jerky due to their lack of fat, but most people will have to settle for beef. Don't get an expensive grade of beef as U.S. Choice and Prime are marbled with fat. Go to a butcher shop where lower grades of beef are available and get a U.S. Good rump roast. Trim off all external fat. Slice as thin as possible across the grain, and cut into strips about 1-in. wide. Finished jerky will weigh about 1/3 as much as the original meat.

Soak strips overnight in marinade (in refrigerator).

Marinade I (keeps very well) for about 7 lbs. meat.

1/2 cup Worcestershire sauce
1/4 cup soy sauce
1½ cups water
1 tsp. seasoned salt
1 tsp. barbecue salt
1/3 tsp. garlic powder
1 Tbs. black pepper
1 tsp. onion powder
1 tsp. M.S.G. (monosodium glutamate)
1 tsp. liquid smoke

Marinade II (harder to keep) for about 7 lbs. meat.

1½ cups beer
4 Tbs. orange marmalade
2 cloves garlic, minced
⅛ tsp. hot pepper sauce
½ tsp. salt
1 Tbs. powdered mustard
1 Tbs. ground ginger

Hang strips from oven racks. Dry at lowest oven temperature with oven door open a few inches (12–24 hr.) until meat is thoroughly dry at the center. Package in sealed plastic bags. Dry, fat free jerky will keep for many months.

BAKED FISH

Fried fresh fish are very good, but have the following drawbacks:

1. Large fish (over 11 in.) don't fry very well, because by the time the inside is thoroughly cooked, the outside is rather dried out.
2. Although the first few fish are a real treat, fried fish can get boring fast.

Baking fish in aluminum foil retains the moisture even of large fish, gives them a different flavor than frying, and makes them at least seem more easily digestible. If you are lucky enough to catch a salmon or steelhead, this is an excellent way to cook it as well as any trout over about 11 in.

Sprinkle the inside or outside of the fish with a little dried soup. Any beef or chicken stock will do but onion is best. Or use minced dried onion and a little salt. Wrap fish well in aluminum foil, and bury in coals. It must have coals on top as well as underneath. Cooking time varies from about 15 min. for an 11-in. fish to 30 min. for a 8 lb. salmon or steelhead.

FISH CHOWDER

This recipe is a great way to use small fish or spread just a few fish out for a large group.

Clean the fish, removing the heads and tails if you are fastidious and place in enough boiling water to cover. Boil for a few minutes. Remove fish and let them cool; save the liquid. Skin the fish (the skin peels off easily), and flake the flesh from the bones. Set meat aside.

Add enough liquid to the fish liquid to give you the desired amount of chowder. Add the dried corn chowder mix available at backpacking stores, and cook according to package directions, adding the cooked fish in the last few minutes.

Or, make your own chowder mix using the following amounts for approximately 4 cups chowder:

1 cup dried milk, added to cooled fish liquid
½–¾ cup dried potato flakes or slices available at grocery stores
1 Tbs. minced dried onions
2 Tbs. parsley flakes available at grocery stores
1 tsp. salt
pepper and spices to taste

Add to about 3½ cups fish liquid, cook until potatoes are nearly done, add fish.

If you are carrying dried milk, dried onions, and spices in your staples bag, and expect to fish, carry one of the little 2-oz. envelopes of potato flakes and you have all the makings for a chowder dinner.

APPENDIX C

Flow and Gradient Data

This appendix is designed to help you find and evaluate two of the key data you need to determine the difficulty of a river that is unknown to you. We have used these ideas and techniques ourselves on a number of rivers we wished to tour. One important ingredient in the success of these techniques however, is a willingness on your part to start gathering information several months in advance of your trip. If you do your intelligence work well in advance, allowing time to get all the necessary data, you will be likely to end up with a party and river that are well matched and a trip that you will enjoy and remember.

Gradient Data

To calculate the gradient, you need both the elevation difference between the points of interest, and the mileage on the river between these points. We will start with the easiest technique for calculating gradient.

River Profile Maps

These maps are published by the U.S. Geological Survey (see Appendix D.4.a for address) and show the elevation along the river bed. Figure C-1 shows a typical segment of a profile map. From this type of map you can not only calculate the gradient of any section, but can also determine whether the river has even gradient or pool and drop character. For example, between RM 115 and RM 107, a distance of 8 mi., the river drops from an elevation of 1,500 ft. to an elevation of 1,340 ft.*

Given this data, we calculate:

$$\text{gradient} = \frac{160 \text{ ft.}}{8 \text{ mi.}} = 20 \frac{\text{ft.}}{\text{mi.}}$$

This is the *average* gradient over the 8-mi. section. Notice, however, that just beyond RM 107 (between RM 107 and RM 106) there is a steep drop of about 36 ft. in about 0.5 mi. or about 72 ft./mi. Thus from the river profile, you might be wise to approach the drop at RM 107 very carefully. For that matter, everything from RM 112 to RM 106 might be nasty. Note also that starting at RM 110 and going downstream to RM 106 there are several pools and several drops, i.e., the river in this section has pool and drop character. So you see that the average 20 ft./mi. gradient might well mislead you very dramatically in your evaluation of the river difficulty.

If you could get a river profile map for every river you planned to run, planning would be easy. Unfortunately there are very few rivers for which profile maps are available. (Those that are available are shown in blue on the state indices to U.S.G.S. topographic maps.) Of the nine tours we have in the guide section, only the Rogue has a profile map available.

In the rather likely event that a profile map is not available for the

*RM stands for "river mile," which is a measure of the number of miles upstream to the station from the point at which the river loses its identity. For example, if the South Fork of the Big River and the North Fork of the Big River join to form the Big River, RM 16 on the South Fork would be 16 mi. upstream from the confluence of the North and South Forks, *not* 16 mi. from the mouth of the Big River.

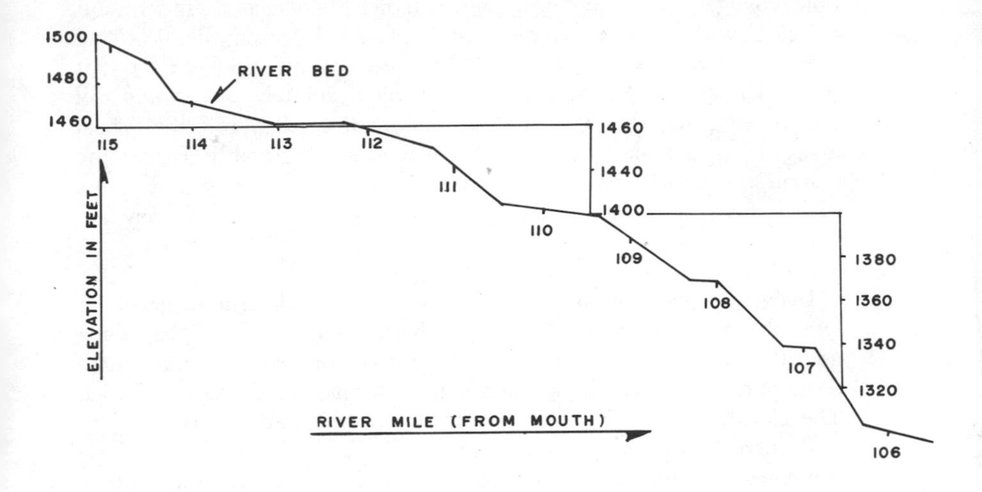

Figure C-1 Typical segment of a river profile map

river you wish to tour, there are several other ways to get gradient information, which we will discuss in the next paragraphs.

Topographic Maps and Gauge Station Descriptions

U.S.G.S. or equivalent topographic maps can be either very useful or nearly useless to determine gradient. Their usefulness depends heavily on the scale and the contour interval of the map. (For information on topographic maps and their interpretation, see Appendix D.3.) In particular, large-area maps with, e.g., a 1:250,000 scale and 200-ft. contour interval are simply too coarse to let you detect 40-ft. waterfalls. However, a map with a 1:62,500 scale and a 25-ft. or 40-ft. contour interval would warn you at least about large falls.

To get gradient information from topographic maps, find elevation contours which cross the river near each end of the section you are investigating. Subtract one elevation from the other to get the elevation change. Next, measure the distance between these contour crossings with a map measurer (see Appendix A for suppliers). Using these two numbers, divide them to get the average gradient for that particular section. To use a map measurer accurately you should roll the wheel along the river, record the reading, then roll the wheel along the map scale to give the same reading. Preferably, repeat the measurement three times to avoid both errors in reading and errors in following the river channel, then average the results if they are reasonably close. If they disagree by more than 10–15 percent, you goofed!

Using gauging station data is another way to determine gradient. Official U.S.G.S. gauges usually have both the elevation of the gauge and the river mile at which it is located contained in the gauge description. For sources of gauge descriptions, see Appendix D.5.a. The elevation is usually given as: Datum of the station is *(elevation)*.

If there is one gauging station near the river section you wish to run, use the description for that station in conjunction with a topographic map. Should this and all the previous methods fail to provide gradient data, then you can try one of the several secondary and usually poor quality sources mentioned in the next paragraph.

Bench Marks, Bridges, and Other Structures

On topographic maps, you see the notation BM (*number*). This is the location of a U.S.G.S. elevation bench mark; the elevation of the marker has been carefully determined. If there are bench marks very close to the river in the section you are examining you may use these to estimate the elevation change. Unfortunately, the bench mark may be several hundred feet above the river, leading to a grotesque value for the gradient.

If all else fails, highway bridges which cross the river and other man-made objects may have known elevations. Write to the builders of such a structure to see whether they know the elevation. When none of these techniques yields information about gradient, and if no other party is known to have run the river, then visual inspection of the canyon from an airplane is strongly recommended before you attempt the tour.

Flow Data

After you've determined the gradient, you still need to know the flow at the time of the tour in order to predict the river difficulty from Figure 1-1. However, when you are planning a tour several months in advance, you won't know what the flow will be at the time of the tour. Thus you must predict the time that will give you a desirable flow. This will allow you to decide on approximate dates for which to schedule vacation time, to know whether to expect cold or warm weather and water, etc. To choose a "desirable" flow that will give a suitable level of difficulty for your party, refer to Figure 1-1 if the river has a fairly even gradient or talk to other people who have run the river at known flows. A note of caution about flow levels is in order here. Below about 300–1,000 c.f.s many rivers simply become unrunnably low. At 300 c.f.s. you can either jump across or wade ankle deep across most streams. In Figure 1-1 we have covered the most common flow ranges at which people undertake whitewater tours, with 5,000–10,000 c.f.s. as a large river, 2,000–5,000 c.f.s. as a medium-sized river, and 500–2,000 c.f.s. as a small river.

In any case you will need to know predicted flows in order to estimate river difficulty and the time to make the trip. Because flow predictions can only be made accurately a month or so in advance, for long-range planning you will need historic flow data, data from preceding years. This will allow you to estimate the approximate dates of the trip; as that time approaches, present and predicted flow data will allow you to pinpoint the dates more precisely.

Historic Flow Data

The best and usually only source of numerical data on flow is the U.S.G.S. or its Canadian counterpart. These data are extremely useful for long-range planning several months before the trip because they allow you to determine both the actual magnitude of the flows and the approximate runoff periods which have occurred in the past. We will look at two rather separate problems. First, how do you decide which gauging station data you need? Second, how do you use these historic records to "guesstimate" the date on which to start the tour?

To decide which gauging station or stations to use in the evaluation, we use several criteria. If there are several gauging stations on the river given in the index publications listed in Appendix D.5.a., pick the gauging station nearest to the end of the tour. This choice yields the highest flow value, and thus, the greatest predicted difficulty for the river; a conservative approach. This approach is not possible if there is only one gauging station and it is above the section in which you are interested. If there are major tributaries or diversions below the station for which you get data, try to get flow data for these tributaries or diversions. If you can get these data, you will be able to tell whether the river changes in size dramatically at these tributary or diversion points. Another criterion that we use is whether data from the gauge is available on a current, daily basis. The availability of daily readings often outweighs all other factors in the choice of a gauging station. For example, on the Rogue (Tour 1), we have chosen to use the Raygold gauge 50 mi. above the put-in rather than the Agness gauge, at the take-out, just for this convenience.

Next, how do you obtain the gauge data and use it to estimate the time to make the tour? Once you have made a choice of gauges for which you want historic data, write to the appropriate state office of the U.S. Geological Survey and request data for one gauge or particular gauges only, rather than the whole book for the state. You should request the most recent three years of data on the gauge. The reason for requesting several years' data is shown graphically in Figure C-2. Several things are worth noting from Figure C-2. A reasonably normal year on the Owyhee was 1969, although 1968 had been a disastrously dry year in which virtually no parties boated the Owyhee and a few walked down it. If you acquire data only from an abnormal year like 1968, you could be badly misled both about the size of the river and about the runoff pattern. Also note the very sharp rise in flow in late March, 1969. In about 10 days the flow went from about 2,000 c.f.s. to 15,000 c.f.s.—a nightmarish time to be boating on the river, with logs, dead animals, and other debris for company. Such behavior is quite typical of rivers that have large drainage areas at a fairly uniform elevation. Most of the snow melts suddenly, pushing the flow to very high levels in a few days. In 1972, a group tried Section II of the Owyhee at just such a time and required a rescue to get out of the canyon.

If you have acquired three years' data from which the flow levels

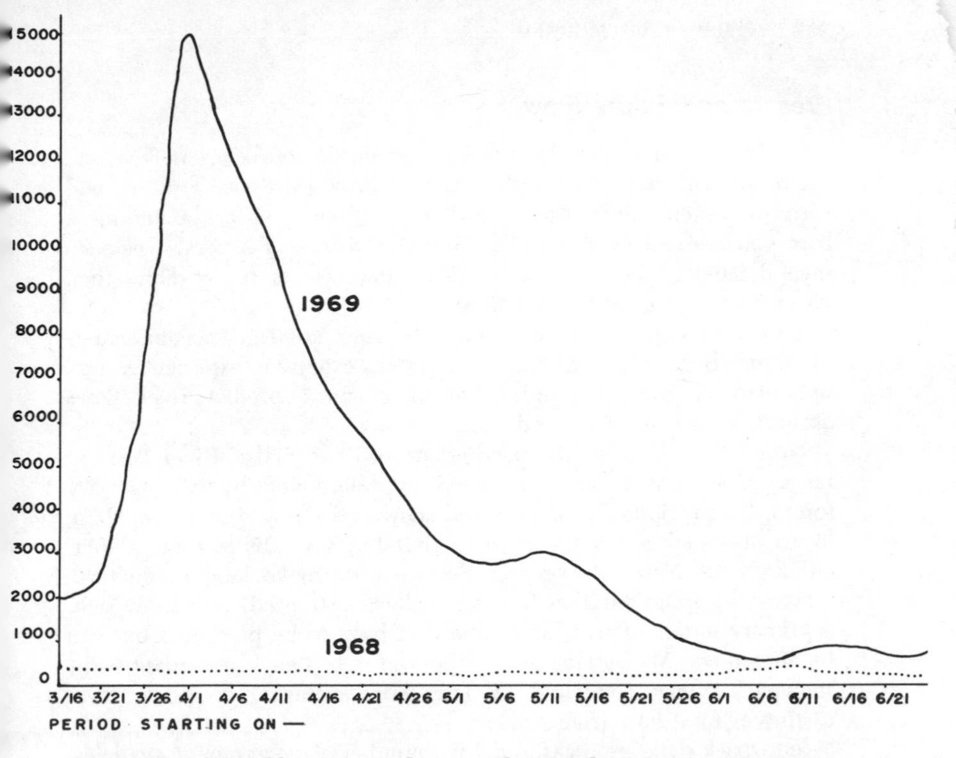

Figure C-2 Weekly average flow on the Owyhee River at Rome for 1968 and 1969 (Source: Water Resources Data for Oregon, *Part I, Surface Water Records)*

and timing of the runoff cycle seem to be fairly consistent, then you can choose an approximate date on which to run the river. For example, using Figure C-2, if you want to run the river at about 2,000 c.f.s., you would expect to be able to find this level during early March or May. Access usually isn't feasible in early March. If you examine several years' data carefully, preferably with a graph such as Figure C-2, you might be able to get a closer guess; e.g., that sometime during the first three weeks of May you would have the desired flow. Even this rather crude estimate of the date for the trip is valuable to establish your probable vacation time and the general sort of weather that would be expected.

Present and Future Flow

To bracket more closely the date at which your chosen flow will occur, we will have to leave ancient history (last year's data) and turn to present and future conditions. When you are planning a trip, you are usually interested in future flow, say several weeks to several months hence. Thus, we will first discuss future flow, then go to the problem of present flow.

To ensure that we are speaking the same language, a comment is in order. Even given a large computer, extensive experience, and unlimited programming aid: You ain't gonna predict river flows *accurately* two months in advance.

Now let's talk about the predictions you *can* make. River flow, as far as river runners are concerned, is determined by two primary forces, the precipitation of rain and snow and the rate at which these forms of water get to the river. Rainfall is very difficult to predict, although the National Weather Service does make long range forecasts of precipitation. Snowfall is equally poorly predicted; snowpack, a primary source of river flow, does not have to be predicted but can be measured. Measurements of the water content and quantity of snowpack, when compared to long-term averages, do allow forecasting of total flow from a river.

Snowpack data are measured by a number of government agencies. These data are used to predict water flows, and the results are published in *Water Supply Outlook*. Write to the agency listed in Appendix D.5.c for a copy of the appropriate regional issue. In fact, ask to have your name put on the mailing list for this publication if you regularly run rivers in an area which the publication covers. *Water Supply Outlook* gives you a fair idea about the amount of potential runoff to expect. For many of the rivers listed the potential for this year is compared (as a percentage) to the long-term average and to the previous year too. The publication is issued monthly through the runoff season from January to June, so you can use it to keep track of the progress of the runoff cycle either for your river or for nearby rivers.

An example is appropriate here. Suppose, starting during the winter the potential runoff is 30 percent above the 15-year average, and that this above-average potential is still present a month or so before you plan to go on the river. You have, of course, already chosen an approximate flow level that you desire for your trip. You were able to make that choice from historical flow records. You may well choose to delay your trip a short time to let the flow drop to the desired level. How long do you delay? One way to guess is to look at the previous runoff cycles for which you have data and determine about how long the flow has taken in the past to decrease 30 percent from some higher level to your desired level. Then delay the trip that length of time. This example, by the way, is a case history. We delayed a trip on the Middle Fork of the Salmon (Tour 5) in 1971 from July 10 to about July 20 for just this reason. Several groups that started about July 10, 1971, came to grief because of the "unexpectedly high" flow level. By July 20, the level was still high but very delightful.

A crude technique? You'd better believe it is! Don't expect to be able to calculate the number of days, hours, and minutes to wait before the river reaches your desired flow. The kind of estimate we have done above may put you on the river within a week of the correct time, and is very useful for adjusting vacation schedules and plans as much as one month before the trip.

If you are very fortunate in your choice of river tours, you may even be able to get a flow forecast for your river. Forecasts are done for some major rivers both for flood warning and for flood control and dam releases are sometimes based on them. We have been quite impressed with the accuracy of flow forecasts on a number of rivers in the guide section. The source of these forecasts is a series of regional River Forecast Centers (see Appendix D.5.c for information about the locations of these centers). Two comments should be made about predicted data from River Forecast Centers. First, the predicted flow values, although often remarkably accurate, are not infallibly correct, as staff members of these centers are prone to point out. Second, the number of rivers on which forecasts are made is too small due to budget limitations. In any case, these methods should give a reasonably precise time to make the trip.

So now the time is almost here—you are scheduled to leave in a few days for the long awaited tour. How do you make a last minute check to be sure that the level is indeed what you anticipated? Now you need present flow data, and getting it is one damn tough game to

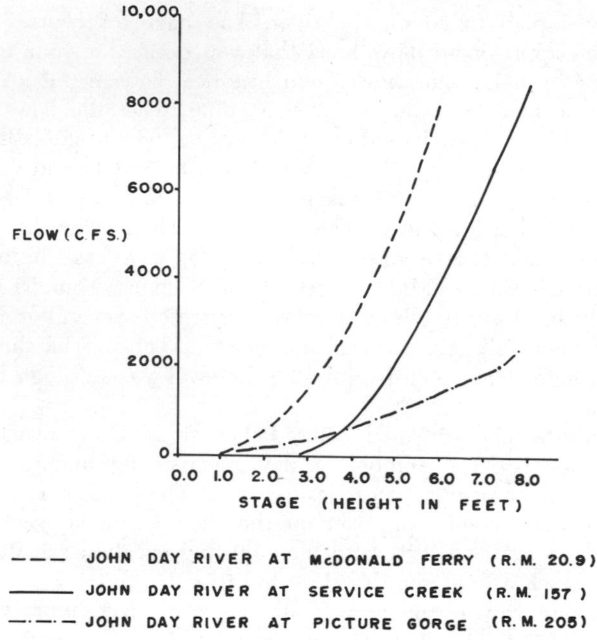

Figure C-3 Flow versus stage for three John Day River gauges—these rating curves have probably changed since 1964, and are used here only for illustration *(Source:* Surface Water Records for Oregon *[1964] pp. 104, 109, 110)*

play for many rivers. If there is a gauge on your river, there are two problems in this game. First, nearly all gauge readings are taken in terms of stage, or height of water at some point on the river, which may or may not be convertible into flow in cubic feet per second. Second, you may not be able to get daily or even weekly readings on the gauge you wish to use. The problems with stage data are well illustrated by Figure C-3; a graph of flow *vs.* stage for three gauging stations on the John Day River in Oregon. These curves are drawn from a rating table, similar to the one shown in Table C-1.

Table C-1 *Rating Table—1964 Data*

John Day River at McDonald Ferry

Gauge height, ft.	*Discharge, c.f.s.*
1.0	64
1.4	195
1.9	490
2.5	1,010
3.0	1,610
4.0	3,200
5.0	5,300

Careful study of these curves suggests a number of rather striking problems with stage data. For example, using the data in Table C-2, we can calculate the change in flow for a one foot change in stage.

Table C-2 *Stage and Flow*

	Flow, c.f.s.		
Station	*At 3.0 ft.*	*At 4.0 ft.*	*At 5.0 ft.*
Picture Gorge	320	620	1,000
Service Creek	150	880	2,250
McDonald Ferry	1,600	3,200	5,300

Table C-3 shows both the change in flow in cubic feet per second and the percent change in flow for a stage change from 3.0 to 4.0 and for a stage change from 4.0 to 5.0.

Table C-3 *Flow Change*

Station	*Flow change, c.f.s. 3.0 to 4.0 ft.*	*%*	*Flow change, c.f.s. 4.0 to 5.0 ft.*	*%*
Picture Gorge	300	+190	380	+160
Service Creek	730	+590	1,370	+250
McDonald Ferry	1,600	+200	2,100	+70

Table C-3 makes you wonder about the meaning of that comment: "The river is up about a foot since yesterday." Where was the reading taken? To what kind of change in flow does this particular one foot of change correspond? Obviously, both these questions can be answered only if a valid rating table is available for the particular gauge on which the reading was taken.

Fortunately for the river runner, most U.S.G.S. gauges are rated for flow in cubic feet per second in terms of stage. These rating tables are the source of the flows that appear in *Surface Water Records for (State)*. Thus, if you are going to use a U.S.G.S. gauge while you are on the river, you perhaps can acquire a rating table for the gauge by writing to the state U.S.G.S. office. Be wary of old rating tables (last year's). Gauge ratings can and do change, e.g., with scouring or siltation of the river bed. Use old ratings if you must, but don't expect high accuracy from them.

The U.S.G.S. data may be available on a current basis if the gauge is telemetered. The telemetered gauges are often read by the River Forecast Service or operators of dams. Thus if there is a U.S.G.S. gauge on your tour, the present flow may be obtained from:

1. The gauge itself if it is accessible by automobile, and you have a rating table.

2. The gauge reader if the gauge is telemetered.

If there isn't a useable U.S.G.S. or Canadian equivalent gauge on the river you are going to tour, you might investigate one of several other sources. If there is a dam on the river, there may be some form of gauge at the dam, and you can try to get readings from the organization that operates the dam. Such gauges may or may not be rated. Similarly, municipal or regional irrigation districts in the western United States sometimes have flow informaton on the rivers which they are drinking.

If none of these types of gauges are available to you, try to find out whether any private individuals maintain gauges on the river and contact them for information, which is virtually always stage data.

If all else fails and no quantitive flow information can be acquired, try the following disaster prevention method. Telephone a bar, gas station, or grocery store, in a town near which the river runs and try the following questions:

1. Have you looked at the river level in the last day or so? If he has, continue; if not, try someone else.
2. Was the river "high" or "low"? Unless the flow is extreme in one direction or another, your informant probably didn't notice.
3. Was the river muddy, or muddier than usual? This question is very important as an indicator of flood conditions, which usually muddy rivers considerably.
4. Have you had much rain or unusually hot weather lately? These questions can suggest the possibility of strongly rising or falling flow.

Needless to say, the quality of information which comes from this source is highly questionable. We call bars simply because most small towns have bars, and often have very interesting, although not necessarily very informative, conversations. You may be able to find out whether the river is in flood by this technique, but you usually don't get much more information than this.

The preceding paragraphs have listed a variety of sources for present flow data. The sources other than U.S. Geological Survey, as you probably noticed, can give you the present flow, but usually only in terms of stage, with all its inherent problems. But at least such information can tell you if the river is rising or falling, which may be all you need if you have pinpointed your time carefully using the other sources in this appendix.

APPENDIX D

Books and Other Information Sources

The books listed below are only a few of the available publications on whitewater and wilderness-related techniques. In our opinion, the books listed are the *best* starting point for a newcomer to whitewater touring.

1. Whitewater Books

A Whitewater Handbook for Canoe and Kayak, John T. Urban (1965, Appalachian Mountain Club, $1.50). This is an excellent introduction to actual boat-handling techniques.

White-water Sport, Peter D. Whitney (1960, The Ronald Press Co., $4.00). Has some sections of considerable value, but some of the book is out-of-date.

Living Canoeing, Alan Byde (1969, Adams and Charles Black Ltd., $4.75). An excellent book on paddling techniques, although some sections will require translation from British English for American readers.

These books will give a beginner in kayak or canoe a sound introduction to effective boat-handling technique. Thoughtful reading and careful experimentation on these techniques can give you a reasonable start on boating skill. If possible, supplement this instruction with help from one of the organized groups listed in Appendix E.

2. Whitewater Periodicals

American Whitewater (quarterly, American Whitewater Affiliation, $3.50/yr.) This excellent little magazine has articles on all phases of kayaking and canoeing. To subscribe contact one of the groups in Appendix E.

Canoe (official bimonthly, published by Sonderegger Publications for the American Canoe Association). This publication features more information than *American Whitewater* on racing and flat water touring with some information on whitewater touring, and is a source of equipment advertising. To subscribe contact one of the groups in Appendix E.

3. General Background Books

Mountaineering: Freedom of the Hills, H. Manning, ed. (1960, The Mountaineers, Seattle, Wash. $7.50). Probably one of the best overall books on back country techniques. Although the slant is toward mountaineering, we believe that anyone planning extended trips in isolated areas should read this book first.

Medicine for Mountaineering, James A. Wilkerson, M.D., ed. (1967, The Mountaineers, Seattle, Wash. $7.50). An excellent book on what to do when the doctor can't come for several days.

Mountaineering Medicine, Fred T. Darvill, M.D. (1967, Skagit Mountain Rescue Unit, Inc. $1.00). This is a brief, lightweight first aid handbook. This book, although far less comprehensive than Wilkerson's book, is very easy to carry and, for most easy first aid problems, quite adequate.

Be Expert with Map and Compass, Bjorn Kjellstrom (1955, American Orienteering Service, New York, $2.95). This is a book published by the manufacturer of Silva compasses to popularize compass use. It is, however, a well done introduction to topographic maps and compasses and their joint or separate use.

Ropes, Knots and Slings for Climbers, W. Wheelock (1960, La Siesta Press, $1.00). This little book has excellent illustrations of nearly all of the common and useful knots needed for whitewater touring. It also has considerable useful and interesting information on ropes.

Outdoor Living—Problems, Solutions (Tacoma Mountain Rescue Council, Tacoma, Wash.).

4. Maps

a. *Topographic Maps*

U.S. Geological Survey

Areas west of Mississippi River:
Distribution Section
United States Geological Survey
Federal Center
Denver, Colo. 80225

Areas east of Mississippi River:
Distribution Section
United States Geological Survey
1200 South Eads St.
Arlington, Va. 22202

Index maps showing the available topographic maps in each state are available from the appropriate Distribution Section. These are free upon request. Available river profile maps are shown in blue on these index maps.

Canadian Topographic Maps:
Map Distribution Office
Dept. of Mines and Technical Surveys
Ottawa, Ontario
Canada

b. Nontopographic Maps

U.S. Forest Service

Forest Supervisor
_____ National Forest
City, State

It is sometimes valuable to include a request in your letter for names of local people familiar with the river as well.

U.S. Bureau of Land Management (B.L.M.)

U.S. Dept. of Interior
Bureau of Land Management
(Local office in state of interest—
usually located in the state's capital city)

County maps
Try state highway departments or private concerns, such as:

Metsker Maps
111 South 10th Street
Tacoma, Wash. 98402

Metsker has maps for Oregon, Washington, Idaho, and California.

Miscellaneous maps
These are sometimes available through the U.S. Bureau of Mines or individual state departments of geology or departments of mines.

c. Aerial Photographs

These are often obtainable, sometimes in stereo pairs, from a variety of government agencies. To obtain information on availability and source of aerial photographs write:

U.S. Geological Survey
Washington, D.C. 20242

and request: *Status of Aerial Photography*, which is free upon request.

5. Water Flow

a. Historical Information

These data are given for States in: *Water Resources Data for (State)*, Part 1, *Surface Water Records* 19—. Write to:

District Chief
Water Resources Division
U.S. Geological Survey
(in the state in which you have interest)

Addresses for the specific states may be obtained through the United States Geological Survey in Washington, D.C. (see 4.c).

These data books are free, but in limited supply, so be conservative in your requests. The books give daily flows at each of the gauging stations in the state for that "water year" (October through September). We would suggest that you request one of these books when you are planning a trip and determine from the book which gauging stations are most useful. Then, to get historic data, request copies of data from *only* that gauge(s) for several years. The data on gauge location listed at the top of these sheets can be quite useful also. Usually, the elevation of the gauge, the drainage area above the gauge, and mean elevation of the drainage are given in this heading.

For historical water flow data on Canadian rivers, individual provincial office addresses may be obtained from:

Water Survey of Canada
Inland Waters Branch
Department of the Environment
Ottawa, Ontario
Canada

Ask for *Surface Water Data* (Province).

For convenience, the western province offices are given below:

District Engineer
Water Survey of Canada
Inland Waters Branch
Department of the Environment
(as listed below)

Alberta and Northwest Territory:
700 Calgary Power Building
110 12th Ave., S.W.
Calgary 3, Alberta

British Columbia and Yukon:
#502 1001 West Pender Street
Vancouver 1, B.C.

Saskatchewan:
G.M.C. Building
1102 8th Avenue
Regina, Saskatchewan

Information on existence and location of gauging stations is in the following publications. For the United States you can obtain the *Index to Surface Water Section,* a catalog of information on water data
U.S. Geological Survey
Washington, D.C. 20242
Attn: Office of Water Data Coordination

This publication contains, for the whole United States, identification and location of gauging stations as well as the frequency of data collection at each station and the agency by which the records are kept for each station.

For Canada ask for the most recent *Surface Water Data Reference Index* when you write to the Water Survey in Ottawa. This publication gives approximately the same information, for Canadian rivers, as the publication above.

b. Current Information

For the United States very recent flow data can be obtained from the *River Forecast Center* in the area (see next section). The U.S. Geological Survey usually does not have recent information as their stations are mostly on a recording basis and the records are collected every few weeks. Usually, if a U.S.G.S. station does have a telemeter for daily monitoring, the reading is taken by the River Forecast Center, or some other agency.

A second possible source of recent data is the company or agency controlling any major dams on a river. Although the flow or stage at such a dam is usually monitored, it is not always available to the public.

In Canada the Water Survey of Canada, District Offices, monitors some gauges daily during the peak runoff period. Contact the relevant office (5.a.) to determine which gauges are monitored daily, during what period of the year they are monitored, and how these data may be obtained. The comments on monitoring at dams is applicable in Canada also.

c. Future Information

An invaluable publication for whitewater tourists is: *Water Supply Outlook for the (region) U.S.* This publication appears monthly from January through June for various regions of the United States (Western, Northeastern, etc.). The data in the publication, predicted *total* runoffs for various rivers, are based on snowpack and moisture, seasonal weather projections, and past history of runoff. These data are invaluable for long range trip planning. To receive this publication, write:

National Weather Service
National Oceanic and Atmospheric Administration
Silver Spring, Maryland 20910
Attn: Office of Hydrology

These are free, upon request. The addresses of the River Forecast Centers in the region are listed in the front of this publication.

A second source of future flow data, predictions for a few days to a month in the future, is the relevant River Forecast Center. Usually, the spring runoff period is the main period of interest to the Centers. Even though they may not have predictions for the river you are interested in, you may be able to obtain some information of value about surrounding drainages from them.

APPENDIX E

Organized Whitewater Groups

The following listing of organized groups gives potential sources of both information and instruction for whitewater novices. The majority of these groups consist of kayakists and canoeists, but in many of the groups at least a few members may be knowledgeable about rafting as well. Wooden drift boats, as used on whitewater, seem to be virtually unknown outside the Pacific Northwest (with a few exceptions). You may be able to get information about drift boaters from Northwest Steelheaders Council, 3226 N. Lombard, Portland, Oregon.

American Whitewater Affiliation members

California

YMCA Whitewater Club
Gary Gray
640 N. Center St.
Stockton, Calif. 95202

Feather River Kayak Club
Mike Schneller
1173 Broadway St.
Marysville, Calif. 95901

Sierra Club
Loma Prieta Paddlers
Ron Williams
84 Blake Ave.
Santa Clara, Calif. 95051

Sierra Club
River Conservation Committee
Gerald Meral, Chmn.
2928-B Fulton
Berkeley, Calif. 94705

Sierra Club
Mother Lode Chapter
Sam Gardali
914 Stanford Ave.
Modesto, Calif. 95350

Sierra Club
San Francisco Chapter
Bob Jack
11 Lynwood Place
Moraga, Calif. 94556

Colorado

Colorado Whitewater Association
Mike O'Brien
2007 Mariposa
Boulder, Colo. 80302

Connecticut

Appalachian Mountain Club
Connecticut Chapter
Christine Papp
Box 285
Bantam, Conn. 06750

Florida

Everglades Canoe Club
Charles Graves
239 NE 20th St.
Delray Beach, Fla. 33440

Georgia

Georgia Canoeing Association
W. D. Crowley, Jr.
5888 O'Hara Drive
Stone Mt., Ga. 30083

American Adventures Club
Horace P. Holden
Box 565
Roswell, Ga. 30075

Explorer Post 49
Mark Reimer
2254 Spring Creek Rd.
Decatur, Ga. 30033

Idaho

Idaho Alpine Club
Dean Hogmann
1953 Melobu
Idaho Falls, Id. 83401

Illinois

Prairie Club Canoeists
George E. Miller
3025 W. 54th Place
Chicago, Ill. 60632

Illinois Paddling Council
Phil Vierling
5949 Ohio St.
Chicago, Illinois 60644

Indiana

Kekoinga Voyageurs
E. Heinz Wahl, Rep.
1818 Kensington Blvd.
Fort Wayne, Indiana 46805

Kansas

Johnson County Canoe Club
Geo. and Joan Weiter
7832 Rosewood Lane
Prairie Village, Kans. 66208

Maryland

Terrapin Trail Club
U. of Md., Kathy Canter
7912—15th Ave. #302
Hyattsville, Md. 20783

Explorer Post 757
Bill Gassawan
3582 Church Road, Box 29
Ellicott City, Md. 21043

Appalachian River Runners Federation
Joe Monohan
Box 1163
Cumberland, Md. 21502

Canoe Cruisers Association
Peggy Harper
384 N. Summit Ave.
Gaithersburg, Md. 20760

Monocacy Canoe Club
Donald G. Schley
Rt. 1, Box 8
Myersville, Md. 21773

Massachusetts

Hampshire College Outdoors Program
Dwight Campbell
Amherst, Mass. 01002

Appalachian Mountain Club Worcester Chapter
Bob Osthues
2 Merrimount Road
W. Boylston, Mass. 05183

Appalachian Mountain Club Boston
Biff Manhard, Rep.
45 Wesley St.
Newton, Mass. 02158

Kayak & Canoe Club of Boston
John Urban, Rep.
55 Jason St.
Arlington, Mass. 02174

Michigan

Kalamazoo Downstreamers
James Tootle
6820 Evergreen
Kalamazoo, Mich. 49002

Raw Strength & Courage Kayakers
Mrs. John Dice
2022 Day St.
Ann Arbor, Mich. 48104

Minnesota

American Youth Hostels, Inc. Minnesota Council
R. Charles Stevens, Rep.
615 E. 22nd St.
Minneapolis, Minn. 55404

Minnesota Canoe Association
Box 14177 University Station
Minneapolis, Minn. 55414

Missouri

American Youth Hostels, Inc. Ozark Area Council
2605 S. Big Bend
St. Louis, Mo. 63143

Meramec River Canoe Club
Al Beletz, Rep.
3636 Oxford Blvd.
Maplewood, Mo. 63143

Central Missouri State College Outing Club
Dr. O. Hawksley, Rep.
Warrensburg, Mo. 64093

Ozark Wilderness Waterways Club
R. Woodward
2209 W. 104th St.
Leawood, Kansas 66206

New Hampshire

Ledyard Canoe Club
Fritz Meyer
Hanover, N.H. 03755

Mad Pemi Canoe Club, Inc.
Dennis F. Keating
93 Realty
Campton, N.H. 03223

New Jersey

Adventures Unlimited
Homer Hicks
Box 186
Belvedere, N.J. 07827

Kayak and Canoe Club of New York
Ed Alexander, Rep.
6 Winslow Ave.
East Brunswick, N.J. 08816

Mohawk Canoe Club
Gerald B. Pidcock, Rep.
Jobstown-Wrightstown Rd.
Jobstown, N.J. 08041

Rutgers Outdoor Club
Robert Markley
RPO—2913—Rutgers
New Brunswick, N.J. 08903

Murray Hill Canoe Club
W. J. Schreibeis
Bell Labs. Rm. 1C-249
Murray Hill, N.J. 07974

New Mexico

Albuquerque Whitewater Club
Glenn A. Fowler, Rep.
804 Warm Sands Drive S.E.
Albuquerque, N.M. 87123

Explorer Post 20
J. H. Fretwell, Rep.
4091 Trinity Drive
Los Alamos, N.M. 87544

New York

Adirondack Mt. Club
Genesee Valley Chapter
Doug Smith, Rep.
769 John Glenn Blvd.
Webster, N.Y. 14580

Appalachian Mountain Club
New York Chapter
John Meirs
Midlane Road, Box 1956
Syosset, N.Y. 11791

North Carolina

Carolina Canoe Club
Bob Stehling
Box 9011
Greensboro, N.C. 27408

Ohio

Keel-Haulers Canoe Club
John A. Kobak, Rep.
American Red Cross Bldg.
2929 W. River Rd. N.
Elyria, Ohio 44035

The Madhatters Canoe Club, Inc.
Christ Wolf
2647 Norway Drive
Perry, Ohio 44081

Oregon

Oregon Kayak & Canoe Club
P.O. Box #92
Portland, Ore. 97204

Pennsylvania

Buck Ridge Ski Club
Hans Buehler, Rep.
1155 Schoolhouse Lane
West Chester, Pa. 19380

Philadelphia Canoe Club
Dr. Paul Liebman
4900 Ridge Ave.
Philadelphia, Pa. 19128

Wildwater Boating Club
Robert L. Martin
LD 179
Bellefonte, Pa. 10823

Penn State Outing Club
John R. Sweet
118 S. Buckhout St.
State College, Pa. 16801

Sylvan Canoe Club
Donald Huecker
Arch St.
Verona, Pa. 15147

Tennessee

Carbide Canoe Club
Herbert Pomerance
104 Ulena Lane
Oak Ridge, Tenn. 37830

East Tennessee Whitewater Club
Don Jared, Rep.
P. O. Box 3074
Oak Ridge, Tenn. 37830

UT Canoe Club
William A. Kruger
Rt. 6, Canton Hollow Rd.
Concord, Tenn. 37720

Bluff City Canoe Club
Jim Goad
Box 4523
Memphis, Tenn. 38104

Tennessee Valley Canoe Club
James C. Mahaney
Box 11125
Chattanooga, Tenn. 37401

Texas

Texas Explorers Club
Bob Burleson, Rep.
Box 844
Temple, Texas 76501

Explorer Post 425
B. Millett
708 Mercedes
Benbrook, Texas 76126

Utah

Wasatch Mountain Club, Inc.
J. Calvin Giddings, Rep.
904 Military Dr.
Salt Lake City, Utah 84108

Vermont

Canoe Cruisers of Northern Vermont
Mrs. Nan Smith
Shelburne Farms
Shelburne, Vt. 05482

Virginia

Explorer Post 999
Thomas J. Ackerman, Rep.
610 Mansion Circle
Hopewell, Va. 23860

University of Virginia Outing Club
Box 101X, Newcomb Hall Sta.
Charlottesville, Va. 22903

Blue Ridge Voyageurs
Ralph T. Smith, Rep.
8119 Hill Crest Drive
Manassas, Va. 22110

Coastal Canoeists
R. L. Sterling, Rep.
309 Mimosa Drive
Newport News, Va. 23606

Washington

Washington Kayak Club
Al Winters, Rep.
8519 California Ave. S.W.
Seattle, Wash. 98116

U. of W. Canoe Club
IMA Bldg
University of Washington
Seattle, Wash. 98105

West Virginia

West Virginia Wildwater Assn.
Idair Smookler, Rep.
2737 Daniels Ave.
South Charleston, W. Va.
25303

Wisconsin

Wisconsin Hoofers Outing Club
Steve Ransburg, Rep.
3009 Hermina St.
Madison, Wisc. 53714

Sierra Club
John Muir Chapter
Jim Senn
10261 N. Sunnycrest Drive
Mequon, Wisc. 53092

Canada

B.C. Kayak & Canoe Club
1200 W. Broadway
Vancouver 9, B.C.

Montreal Voyageurs
Rene Bureaud, Rep.
360 Barberry Place
Dollard des Ormeaux
Montreal 960, Quebec
Canada

Index